WITHDRAWN
FOR SALE

Sir Percy Sillitoe

A. W. COCKERILL

W. H. Allen · London
A division of Howard & Wyndham Ltd
1975

© A. W. COCKERILL 1975

PRINTED AND BOUND IN GREAT BRITAIN FOR THE PUBLISHERS
W. H. ALLEN & CO. LTD, 44 HILL STREET, LONDON W1X 8LB
BY BUTLER & TANNER LTD, FROME AND LONDON

ISBN 0 491 01702 2

ALL RIGHTS RESERVED, INCLUDING THE RIGHT OF REPRODUCTION
IN WHOLE OR IN PART IN ANY FORM WHATSOEVER

FIRST PUBLISHED 1975

Contents

Acknowledgments	ix
1. The Chorister and the Skeleton	1
2. Private Trooper	11
3. Bwana Lieutenant	23
4. The Askari War	32
5. Political Officer	43
6. Rock Bottom	56
7. A Different Kind of Policeman	61
8. Country Policeman	70
9. Sheffield Fine Steel	75
10. Sillitoe's Gauntlet	87
11. The Sillitoe Tartan	101
12. 'Just for the Joy-Ride'	114
13. C Division Specials	126
14. Gangsters and Barking Dogs	139
15. The Common Touch	155
16. Man of Kent	167
17. The Muttonhead Institute	178
18. The Diamond Syndicate	192
19. Endgame	205
Appendix	213
Bibliography and Sources	217
Index	219

Acknowledgments

Sir Percy Sillitoe was by no means a literary man. If, therefore, one had to rely on any 'Sillitoe papers', this book would never have been written. On the other hand, the nature of Sillitoe's work, the fact that he lived in a number of countries, and the international scope of his operational area during the latter part of his life presented considerable difficulty in the gathering of material. During the early years of his life he lived in Rhodesia, Tanganyika (the present-day Tanzania) and what is now Zambia. Later he travelled extensively in connection with his MI5 work—to North and South America, the Far East, Middle East, and to most of the countries of the British Commonwealth. In the task of gathering information, I therefore found it necessary to recruit a team of research assistants, and readers must judge for themselves the fruits of their work. However, I must make it clear that I accept full responsibility for this book's contents.

Miss Enetia Vasselitos and Professor R. S. Roberts of the University of Rhodesia helped provide information on the period during which Sillitoe served with the British South Africa Police; Assistant Commissioner Jouning of the BSAP, Salisbury, was a source of information not available elsewhere; Mrs Vanessa Neave researched material in East Yorkshire; Mrs Pamela Eastaff travelled extensively in Yorkshire, London and Kent for information and to conduct personal interviews; and Mr James McGlinchey covered the period during which Sillitoe was Chief Constable of Glasgow; research in Canada and the United States was handled by myself.

There is, however, one important source of information that requires a special word of explanation. This concerned the period when Sillitoe was Director General of British Security Services, MI5. A number of former secret service operators (not all of the British cloak-and-dagger department) provided information, but

ACKNOWLEDGMENTS

they were, to a man (or woman—to be devious), unwilling to be identified. One feels obliged to respect this confidence. This is an added difficulty, one realises, when one is unable to substantiate statements or to qualify opinions, yet, as this is a biography and not an exposé of any secret service, the question of 'delicate material' hardly arises.

In addition to the research team and those unnamed sources, numerous organisations, police departments and institutions were generous in supplying information. Their more specific contributions are acknowledged in the chapter notes. However, in general order of reference in the text, they are listed as follows:

St Paul's Cathedral Choir School, London, England
The Canadian Royal Military Institute, Toronto, Canada
Northamptonshire Comrades Association, Northampton, England
The National Archives of Rhodesia, Salisbury, Rhodesia
The British South Africa Police, Salisbury, Rhodesia
The Institute of Commonwealth Studies, Oxford, England
Borough Council of Whitley Bay, Northumberland, England
The Star, Sheffield, England
Sheffield and Rotherham Constabulary, Sheffield, England
East and North Yorks Constabulary, Beverley, England
The Sunday Mail, Glasgow, Scotland
The Chicago Police, Chicago, Illinois, USA
The Bancroft Library, University of California, Los Angeles, California, USA
Beverley Police Department, Beverley, California, USA
The International Association of Chiefs of Police, Gaithersburg, Maryland, USA
Federal Bureau of Investigation, Washington, DC, USA
Kent County Constabulary, Maidstone, Kent, England
Die Transvaaler, Johannesburg, South Africa
De Beers Consolidated Mines Ltd, Johannesburg, South Africa
The *Rand Daily Mail*, South Africa
Anglo American Corp. of SA, Johannesburg, South Africa
The *Daily Express*, London, England
The Times, London, England
The Jewelry Council of South Africa, Johannesburg, South Africa
De La Rue Ltd, London, England

ACKNOWLEDGMENTS

To David Higham Associates Ltd, copyright holders of *Diamonds Are Dangerous* by J. H. du Plessis and published by Cassell & Co., London; to Jonathan Cape Ltd and MacMillan Publishing Co. Inc., publishers of Ian Fleming's *Diamonds Are Forever* (© Glidrose Productions Ltd 1956) and *The Diamond Smugglers* (© Glidrose Productions Ltd 1957, 1958), I am grateful for permission to quote from these works.

To Richard Sillitoe I am grateful for immense help on the domestic front and for providing his collection of photographs and a comprehensive scrapbook for my use; to Mr J. H. Clarke for his expert opinion on certain legal aspects of various cases cited; to Dr J. F. Leeson and Dr T. G. S. Wilson for their medical opinions; to my wife, Charlotte, for her helpful advice; and to Mrs W. E. Barr and the staff of Cobourg Public Library for never once failing to locate a required work of reference. Lastly, to my editor, Mr Adrian Shire, without whose help and encouragement my book would not have found its way to the printer, my sincere thanks are due.

If this book is to be dedicated to anyone, it must be to those legions of constables, askaris, troopers and patrolmen, wherever they may be, who pound the beat, guardians of the collective wisdom of their respective societies.

A. W. COCKERILL
Cobourg: 1973

Chapter One

The Chorister and the Skeleton

It is not widely known that Ian Fleming's best-selling novel *Diamonds Are Forever* was partly based on an actual criminal case—that of the Rand diamond smuggling ring. The man who substantially solved this case, and brought it to a successful conclusion was Sir Percy Joseph Sillitoe, former Director General of MI5—the British counter-espionage service. The connection between Fleming's novel and the real-life ring of international diamond smugglers becomes clearer when one learns that the author had himself spent a number of years in the service of British Naval Intelligence, and that after he left the Navy, and Sillitoe the service of MI5, the two men enjoyed an abiding friendship. How Sillitoe became involved in the case, the manner in which he set about his investigation, and the speed with which he cracked it, will be dealt with in their due place in this biography. Suffice it to say here that the real events are as thrilling, as complex, and as extraordinary as those depicted by Ian Fleming.

Sillitoe's career, from his enlistment as a trooper in one of the toughest police forces in the western world—the British South Africa Force—to his becoming Director General of MI5, spanned almost half a century. There was no spectacular leap from trooper to Director General; no magic transition brought him from anonymity into the limelight. Public recognition and the honours bestowed on him were earned by hard work, through dedication to his job, to the traditions and values in which he believed, and by the solid contribution he made during his career to the institution of British constabulary.

Sillitoe's early life is something of a mystery. It is the one period of his life he refused to discuss in any detail—even with his children—until the day he died. He mentions something of it in his autobiography, *Cloak Without Dagger*,* but only briefly, to serve as an introduction, and with an air so apologetic as to border on embarrassment. He kept few photographs, and no family papers, letters or memorabilia of any description at all. Nevertheless, a picture does emerge from the few scraps of information available. Most of these have been gleaned secondhand from his son, Richard Sillitoe, from relatives, former acquaintances, and by pondering on what little he said of himself. Considered separately, such clues are insignificant enough. Put together, they give us a fairly clear picture, which goes a long way to revealing the foundation on which he built his successful career.

Percy Joseph Sillitoe was born at Tulse Hill, in South London, on 22nd May 1888, the second son of Joseph Henry and Bertha Leontine Sillitoe, née Smith. His brother, later the Reverend Hubert John Sillitoe, was two years older and he also had a sister, Bertha Louisa, ten years his junior.

The Sillitoes originally came from Shropshire. In a family tree compiled by Percy's brother, their surname is traced back to the fourteenth century, but the amateur genealogist, despite his loyalty to the family, was unable to prove a connection between the Shropshire Sillitoes and those recorded in the Yorkshire Poll Tax Records of 1379 and 1397–8. Sillitoes had nevertheless been well established in the Newport district of Shropshire for centuries. Pell Wall House, Staffs, near Market Drayton, Shropshire, was built for Pursey Sillitoe (1772–1855) (and was, incidentally, the last private house to be designed by Sir John Soane).

Percy Sillitoe's mother was a native of Tulse Hill. Little is known of her background except that her parents were people of property, and enjoyed a middle-class standard of living. They employed servants and had the necessary means to provide their daughter with a genteel upbringing. In keeping with the standards of the age, she learned nothing that might be described as useful in earning her own living. She read little though she was a good conversationalist and, in common with other young women of her class at that period, was trained to head firmly towards marital status. She reached her goal, in the shape of Joseph Henry Sillitoe, but their union was not to be the voyage of unruffled calm that she had been educated to expect. Sillitoe senior was, to

* Cassell & Co. Ltd, London, 1955.

take the most charitable view, a philanderer and, as he was later to be described by his daughter-in-law, Dorothy Mary Sillitoe, a 'ne'er-do-well'. Consequently, there was never enough money for his family to live an 'ordinary' life. He brought a modest fortune to his marriage but, following a series of disastrous investments, was obliged to live by his wits. Percy Sillitoe records in his autobiography that his father became an average adjuster in marine insurance after his final sortie into the stock market, but he probably never had a regular job. He was an inveterate gambler, spent a great deal of time away from home, and generally existed on his charm, of which there appears to have been much to spare; he was tall and handsome, which doubtless helped snare Bertha Leontine into the marriage. It is not known for sure, but he is reputed even to have been in and out of jail on one vagrancy charge or another (it was probably drunkenness—there is no evidence to suggest that his misdemeanours were of a criminal nature). He certainly ended his days in the workhouse, or some such establishment, because we know that Percy later sent his mother money for his father's maintenance. Obviously Sillitoe senior is the skeleton in the Sillitoe cupboard, and perhaps the fundamental reason for Percy Sillitoe's developing a phobia about his childhood.

Nevertheless, the picture should not be painted all black. His childhood had at least one redeeming feature, and that a very significant one. His salvation, for such it was, stemmed from his mother's love of music.

Among her accomplishments, Mrs Bertha Sillitoe had some talent as a pianist. She also loved to sing and had a tolerably good voice. More important, she passed this love on to her children in the hours they spent together, clustered about the piano in their rather threadbare drawing room.

This recreation was to bear fruit in a practical way, for it helped solve the difficult question of the children's education. The elder boy, with assistance from a relative, a Governor of Christ's Hospital, gained an award for entry to the Hospital School. The same course was not available to his younger brother, Percy, but that problem was solved a short time later, for his singing voice was found to be good enough to gain him acceptance into the choir of St Paul's and thereby to ensure him, in the Cathedral Choir School, the kind of education he would otherwise have been denied. Obviously there would be no public-school education for the Sillitoe offspring, and attendance at one of the 'penny-schools', as they were then known, would naturally have been beneath the family's consideration. Entry into the Choir school assured him of many things, including such basics as food, clothing, shelter and, of course, education. At the same time his mother, who never worked a day in her life outside the home, was relieved of the burden of his upkeep.

Thus was determined for some years to come the life-style of the Sillitoe family, a plight universal to the genteel poor; the slightly shoddy appearance of the parents, with their out-of-date and sometimes well-worn clothes; the children's crisp uniforms, supplied by the institution to which they have been (albeit reluctantly) consigned; the polishing up of the family plate, those steel knives and forks burnished to a gleaming, pristine brightness with the aid of a wet rag and scouring powder, for every happy homecoming; the sometimes familiar, sometimes distant nods of acquaintances when the reunited family are out on their Sunday walk.

Perhaps more than anything else, Percy's experience as a St Paul's chorister gave him his first taste of detached discipline—a discipline, that is, distinct from that he had at home. It goes without saying that the latter was all but absent on the paternal side, what little effort his father might have made to exert some authority being nullified by the example he set.

This is an interesting and major aspect of Sillitoe's personality, because he developed into a stern disciplinarian. Indeed, of his two dominant characteristics—the other being a strong humanitarianism—his obsession with discipline formed the cornerstone of his success.

It is fairly certain that Percy eventually came to despise his father, both for his cavalier treatment of Percy's mother and for his unwillingness or inability to give the boy a sense of those values he instinctively knew to be of importance. Expert opinion may be divided on the question of parental discipline, but there is general agreement that children do sense a need for it, interpreting it subconsciously as evidence of whether or not their parents care for them. So it is not mere conjecture to suggest that the pressure of resentment built up to a point where it became a mental block so far as his father was concerned. Certainly, once he reached manhood he almost never spoke of his father again. It also helps explain why he readily accepted the rules imposed by the staff of St Paul's, developed a strong sense of self-discipline and made imposed, authoritarian discipline one of the main underlying principles of his life. The unhappy relationship with his father undoubtedly contributed, too, to the attitudes he developed in the important formative years of his youth; his kind but distant attitude to his own children, his lack of ease in the presence of young people, his remoteness and the tendency to keep to himself. We should have no hesitation in placing at Sillitoe senior's door the responsibility for his son's susceptibility in childhood and teenage to accept other influences. Fortunately, the influence which figured in the moulding of Percy's character were good ones.

One of them was his physical appearance. As he grew into his middle teens he shot up tall and straight, becoming in appearance more and more like his father. He developed the strong, questing nose and square, thrusting chin which gave his face strength, the 'intense blue eyes' (repeatedly noted by reporters in later years), and the abundance of blond, wavy hair which softened his appearance.

He had, too, an important asset which could only be seen in retrospect, and that was good fortune. Luck is as much an ingredient in the making of a successful career as intelligence, native ability, imagination, and outright talent. Nor is the saying 'It's not what you know but who you know that counts' any less apposite today than it was at the turn of the century. Good fortune came to Percy Sillitoe in the shape of Colonel Hugh Sinclair, brother of one Dr Sinclair, the Archdeacon of London who, in turn, had got to know Percy as a chorister.

What special reason Colonel Sinclair had for singling out Percy from among the many choirboys at St Paul's is not known, but he undoubtedly took a special interest in him. It is equally certain that he made a deep impression on the boy, who regarded him with something approaching hero worship. To the excitement of meeting an important adult was added the far more thrilling fact that he was a soldier, indeed an officer.

The end of the nineteenth century (the two met in 1898–9) saw the British Empire at the pinnacle of its splendour and glory. The British Navy was mistress of the seven seas, the Empire was still being pushed to new frontiers, foreign trade was expanding, international affairs were under the all-pervading influence—and control, it seemed at the time—of the most competent government the country had ever elected. True, there was a spot of bother brewing among the Boer settlers in South Africa, but it was considered minor in comparison with other difficulties which the realm had dealt with in the past fifty years: the Crimean War, the Indian Mutiny, the Boxer Rebellions. A respect for tradition, for national heritage, virtue, a sense of right and wrong, was ingrained in the heart of every young Englishman. Percy may have known that a distant relative, Lieutenant William Sandy, RN, served on the man-o'-war HMS *Polyphemus*, which brought home Lord Nelson's body after the Battle of Trafalgar, and of the exploits of other illustrious members of the Sillitoe line. It is not difficult to imagine what impact the friendship of an active army colonel would have on him. Can we doubt that the qualities he recognised in Colonel Sinclair were the very ones he failed to see in his own father?

Sinclair's colonelcy was a brevet rank—a rank, that is, without pay. According to the Army List for 1902, he had been a major in the Corps of Royal Engineers, and served as Commanding Royal Engineer with the expedition to Ashanti under Sir Francis Scott in 1895, and was mentioned in despatches. With the outbreak of the Boer War, Sinclair left the country and sailed for South Africa, probably as a seconded officer to the City Imperial Volunteers of London. This was a mounted infantry regiment of gentlemen about town, raised for the South African campaign in 1899 and disbanded in 1901. It was a fairly common practice at about the turn of the century to raise units for small 'firefighting' actions, and to disband them a short time afterwards. The City Imperial Volunteers was a typical unit of this type, for it spent only from February until June in the field before being returned to England. The next time Sinclair and Sillitoe met was in fact on the occasion of the Thanksgiving Service held in St Paul's following the return of the City Imperial Volunteers. Percy records that he was fascinated by the spears, assegais and other mementoes the Regiment brought home.

In 1902, he left St Paul's (his voice had broken) and returned home to live with his parents at Tulse Hill. For the next three years he remained at home, studying for the Indian Police Examination with the help of a private tutor, which suggests that the family was by no means entirely impoverished at that time. Mrs Sillitoe had inherited a little money, and this she used carefully to supplement the occasional monies her husband earned.

During that period—the last time he was to live with his mother for any length of time—Percy led a very active life. He enjoyed field sports, played cricket, bicycled, and generally inclined to a physical existence. He says that he read a considerable number of books, but how serious his interest was is not certain; he was by no means an avid reader in later life. Moreover, while he recognised the value of books and encouraged his children to read, the one type of person he disliked intensely—and he made no bones about it—was the book-learned intellectual. He himself acquired all his education without benefit of college or university, or even of one of those certificates considered essential to the school-leaver today. But he was a keen observer of people and of life, and his curiosity never slackened. For instance, the descriptions of African wildlife and of the habits of tropical birds, which he later gave at public lectures in Chesterfield, Beverley and Glasgow, were masterpieces of perceptive observation.

He also had the rare gift of an extraordinarily retentive mind. He gave an early demonstration of this ability by committing to memory as a St Paul's chorister the entire score of Handel's Messiah, both words and music, and for the rest of his life he was capable of instant recall of any part of the magnificent work. It is hard to say whether this was entirely a gift, or in part a developed talent stemming from the discipline imposed by the cathedral choirmaster. In any case, that basic training and his capacity for recall added to the strength of his personality.

During the period he lived at Tulse Hill, he maintained contact with Colonel Sinclair, and at the age of seventeen he left home and went to live with the Colonel. Sinclair was by that time an Assistant Quartermaster General, a competent and widely-respected officer living in the City of London. His wife was the daughter of Sir John Jackson, a prominent financier with important connections in a number of city and foreign commercial enterprises, including the British South Africa Company, which was to figure largely in Sillitoe's life over the next few years. Sinclair was clearly a man of some influence, for he was instrumental in obtaining for the seventeen-year-old Percy a junior position with the Anglo-American Oil Company, where he apparently worked for the next two years.

Given Sinclair's and Sir John Jackson's connections and their wide circle of friends, Percy thus had ample opportunity to mix with the kind of people on whom the day-to-day affairs of the

Empire depended. It was a dashing era in which he lived, too, and there were heroes aplenty for the young to admire. The Boer War generals, thick as flies about the War Office, were still being toasted, feasted and cast in bronze; Captain Robert Falcon Scott, RN, had just set sail on his ill-fated expedition to Antarctica, hoping to beat his Norwegian rival, Amundsen, to the South Pole; yet another explorer, H. Hesketh Prichard, with less fanfare and far more modest means, was preparing to trek across the unknown interior of Labrador with only two companions; the clipper ships were in their heyday; and the Port of London still bristled with a forest of wooden masts, despite the inroads being made by steam; India, the Far East, South America and the New World all beckoned furiously to the young, and especially to those such as Percy Sillitoe who lived at the hub of the encircling and expanding Empire.

There is some evidence that in the company of Colonel and Mrs Sinclair, Sir John Jackson and their acquaintances, Percy made contact with a number of adventurers and explorers of the day. In the meanwhile, he enjoyed the good life with Sinclair, who was himself a hard-riding, sporty type of officer. He ran his own stables and spent a great deal of time teaching Sillitoe horsemanship, which led indirectly to the latter acquiring the nickname 'Tod'. Sillitoe evidently liked the name, because he used it to introduce himself throughout his life, though not everyone felt the same way; his elder brother, Hubert, was one. Recalling how the name arose, Hubert said, 'As far as I remember, the name "Tod" was first jokingly given [to Percy] in the garden on a summer day "tea" there [Tulse Hill] about 1905 or 1906—after our schooldays. There was some joking reference to Tod Sloane, the then famous American jockey and, as so often, it stuck, as pet names thoughtlessly used to. Candidly, I never used the name "Tod"—it always irritated me, as I felt it both stupid and inappropriate, as such names usually are.'*

The first overt move of Percy's police career was made in 1908, when he left for Salisbury, capital of what was then Southern Rhodesia. I have mentioned that from fourteen to seventeen he studied for the Indian Police Examination under a private tutor because, as he relates in his autobiography, it was decided he should seek a police career. The decision to enlist in the British South Africa Police was made over a meal with an acquaintance,

* In a letter from Hubert Sillitoe to Richard Sillitoe, 18th August 1972.

an ex-St Paul's chorister, who was Secretary for Native Affairs in north-eastern Rhodesia, and then in England on a spell of home leave.

In an interview which Percy gave to the *Glasgow Weekly Herald* when he was Chief Constable of Glasgow in the early thirties, however, we find:

> His tutoring complete, there was considerable indecision as to whether the 'Man You Know' should join the army or become a doctor.

No mention was made in the article of plans to follow a police career, either on his mother's part or his own. Moreover, given his association and strong ties with Colonel Sinclair at that period, it is more than likely that he did seriously consider joining the army. As for becoming a doctor, it would seem fairly obvious that his lack of higher education and the family's limited means reduced to a minimum his chances of joining the medical profession—perhaps he was indulging in wishful thinking in the Glasgow interview.

So although his autobiography states that it had already been decided for him that he was to pursue a police career, there is some question in my mind that such a decision had yet been made.

His wife, Dorothy, often discussed her husband's childhood with the children in later years. She was, of course, not bound by the same inhibitions of conscience to maintain a silence on the subject, though her knowledge of events before June 1912, when they met, must perforce be second hand. However, Richard Sillitoe reports that his mother was adamant about his father's reasons for choosing a police career. She said that Percy's first and foremost reason was to earn enough money to help support his mother. This seems logical, especially since during the whole period he served in South Africa he regularly sent her an allowance. It may be significant that the pay scale of the British South African Police was higher than that of the British Army. A second reason for his choice was an ardent desire to travel.

On the other hand, Richard Sillitoe has said that his father told him on more than one occasion that he had no particular desire to join the police, but that it seemed to be the best thing to do at the time.

This discussion may seem to emphasise an apparently trivial matter, but the skeleton in the Sillitoe cupboard is of some importance. Percy was extremely attached to his mother—as will be shown later—and felt a great need to help her. He was not blind to her difficulties. Therefore, if the explanation put forward here for his decision is more plausible than his own, how is his version to be explained? The answer, I think, is to be found in his desire to keep a very distasteful subject hidden from public view. No one is disposed to reveal family skeletons, least of all eminent chief constables. From the very outset he glossed over any subject which might bear on his father, presenting as charitable an account as he was able—and then only barely sufficient to get his story started. Also, it should be remembered he was still active in public life when *Cloak Without Dagger* was published. His reluctance to reveal what, even in later life, was still a painful memory is understandable also in terms of his responsibilities.

All this is not to imply that he was guilty of conscious deceit. Indeed, he probably thrust the matter of his relationship with his father so far into his subconsciousness that he was beyond considering it in perspective.

Though so little is known of Sillitoe's early life, one thing is certain: in 1908, at the age of twenty, when he left England for Salisbury, Rhodesia, he had little or no money. Like any other young man on the threshold of life, he was intent on seeing the world and eager for adventure. Furthermore, he knew what he was letting himself in for by enlisting in the British South Africa Police; even at that time its reputation as one of the toughest police forces in the world was already well established. He had the talents to lead him to success—and the strongest motivations.

Chapter Two

Private Trooper

Sillitoe arrived in Rhodesia six years after the death of its founder, Cecil John Rhodes. The British South Africa Police, in which Sillitoe had signed to serve for a three-year term, was the instrument of authority of the British South African Company. This Company, formed by Rhodes and Alfred Beit, was incorporated in 1889 under a Royal Charter by which British rule was extended over central Africa without involving the British Government in either expense or direct responsibility.

One must understand the events which led to the establishment of that rule in this part of the world in order to appreciate the frontier atmosphere of the country Sillitoe served for the next few years and the subsequent events in which he took part. They were to be crucial, formative years which toughened him physically and sharpened his perception. The long periods of isolation, privation and loneliness that they inflicted on him turned out to be just what he needed to acquire and develop the skills essential to a successful policeman.

Salisbury, where he reported for recruit training, is located on the fringe of Matabeleland (what is at present south-western Rhodesia, although the exact extent of Matabeleland in the nineteenth century is still historically controversial). Long before the arrival of British and Afrikaner settlers, this great tract of territory had had a turbulent history at the warlike hands of the Matabele people. The Matabele (also known as the Ndebele),* or northern Zulus, were themselves invaders who had conquered the territory in a northern drive in the early nineteenth century. For ferocity, the Matabele have been justly compared with the

---

* The word Matabele is used in preference to Ndebele in referring to the followers of Chief Lobengula in Matabeleland.

Masai of Kenya and the Ashanti of West Africa. They spent the next sixty years making war on the indigenous Shona-speaking peoples and extending their kingdom. At the time of Cecil Rhodes's arrival on the scene, the Matabele were ruled by a strong leader, Chief Lobengula. In 1888, Sir Sidney Shippard, Assistant Administrator of the Protectorate of Bechuanaland, despatched J. S. Moffat to negotiate with the Matabele, and he was successful in obtaining the Moffat Treaty, by which Lobengula agreed not to make other treaties with foreign powers without British sanction. The Moffat Treaty was in effect a declaration of a sphere of influence in Lobengula's territory. It kept other people out, but did not guarantee British direct rule. Later the same year the equally-important Rudd Concession (Rudd being one of the three negotiators) was obtained. This concession granted mining rights to white settlers in exchange for 'one hundred pounds a month, a thousand rifles and an armed steamer on the Zambesi River'—the latter, presumably, to protect Matabele interests. Together, the two treaties allowed settlers to establish Fort Salisbury (named after Lord Salisbury) without molestation from the neighbouring Matabele. It was as a direct result of Rhodes's diplomatic successes (he persuaded Sir Sidney Shippard to despatch the negotiators) that the British South Africa Company was granted its Royal Charter. Rhodesia was described in the Charter under Clause One as 'the region of southern Africa lying immediately to the north of British Bechuanaland and to the north and west of the Portuguese dominions'.

With the arrival of white settlers, the Matabele discovered that they were no longer free to pursue their favourite pastime of raiding neighbouring Shona villages for pillage and plunder. The influx of further settlers meant that more and more raiding grounds were cut off and, because the raiding system was important enough to the Matabele way of life, this precipitated tension with the newcomers. A small incident in 1893 in which settlers sheltered Shona tribesmen from pursuing Matabele *impis* led to the Matabele War—a war mainly in name, for by modern standards it was hardly more than a series of skirmishes. In the ensuing conflict, there were successes and failures on both sides, but, in the main, the Matabele, despite superior knowledge of the terrain and possession of modern firearms of the day, were out-manœuvred, out-fought, hunted down and given no quarter. The bloody contest was not without its moments of glory.

Major Wilson and thirty-six troopers of the British South Africa Company's private army, pursuing a large band of warriors, found themselves cut off by flood waters at the Shangani River, and outnumbered. They were killed to the last man. In paying homage to the bodies of their foes, the attacking warriors proved that they were not incapable of appreciating gallantry. A large painting, hanging in the Salisbury mess of the British South Africa Police, and depicting Major Wilson's last stand (shades of General Custer), inspired generations of new recruits to the BSAP. Rhodes, who was in England at the outbreak of hostilities, set off immediately on receiving the news. Alone and unarmed, he met with the Matabele leaders, the Indunas, outside Bulawayo and restored the peace.

Contrary to popular misconception, the Matabele were not out-and-out savages—there is a parallel in the conquest of Rhodesia with the saga of the American West and the Plains Indians. Ferocious as the Matabele were, they were a proud and intelligent people with a code of ethics suited to their social organisation. Immorality was practically unknown among them; they took care of their old and treated them with respect; the young were taught to honour their elders and there were few cases of parental neglect or cruelty. In every kraal, or village, a hut was set aside for travellers; they were hospitable people, refusing no one food and shelter.

Between the Matabele War and the final conflict which followed in 1896 there was a period of relative calm, during which the new invaders established themselves and consolidated their gains. Conquest strengthened the confidence of the Company, native police were recruited and native labour for the mines. A hut tax was imposed and—what with seizure of large numbers of native cattle, sheep and goats by the Europeans, and competition with African justice by European authority—a Matabele uprising was, in retrospect, inevitable. The remnants of Lobengula's warriors took up arms and descended on Bulawayo, the former Matabele capital (occupied since the War by settlers), where a few years earlier Lobengula had experimented with his new rifle (courtesy of the Rudd Concession) on his own subjects. (The old *indaba* tree under which he held court and meted out his own brand of justice was still standing in 1960.) It was only natural that the ten thousand warriors, resplendent in black ostrich feathers and white cow-tail kneelets, should assemble at Bulawayo to settle matters with spear and shield. Though put down by the new regime without much difficulty, the revolt was a magnificent but futile gesture and has come to be regarded as a determined effort to preserve the African way of life.

In 1908, when Sillitoe joined them, the British South Africa Police had all but completed the process of being turned from a private army into a proper peace-keeping arm of civil government. The force was at that time responsible to, and maintained by, the British South Africa Company (hence the slightly higher pay scale than that of, say, the Indian Police). It was an extremely tough, disciplined force under the harsh leadership of Colonel (Billy) Bodle, who had gained something of a reputation in the Matabele Uprising. From the BSAP's ranks had been drawn the five hundred troopers whom Leander Star Jameson had led in the famous 'Jameson Raid', which had led to the South African War—the Boer War. Following that conflict there had been a further influx of settlers, as a result of which a number of ex-servicemen were absorbed into the British South Africa Police. Ceremonial dress was a blue and khaki uniform with riding breeches, khaki shirt, and a khaki bush hat similar to the headgear of the Canadian Mounties.

Recruits were subjected to a rigorous six-month period of training which included foot-drill, musketry, riding and lectures on those subjects needed for survival in the bush—first aid, cooking, hunting. Apart from such specialist instruction, their training followed the pattern of any military unit, garnished with the heavy sarcasm of veteran sergeants.

Like any mounted force, the first care of the troopers was their horses. First light found them in the stables grooming their horses and polishing saddlery. Tod Sillitoe had been fortunate in being taught to ride by Colonel Sinclair. He was already in good enough physical shape to be able to join the best riders of the swashbuckling corps of troopers, and he took to the life with ease. He was no complainer, but enjoyed the tough life of a BSAP recruit and wrote enthusiastically to his brother, Hubert, of the experience.

He neither smoked nor drank at that time, and was therefore able to send his mother a regular allowance from his trooper's pay. According to his wife, Dorothy, some years later, his payments to his mother were not only regular but, by the standards of the day, substantial.

At the end of recruit training, Sillitoe was posted to Bulawayo as troop clerk, under the command of another veteran of the '96 uprising, a Captain St John. Bulawayo, like Salisbury, was a thriving frontier town in 1908, as rough and tough as anything the Americans had to offer in the wild west. Its streets were—in accordance with Rhodes's specifications—wide enough to give turning room to a trek wagon drawn by a full span of sixteen oxen. With the opening of the railway line to Victoria Falls, the town became an important railway junction.

Bulawayo had a well-deserved reputation as a central meeting place for miners, fortune-seekers and opportunists, attracting to its bosom as bawdy and brawling a mob of adventurers as any imaginable. The trooper constables of the BSAP had to be equal to, and better than, the hardy crowd among which they maintained some semblance of law and order. It was therefore important that they should not only maintain discipline amongst themselves but also an *esprit de corps*. That on occasions they failed to do so led to one incident, during his first Christmas away from home, which left young Sillitoe dispirited and low.

When he first went to Bulawayo, he befriended an itinerant Australian down on his luck and, in return for providing him with quarters, was given boxing lessons. To entertain the other troopers and officers of the Bulawayo detachment, the two men agreed to a sparring match. At its conclusion another trooper, who fancied himself and rather disliked the cocky Sillitoe, challenged him to a fight. Primed with liquor and spoiling to see a fight, the officers and men goaded Sillitoe into accepting the challenge. But even though all the trappings necessary for a boxing match were there—gloves, ring and seconds—there was the climate for a brawl, and that is what it turned out to be. The whole incident was upsetting to Sillitoe, even though he succeeded in knocking his opponent out for the count, for it offended his sense of decency and noble ideals.

'Is this,' he must have thought, 'all it means to be a trooper of the BSAP? No better than the drunken, brawling miners we're supposed to police?' It was a lesson he never forgot when he later came to command men himself.

He was thankful a short time later to be posted to an independent detachment at Nyamandhlova, thirty miles north of Bulawayo along the Victoria Falls railway line. Situated in a monotonous area of brush broken only by baobabs of all sizes and ages, Nyamandhlova lies near the Gwaai River, a tributary of the Zambesi. At home on his detachment station, he lived in the same type of dwelling as the Africans. This, in the kraal, was a round house with a conical roof and single entrance, constructed of veldt grass. It was ideal for the equatorial climate, cool in the hot African sun and warm during the chilly nights.

Considering the fact that this was the heart of Matabeleland, where just over a decade earlier fierce warriors had roamed freely, there was remarkably little for Sillitoe to do. The Matabele had long since been transformed into law-abiding citizens; and now small groups, deprived of their traditional way of life by the inexorable march of civilisation, hugged the white man's lifeline, the railway track. One has only to compare the colourful warriors of the late nineteenth century with the shoddily-dressed and colourless specimens of Sillitoe's day to realise what a traumatic experience they had been through. Writing in *Rhodesian Patrol** of his journey by train to join the BSAP, F. E. Lloyd says, 'When we stopped, as if by magic, hordes of Africans in torn and tattered clothing closed on the train offering skins and carved curios for sale.' J. S. Moffat (negotiator for the Moffat Treaty), who became resident agent of the British Government and Deputy Administrator to Sir Sidney Shippard, made a prophetic statement in a letter dated 29th May 1892 when he observed of Matabele society, 'There is a process of deterioration and of, I think, disintegration going on: it is possible, though perhaps not probable, that there will be an explosion one of these days, breaking up the whole affair; but, even if not, the slower process is gradually at work.'

The BSAP were concerned with three distinct categories of law and order. The protection of company property, its interests and its production output formed part of their work (since this happened to be principally gold, the police were always on the lookout for gold smugglers). They were also responsible for the maintenance of order according to the white man's imported laws (though there were enlightened police officers—and Sillitoe turned out to be one—who interpreted the law according to the established customs of local African society. Lastly, the police were concerned with the protection of the native peoples against exploitation by such groups as mine operators and biltong traders.

* Arthur H. Stockwell Ltd, London, 1965.

Biltong was the name given to game meat cut into strips and dried over a fire—a technique of preserving the meat common to many pre-industrial hunting peoples. Europeans who engaged in the illicit sale of biltong were considered serious offenders because biltong was made from game, and game poaching was strictly illegal.

It was in connection with the biltong trade that Sillitoe made his first arrest. Assigned to the trail of an Afrikaner wanted for engaging in the trade, he set off in pursuit and succeeded in catching him. Naïvely, Trooper Sillitoe took the man's word of honour that he would not attempt to escape if handcuffs were not used. It was a mistake. The prisoner fled that night—with his captor's horse. Sillitoe had no other course but to give chase again, this time on foot. He caught the Boer again, and made the sixty miles back to Nyamandhlova with the prisoner handcuffed to his stirrup. For him it was a matter of pride that he 'got his man'.

Only rarely was Sillitoe's stay at Nyamandhlova punctuated by such exciting incidents. For the most part, he was thrown on his own resources during long periods when he saw no one of his own kind. He patrolled the up-country bush for days on end, his only company an African constable and a servant to do the cooking and take care of the pack mules, which Sillitoe found more suited to the climate and country than a horse. When he was off duty, too, there were long idle days to contend with and, although there were frequent reports to submit to Bulawayo troop headquarters, they were hardly sufficient to keep him occupied. During this period he learned to speak Sindebele, the language of the locale. His fluent mastery of it was to be of inestimable value to him later in his career. His other major interest was a fascination with the teeming wild life in the vicinity. In a short time he acquired a remarkable knowledge of the habits of the local birds and animals which, requiring patient observation and intelligent reasoning, helped to develop in him those characteristics that were to make him a successful policeman.

A picture of Sillitoe, the future chief constable and spycatcher, picking his way through the African bush on the trail of a honey bird or patiently watching the behaviour of a blue-jay, seems more suited to the pages of an African Audubon, yet it is a clue to the workings of his mind. If he made written notes of his observations, and this is doubtful, none has survived. It is far more likely that he relied on his prodigious memory; lecturing on his African experiences many years later, he was able to recall his activities in minute detail.

After five months at Nyamandhlova he was posted to Victoria Falls, which must have come as a welcome change for him. Fed by the towering vapour plume which local Africans called 'Mosi-oa-tunya', meaning 'smoke that thunders', the immediate area around Victoria Falls was a veritable rain-forest of lush vegetation supporting an abundance of wild life. The area under the canopy of Mosi-oa-tunya, a matter of several acres, was constantly bathed by spray, and the hot African sun and profusion of colour made it a place of unparalleled beauty. Here were to be found the giraffe, antelope, buck and lion. At the point where the Falls occur, the water plunges into a chasm four hundred and twenty feet deep. Directly opposite the Falls are precipitous cliffs through which there is a narrow opening known as the Boiling Pot, through which the turbulent waters rush. Below the Falls, for a distance of forty miles, the river follows a narrow zigzag gorge. For a considerable distance upstream of the Falls, the river flows over a level sheet of basalt. Smooth as plate glass, the clear blue waters are dotted with numerous islands which increase in number as the river reaches its greatest width, a mile across, before plunging over the precipice.

Another attraction of the Falls was the opportunity it provided of enjoying a civilised social life. Since the opening of the railway three years earlier, and of the great railway bridge across the Zambesi River, a steady stream of European sightseers 'doing the east' flowed to Victoria Falls. Guidebooks to describe their magnificence did not exist in the 1908–12 period, but word of their grandeur had quickly spread through the drawing rooms of Edwardian England, so that it was here, after the exhausting journey from Johannesburg and beyond, that pith-helmeted travellers came to rest.

A hotel, well equipped with red-plush Edwardian furniture, had been built within walking distance of the Falls. It consisted of a collection of buildings raised on wooden stilts some four feet from the ground and constructed of wood and corrugated iron. The dining room was originally an old engine shed with a verandah running along its length. Here, as old photographs show, lunch would be served. When they were refreshed, the ladies wielding their parasols and the gentlemen their ivory-handled fly-whisks, travellers might follow the hotel guides to their first stunning sight of this natural wonder.

The Edwardian tourists were provided with plenty of other entertainments. There were boat trips on the river, local beauty spots to visit, picnics, safaris for the men. According to Richard Sillitoe who recalled his father reminiscing about this period, had these facilities not been available to ensure the comfort and pleasure of visitors, thereby maintaining the flow, Sillitoe might not have had the helping hand of brother fortune in the pursuit of his career about this time.

In the meantime, and until the right moment arrived, he went about his duties. The quarters of the Victoria Falls detachment, in contrast with the chintzy décor of the hotel, were not much different from those at Nyamandhlova. He rather enjoyed the spartan and primitive African round houses, and had grown used to them. When he was not on patrol in the bush he mixed with the patrons of the hotel, visited his colleagues of the Northern Rhodesia Police in Livingstone, and got to know some of the officers.

Livingstone was a larger, more developed community, twelve miles from Victoria Falls, and was the seat of the NRP headquarters. This force was run on slightly different lines from the BSAP. For example, the Europeans were mostly commissioned officers; a small number were NCOs, and the constables were all African askaris. Like the BSAP, it was a para-military force. It had more prestige, though, and Trooper Sillitoe considered transferring to the NRP. However, he was young, unknown and without influence; he realised as well as anyone how important it was to have connections. Besides, there was ample opportunity for excitement in doing the job he was doing; he enjoyed telling the story of his brush with a lion during this period.

This occurred on one of his many patrols to the Matetsi station, thirty miles south of Victoria Falls. Approaching the station, mounted on a mule, he mistook the frantic signals of a farmer for an enthusiastic welcome. Suddenly, five hundred pounds of African lion hurled itself at him from the cover of the brush. His startled mule plunged, reared across a stream and threw its rider. Sillitoe graphically describes the encounter. He is sent sprawling—his rifle falls some distance from him—he, the lion (which had earlier been wounded by the farmer) and the rifle form three points of an equilateral triangle—Sillitoe spits out a mouthful of dirt—the lion measures its foe—Sillitoe eyes the rifle—stalemate—suddenly there is a clatter of cooking pots and pans as Jim, his carrier, blunders on to the scene. The lion, unnerved, scurries into the safety of the bush. Once again Sillitoe demonstrates his tenacity by setting off to stalk his quarry after meeting up with the farmer. Needless to say, he succeeds in killing the lion and returning to the Falls with its pelt.

A few weeks after this incident, his stay in Victoria Falls was interrupted by a temporary posting back to Bulawayo, where he received his promotion to corporal. He was immensely proud of his promotion—far more, he later admitted, than of any other promotion or appointment of his entire career. This was understandable, for there is no question that he achieved the recognition entirely on his own merit.

When he was given the opportunity of choosing his next posting, he elected to return to Victoria Falls to lead the detachment there. His first move on his return was to reorganise his small command by making better use of his European troopers and African constables. He improved efficiency by setting up an information-gathering system in his district. He spruced up the police compound to set his little collection of huts apart from the rest of the community; his carefully mounted collection of photographs shows lines of white-washed stones delineating the paths and a carefully painted signpost reading 'BSAP ENQUIRIES AND CHARGE OFFICE'. It became a matter of pride for him, because he considered the post an important station in view of the impression it created among important visitors and tourists.

Even at this early stage (he was only twenty-one when he was promoted) he developed an unmistakable reserve. He was friendly but aloof, and one gets the impression from his photograph album that he hardly seemed to relax at all. He seems to be constantly on guard, ready to leap into action at a moment's notice; his expression is one of charming and rather superior reserve—like a leopard. But there was another side to his nature, and it showed in his deep concern for the native people among whom he lived and worked. The fact that he learned to speak their language so quickly is enough to indicate his efficiency and desire to communicate with them on equal terms.

Being an active sportsman himself, it was natural that he should introduce the Africans to soccer and cricket. Also, he probably had a hand in organising the Zambesi Regatta in 1910. This was a grand affair, in which everyone took part, and spectators for miles around flocked to the banks of the river for the occasion. The arrow-like boats of the local fishermen, seating four-man crews and more, were swift craft which sped like the wind. For the expatriate English it was a bizarre sight, the sweating crews angling their paddles through the blue waters to the rhythm of their ancient tribal chants.

All this time, he maintained a regular correspondence with Hubert, his brother, and kept in touch with Colonel Sinclair. From Sinclair he learned that an important visitor was coming to the Falls—Sir John Jackson, Sinclair's father-in-law. Jackson must have appeared as a welcome lifeline to Sillitoe, engulfed as he was in the stormy waters of competition. A meeting between the two is easily imagined: Sir John, making the long journey from England, anticipating the meeting with the young man he had known as a member of his son-in-law's household, pleased to have someone he knew waiting for him at the journey's end; Sillitoe, equally pleased to meet a link with home.

When they met, Sir John was suitably impressed with the progress young Sillitoe had made. He asked if there was anything he could do to be of service, and Sillitoe replied that he would very much like a commission in the Northern Rhodesia Police. The territory of Northern Rhodesia, like neighbouring Southern Rhodesia, was at that time administered under Royal Charter by the British South Africa Company. Sillitoe may or may not have known of Sir John's connections with the Company's board of directors, but he was more than satisfied when his patron promised to write to one of his acquaintances on the board and to make a recommendation.

Jackson kept his promise and Sillitoe's commission was granted without delay. He became a second lieutenant in the Barotse Native Police, centred in the Livingstone district.

On his discharge certificate from the British South Africa Police, it was noted that he had served the force for almost three years. It also reports him as being six feet in height, with light brown hair and grey eyes, and of fair complexion. (Either his eyes changed colour later to the 'intense blue' noted by reporters, or his principals in the BSAP were not very observant.) His character reference on his discharge document is uncommonly brief and to the point. It listed only four categories: education, sobriety, efficiency and general character. There were, however, five gradings to choose from—very good, good, fair, indifferent and bad. Corporal Sillitoe was rated 'very good' in all categories.

Chapter Three

Bwana Lieutenant

Gone were the bush hat, the riding boots and breeches, the rifle and bicycle with its leather gun case slung under the cross bar. In place of them, Second Lieutenant Sillitoe wore stove-pipe trousers, a black tie and narrow-collared white shirt, a smart jacket and pith helmet, and carried a new symbol of authority—a thin black walking stick. He had been transformed overnight, and how he enjoyed his new role! The modern brick buildings of the police barracks, the facilities and services available in Livingstone were in sharp contrast to the makeshift huts and primitive life of Victoria Falls. In a word, he found himself in civilised surroundings. Here there was unexcelled comfort, fine food, servants, fishing, hunting, all the amenities a young commissioned officer could wish for.

As a single man, his quarters were in the officers' mess. This was a large ugly building, though imposing to look at from a distance, and set apart from the other buildings in the barracks. The architect had attempted to give it a handsome appearance by adorning the entrance with an abnormally high arch with white stone facing, flanked on either side by a narrower arch to give balance. In fact, this was little more than a façade, because immediately to its rear the body of the building was of single-storey construction, reminding one of the grand-looking saloons of the early days of the American West. Any architectural beauty it might have possessed was dissipated by a great assortment of containers, stuffed with geraniums, that festooned the entrance. The pots were of all shapes and sizes—tin cans, a wooden barrel, stone jars of local manufacture. The hot African sun and daily watering kept the plants constantly in bloom, but despite all attempts to brighten things up, the building was as characterless as anything the pukka-sahibs of India could devise.

The mess stood on one side of the dusty barracks square. On the opposite side there nestled a conglomeration of long, low buildings housing the native police constables, offices, stores and stables. There was also a band-room. The Northern Rhodesia Police headquarters at Livingstone boasted a thirty-piece band which played at mess functions, on parade and, occasionally, for the public pleasure at events such as the Zambesi Regatta.

Sillitoe's new position enabled him to make new and influential friends, including his new commanding officer, Major Stennett. Major and Mrs Stennett were persons of importance in the community, but they went out of their way to take the newly-commissioned officer under their care, and so Percy became a frequent visitor to the Stennett residence. Major (later Lt-Colonel) Stennett and Sillitoe were to play an important part in the crucial moves of the coming East African Campaign. When Percy first met Stennett, the latter was in his early forties. He was a heavy man out of his prime who, by his appearance, betrayed a lack of physical exercise. If exercise he did take it must have been more cerebral than physical. Nevertheless, he was a kind and hospitable man who enjoyed the liking and respect of his subordinate officers. Mrs Stennett was a charming and vivacious little woman, a few years her husband's junior. She dressed trimly with throat-clutching necklines and full-length sleeves. Wherever she went she carried a parasol, and she adored posing with the handsome junior officers for her snapshot.

Sillitoe got on well and impressed Major Stennett with his keenness and devotion to his job. The major was undoubtedly responsible for recommending Sillitoe's appointment as escort officer to the Anglo-Belgian Boundary Commission which had been formed to determine the border between Northern Rhodesia and the Belgium Congo. So it was that in October 1911 2nd Lt Sillitoe, commanding a protective force of askaris, accompanied a large party north to Katanga Province. The company consisted of surveyors, political officers, a doctor, and the usual large contingent of porters, carriers, servants and cooks.

Travelling north from Livingstone to the area now known as the Copper Belt, in the general area of Ndola, the woodland country is typical of that to be found in the greater part of central Africa. It is rolling country with many deciduous trees, their canopies of leaves touching yet allowing sufficient light to penetrate to permit an undergrowth of grass, herbs and shrubs to grow. In places, woodland gives way to savannah in which tall grass becomes the dominant vegetation, and what trees there are lie widely spaced. Termite mounds are common, rising to heights of fifteen feet or more, like grotesque carbuncles on the landscape.

Sillitoe was in his element. He had an independent command, and he was leading the outdoor life which he loved, the camping, hunting and chance to explore. For the next year he conducted his party through the border country, and had every opportunity to study primitive tribesmen in territory virtually untouched by the white man. It was from these local tribesmen that Sillitoe learned the native art of elephant hunting.

They first chose a spot to which an animal might be lured, and there constructed an ingenious trap out of a pair of suitably-placed trees, and a mechanism consisting of a huge stake secured in an elevated position by lengths of twisted vine. The whole contraption had a built-in spring effect when triggered. When the unsuspecting elephant, decoyed from the herd, charged between the trees, it released the trigger mechanism. The suspended stake then swung down with great force to strike the beast at the back of the head, piercing its spine with unerring accuracy. Sillitoe records that he never heard of a native elephant trap failing.

It may seem facetious to draw a parallel between a big game hunter and a policeman but, in Sillitoe's case, there is a significance which should not be overlooked. He was obsessed with hunting. The enthusiasm with which he flung himself into the chase was one of calculated efficiency and determination. He was also agile, brave and quick-witted.

Describing his first hunt, when he bagged two elephants with a single-loading Martini-Enfield, he said:

'When I shot my first elephant there came up a big crowd of elephants, including one of those dangerous tuskless bulls called tondes. This tonde nosed round me, as it doubtless thought I had done an injustice to one of its mates, and I was in a bit of a sweat. The best thing I could think of doing was to lie behind the body of one of the elephants I had shot. I had an uncanny experience. Although the elephant was dead, its nerves were not, and, an elephant's nerves being pretty big, were capable of causing considerable twitches and lurchings of the brute's body. Every moment I fancied the animal would roll over on top of me. The tonde kept looking for me until I thought it was up with me but, ultimately, it got tired and went without discovering me.'

The Boundary Commission had enough work ahead of it to last two or three years, but Sillitoe's connections with it were abruptly severed when he contracted blackwater fever. This malady, a virulent form of malaria, is entirely confined to the white races and in 1911—and for many years to come—had a high mortality rate. Sillitoe was one of the lucky ones. After a long spell in Livingstone hospital, he returned to England to recuperate, In June 1913, on his way back to Africa on board the *Gloucester Castle* he met Dorothy Watson who, with her parents and brother, Cecil, was making the Grand Tour or rather as earlier noted, that version of it known as 'doing the east'.

The Watsons were a Yorkshire family from Elloughton, Brough, near Hull, John Watson being senior partner in the Hull architectural firm of Watson & Carter. He was well known in the city as a magistrate and, for his work connected with the welfare and housing of old people, he was awarded the MBE. There were three children. The eldest, Bernard, had emigrated to South Africa in 1911 to start a sugar plantation with capital provided by his father. Then there was Dorothy, a brunette nineteen years old in 1913, and Cecil, a year younger.

John Watson was a prosperous, tight-fisted businessman, then in his mid-fifties. He was a staid, conservative man, fully conscious of his importance in the community. Bluff, gruff and rigidly set in his ways, he conducted himself with the air of the patrician he was. His uncompromising inflexibility was to lead to difficulties in his relationship with his future son-in-law but, in June 1913, that was in the nebulous future. His primary purpose in making this journey was to visit Bernard and find out for himself how well his son was doing with the investment. Two years, he considered, was ample time to clear the land and plant a crop. Also, being an admirer of Cecil Rhodes, magistrate Watson was intent on touring the fabulous Rhodes empire.

It was perfect weather when the ship weighed anchor for sailing down the Solent. Mrs Watson was not a talkative woman, deferring to her husband in all things, but she remarked how wise Papa had been to decline the pressing offers of friends to see them off. 'How one can recognise people in that sea of faces is beyond me,' she remarked loftily as the lines were slipped and the liner got under way.

Dorothy, sitting at the end of the bench which accommodated the four of them, had eyed every young man mounting the companionway with lively interest. Mrs Watson was rather fussy about her children's behaviour in public and once, when she thought Dorothy was too inquisitive, said ,'Dorothy, I think you would be better occupied reading like the rest of us.'

Suddenly, Sillitoe was standing beside her with a quoit in his hand and wearing a broad, impudent grin. She hadn't noticed his coming. She returned the grin with a smile, the merest flicker of amusement in her eyes.

'Do you play quoits?' he asked.

'A little,' she said, immediately standing up, 'but not very well.' Her mother and father were both looking at her with expressions of shock, and Cecil, who was sitting at the far end of the bench, was too embarrassed for words and got up to lean over the railing, thereby excluding himself from the confrontation. Papa Watson made a noise in his throat, and Percy thought it about time he introduced himself. Many times in the years to come, Dollie laughed about this first meeting, and said how much it upset her parents. Her father thought it a most impudent way of introducing oneself to strangers, while her mother wondered what in the world the manners of young people were coming to. But Dollie did something she had never done before; without so much as a 'by your leave', she went off to play quoits.

Percy had introduced himself as 'Tod' and Dorothy had called herself 'Dollie'. He was tall and handsome and she admired his boldness. To his way of thinking she was an extremely uncomplicated type of girl with an appealing vitality. They kept close company from then on, and in the dining room, with her father's permission, Tod shared the Watson table. Their friendship was quickly recognised for what it was, a shipboard romance, but neither minded the gossip in the least. In the evenings, when most of the younger people gathered in the saloon, Dollie accompanied on the piano while Tod sang. They had a favourite song, the Edwardian ballad, 'She was only a Bird in a Gilded Cage', which would be called for nightly amid the hoots and banter of the other young passengers. For Dollie and Tod it had a special meaning.

It was natural that they should discuss their respective families. Tod, who felt the Watsons kept an unnecessarily close watch on Dorothy particularly where he was concerned, asked one day, 'Do you ever get out of the cage they keep you in?'

She gave him a conspiratorial laugh, 'With your connivance they might open it and let me fly.'

By the time they reached their destination, Durban, the two were engaged, though not without considerable reservations on John Watson's part. Mama once more deferred, no doubt, to her husband's opinion. It was not enough that his daughter should fall in love with a police lieutenant about whom he knew next to nothing. They had not met the Sillitoe family, the young man had nothing but his own word to recommend him; he could be an utter scoundrel, for all John Watson could tell, and to give consent to the marriage at this stage would have been like investing hard-earned capital in penny stocks. Therefore, until he knew much more about Tod Sillitoe, the engagement was to be considered strictly tentative. For this reason there was a change in plan: the whole family would visit Livingstone. Meanwhile after the Watsons had visited Bernard in Durban, Tod continued his journey to Livingstone to report for duty.

From Durban, where they took time off to visit Bernard's sugar plantation at Ifafa, the Watsons travelled north to Bulawayo and Salisbury. In Rhodesia they visited Rhodes's grave at Matipos, the monument to Major Wilson, of Shangani River fame, and then made their leisurely way north to Victoria Falls where accommodation had been booked for them at the hotel.

Tod wangled some leave to be with them at Victoria Falls, and to conduct them personally around the local tourist sights. The Stennetts were delighted to meet the Watsons and invited them to spend a few days with them in Livingstone. Mrs Stennett, the perfect hostess, arranged dinner parties and lively entertainment for the visitors so that nothing should mar their stay. Despite the warmth of their reception and the unstinting hospitality, Dollie found the heat intolerable, the flies and insects abominable, and the primitive conditions completely foreign to her tastes. She was not pioneer material, but with admirable forbearance she kept her true feelings submerged. Her father was still unable to hit it off with Tod, but, like her disenchantment with Africa, he managed for her sake to keep his feelings below the surface. He thought the young man a little too 'bold' for his own good, by which he meant too spirited and sure of himself, and considered that Percy could do with taking down a peg or two. The feelings were mutual, as a matter of fact, but suitably disguised also by Percy, who thought Dollie's father nothing but an old fuddy-duddy and as cantankerous as a bear. Despite these opinions, Dollie adored her police lieutenant, and Papa Watson was considerate enough to give his consent to the marriage before the family bid the Stennetts and Tod Sillitoe goodbye and continued their journey.

On her return to England, Dollie met a very personable young man who lost no time in pursuing her—she was a very attractive girl. World events conspired to keep her and Tod apart for the next seven years, and she was tempted many times to throw Tod over and marry his rival, but each time she relented.

Unaware of this fierce competition so far away, Sillitoe undertook a new task. He was to open up a police post at Lusaka, a place halfway to the copper belt. Destined to become the capital of present-day Zambia, in those days it was nothing more than a railway halt with a few huts, stores and blacksmith's forge to mark its location. Sillitoe's party consisted of himself, two European sergeants, half a dozen askaris and a civilian works engineer, Charlie Warriner.

Warriner's task was to sink a well, by all accounts a formidable undertaking, since it required the use of explosives. The works engineer was typical of a certain type of Englishman that one meets in the oddest corners of the world: Jack-of-all-trades, prepared to work all hours of the day and night in return for a nominal wage and 'consideration' from his employers. Generally single, such men are not averse to 'going native' for the duration of the job but, while they are easy to get along with, they are generally oblivious to any kind of authority. To this, Charlie Warriner was no exception. He was outspoken and treated all men with equal candour. Sillitoe had enormous respect for him and they got along well together.

Charlie's attitude to authority and his outspoken temperament gave rise to an incident which tested his superior's power of persuasion to the elastic limit. The Acting Administrator, a man named McKinnon paid a site visit with his ADC in tow. He was unwise and self-important enough to tell the works engineer he didn't think the job was going fast enough.

'If you don't think I'm doing it fast enough, mister,' Charlie replied, 'then you'd better bloody well do it yourself.'

The administrator was outraged, stamped off in high dudgeon and, directly he reached Livingstone, had Warriner dismissed for insubordination. Sillitoe was in a dilemma. It was not his place to resist the heavy hand of authority, but first-rate engineers, however unyielding, were a rarity. The messages began to fly while Charlie, impervious to the storm raging above his head, continued work on the well. What did he care? He shrugged his shoulders while the lieutenant petitioned his superiors, cajoling them to reconsider the decision. Without Warriner, the job would have to come to a standstill; besides, he was too good a man to lose. In the end he managed to have the decision reversed and the works engineer stayed. In itself this was a small incident, but it was destined to be repeated many times during his career. Sillitoe's willingness to stand up to those above him on behalf of those under his command was one of his most admirable traits and marked him out early as a leader of men.

The rest of Sillitoe's time in Lusaka followed a familiar pattern, with frequent patrols in the bush, the settling of disputes among the settlers and tribesmen, and chasing after diamond smugglers. The highlight of his stay there was a visit paid to the area by Sir Leander Starr Jameson. Dr 'Jim' Jameson, Prime Minister of the Cape Colony from 1904 to 1908, had become President of the British South Africa Company following the death of the Duke of Abercorn. He had become frail, and spent most of his time in England. His visit to the Lusaka District, to talk to the settlers and to learn at first hand how things were going at the north end of the company's private empire, was to be his last to Africa. As one who had been a close companion and confident of Cecil Rhodes, Jameson made a great impression on Sillitoe; he was one of those men who had the rare distinction of being a legend in his own lifetime. He and his party remained in Lusaka for three days, and while there is no record of what he thought of Sillitoe, he was impressed enough with the job the latter was doing to promise the loan of three BSAP troopers from Southern Rhodesia to lend a hand. He kept his word and the three troopers arrived a short time later.

The last part of 1913 and first half of 1914 was a happy period for Percy. He had risen from the ranks, learned to speak two difficult African languages, helped open up a great deal of new territory, and walked over much of the unknown face of central Africa. He had achieved more in five years than most men achieve in a lifetime. He had a little money saved and his future seemed as safe and secure as British Consuls. And then there was Dollie. They discussed plans for their coming marriage in every letter they exchanged. With home leave due at the end of the year,

Percy was the happiest of men. Oblivious to the approaching storm, he had not the slightest inkling that before the year was out he would be involved in the fiercest holocaust of all time.

Chapter Four

The Askari War

Sillitoe was still at Lusaka at the outbreak of the First World War. In common with his compatriots scattered over a hundred thousand square miles of territory, he had little idea of what was going on in Europe, but it was not long at all before he was deeply involved in the East African campaign.

German East Africa—Tanganyika—corresponding to present-day Tanzania, was securely boxed in. To the north lay Kenya and Uganda, under British control and influence; to the south, Nyasaland, a British protectorate, and the two Rhodesias; to the west was Lake Tanganyika, forming a natural barrier, and the Belgian Congo; and to the east, the Indian Ocean. On the other hand, the German command began the conflict with every advantage—weapons, supplies, a comparatively large fighting force, and a cadre of professional officers. According to his own account the German commander, Colonel (later General) von Lettaw-Vorbeck, had 216 European officers and service men, 45 European police, 2,150 askari policemen and 2,540 askari soldiers —almost 5,000 men under arms.

The railway networks, in both German- and British-held territories, were strategically important to the antagonists as communication and supply routes. For these reasons, the railways became prime targets for capture and control by the opposing forces. In Kenya the British had constructed a line from Mombasa to Kisumu. In the south, the railhead had been pushed from Livingstone to Broken Hill, a small mining community situated mid-way between Livingstone and Lake Tanganyika. This same line was to be extended to Elizabethville and Fungurume by the summer of 1915. A German railway system, one thousand miles long, connected Dar-es-Salaam on the coast with Kigoma on

Lake Tanganyika, and this became the spinal cord of German East Africa. The German engineers had enormous difficulties to contend with in building the line—far more than the British in the Rhodesian railway system. Quite apart from technical and administrative problems, the Germans had to deal with hostile tribesmen over whose territory the track was constructed. In spite of all this, the central railway was completed and opened for traffic in July 1914. Edmund Dane, in *British Campaigns in Africa and the Pacific*,* says, 'Whether by design or accident, there were in the colony a number of German officers who had come out to assist in the celebration of the opening.'

In addition to their railway, and with the exception of Lake Nyasa, the Germans had control of all the inland waterways. In particular, they controlled Lake Tanganyika by means of the armed steamer *Hedwig von Wissmann*, a factor which figured prominently in German strategy. There was also the 1,500-ton *Graf von Götzen* under construction at Kigoma, which we will come to shortly. A factor which must not be overlooked was the presence of the German cruiser, *Königsberg*, in the Indian Ocean; this, however, was opposed by a British naval force consisting of two old cruisers, the *Astroe* and *Pegasus*, and a number of smaller guard ships.

Lettaw-Vorbeck's plan of offensive was simple. Believing his countrymen would have a swift success in Europe and, as a result, would solve his re-provisioning problems, he split his forces into three commands, with the idea of slicing into the enemy in a single, three-pronged, lightning attack. By electing to fight on three widely-separated fronts, he deprived his commanders of the strength that comes from mutual support. If any one striking force ran into difficulties, there was little hope of its receiving help from either of the other two. This dissipation of strength served to weaken Lettaw-Vorbeck's position from the very beginning of the East Africa campaign. One prong was directed north into Kenya to occupy Nairobi and Mombasa and to seize the Mombasa–Kisumu railway. The second was to move along the spinal cord, strike north along the shores of Lake Victoria Nyanza, and invade Uganda. The third and southern prong, under the command of Count von Falkenstein, was to pierce the border with British territory in the south with the idea of cutting off all communication between South Africa and the

* Hodder & Stoughton, London, 1919.

central Africa lake region: with control of Lake Tanganyika, von Falkenstein stood a very good chance of striking through Northern Rhodesia to link up with German South West Africa and so achieve his commander's objective. To move through Northern Rhodesia, von Falkenstein first had to protect his eastern flank by gaining control of Lake Nyasa. By the time Lettaw-Vorbeck had set his three-pronged attack in motion, the *Königsberg* had relieved pressure on the seaward flank by routing the British naval force—for a time at any rate—and was steaming north to harass allied merchant ships. These opening manœuvres occurred within a month of the outbreak of hostilities.

Compared with the British forces opposing him in the south, von Falkenstein had a formidable army consisting of 700 rifles, 8 Maxim machine guns, and a battery of field guns all of which he assembled at New Langenburg, a strong base in German territory. It was a good opening move.

The British defence of the border with Tanganyika was the responsibility of two commands. The first, in Nyasaland, was headed by Captain Barton of the Northamptonshire Regiment (48th of Foot), seconded to the King's African Rifles. He had two companies under his command. To this scratch force he was able to add a number of volunteers, a staff of colonial officials and some European officers. Barton's first move was to commandeer an assorted flotilla of small craft, transport his 'army' from Zomba to Karonga, a village on the north-east shore of Lake Nyasa, and there consider what to do next.

The other command was in Northern Rhodesia, where, on 14th August 1914, they were totally unprepared for war. The authorities in Livingstone reacted quickly enough, and mobilised the available forces in a week, but the Livingstone command, such as it was, had to split its force in two. Considering the possible threat from German South West Africa, there was no other course but to despatch the largest contingent, a combined force of BSAP and NRP mounted troopers and askari rifles, to occupy the Caprivi Strip with all haste. Colonel Stennett (recently promoted) meanwhile took command of the smaller column and headed for the north-east border. His objective was Abercorn, a small outpost some fourteen miles from the southern edge of Lake Tanganyika, and then occupied by a handful of police and askaris. At this juncture, Lieutenant Sillitoe came into the picture.

At the outbreak of hostilities the forces of both Rhodesia and the Nyasaland Protectorate were equipped with little more than small arms, including a few machine guns. There was no artillery. A panic call to Southern Rhodesia revealed that a screw gun, together with two hundred rounds of ammunition and a supply of black powder, was in working order and available. Sillitoe was therefore ordered to leave his post at Lusaka and go to Broken Hill, there to await the arrival of the field-piece.

The screw gun, referred to in Sillitoe's autobiography as 'an ancient museum piece', was a rifled 2·5-inch muzzle-loading mountain gun which was used by the British Army until 1896, when it was replaced by the 10-pounder breech-loader mountain gun. The screw gun got its name from the fact that the muzzle and breech sections, held together by means of threaded steel jacket, could be dismantled. The carriage, wheels and axle could also be taken apart for transportation by mules. No single piece weighed more than two hundred pounds, and for this reason the weapon was considered ideal by artillerymen for military operations in remote and mountainous regions. The effective range of the screw gun was about 2,500 yards, but its main disadvantage was in the use of black powder as the charge. When a shot was fired it produced a considerable volume of black smoke, an obvious drawback if enemy artillery was within range. Sillitoe arranged for 600 native carriers to assemble at Broken Hill to carry the contraption, its powder and ammunition to Abercorn. Meanwhile, action was about to begin at the front.

Barton had no idea where the enemy would strike, but had a shrewd idea they would try to take Karonga. He also knew that it would be foolhardy to concentrate his entire force in one spot in that type of country. The border was wide open, giving a resourceful enemy an equally open invitation to cross at a convenient place and encircle them. He therefore split his force and moved into the bush country, keeping within striking distance of Karonga in case it should come under attack. Taking care to maintain good communications with the two companies of askaris remaining in Karonga, he cautiously reconnoitred as wide a front as his slender strength allowed.

Barton was correct in supposing that von Falkenstein had his eye on Karonga. To have possession of the village, with its facilities on Lake Nyasa, would be no small achievement: it would mean that the only German ship operating on the lake, the *Hermann von Wissman* (not to be confused with the *Hedwig von*

Wissmann on Lake Tanganyika) would have a safe base from which to operate. Von Falkenstein attacked Karonga during Barton's absence in the last week of August, but met unexpected resistance. Astonishingly, Barton's two companies of African Rifles offered such a strong resistance that they sent the attackers scurrying back in the direction of their own territory. Barton was returning to lend a hand when he heard the news of the successful repulse. He also received a lead on the direction in which von Falkenstein was heading. He therefore did a smart about-turn and hurried his contingent to the Kasoa River, where he laid an ambush. Luck, a cool head and decisive action counted in his favour. Within a few hours, von Falkenstein's column, still licking its wounds from the earlier encounter, drove smack into the trap. Barton's haul of booty from this little adventure netted 10,000 rounds of ammunition, two field-guns, a couple of Maxim machine guns and a large quantity of stores and provisions. The enemy retreated, for the second time in disarray, and, unpursued, disappeared into the Tanganyika bush, battered and bruised, but not demolished.

Von Falkenstein evidently decided to try his luck at the Lake Tanganyika end of the border. Instead of driving his column through the unprotected border and heading for the Chinganzi River, and thence curving north to join with his compatriots on the Lake east of Abercorn, he chose to retreat into home ground and execute a manœuvre which brought him before the Abercorn police outpost. The movement of men and equipment, however, kept the Germans occupied from late August until well into September.

During this same period Stennett's column was moving north, struggling through an unseasonable rain storm to reach Abercorn. By 8th September it would be a beleaguered outpost. And where was Lt. Sillitoe during the period when the opposing forces were moving into position?

The screw gun had arrived at Broken Hill about mid-August, accompanied by Corporal Horton and three troopers of the British South Africa Police who, because they had some knowledge of artillery, were to attend the gun. Sillitoe scratched his head and wondered how to deal with the thing, massive and dripping with thick preservative grease in the hot sun. It is curious that with his knowledge of mules, and the fact that the gun was especially adapted to this mode of transport, he chose instead to employ native porters. With the help of the troopers the gun was dismantled, while Corporal Horton built a cradle for carrying the barrel which, weighing two hundred pounds, was the largest single piece. Carried stretcher fashion by four porters, it was a comfortable load—for no more than a hundred yards at a time.

Sillitoe knew the watercourses would soon be in flood. He therefore decided to choose a route which followed higher ground. This meant veering slightly to the east for about one-third of the march, then striking north instead of moving in a direct line for Abercorn. Because he was to travel in unfamiliar country, he used his Barotse tribesmen as guides along the well-trodden paths connecting village to village.

The community of Broken Hill turned out *en masse* to cheer them on their way, and watched until the last carrier in the straggling line, a mile or more in length, disappeared from sight.

It was an exhausting march from the outset. Winding through villages, skirting escarpments, and lugging the dismembered weapon up steep bluffs was heavy work yet, under Sillitoe's leadership, the sweating carriers kept up a gruelling pace which averaged eighteen miles a day. Snaking over the hills, Sillitoe's thin black line of carriers chanted a rhythmic song in praise of the precious load they carried, needing no urging from Bwana Sillitoe to get a move on. Being paid for making war was a novelty to them.

Meanwhile, there was not a word of von Falkenstein. Captain Barton had sent news of his successes south, and native drums spread the message far and wide, but in Livingstone there persisted an understandable anxiety. They did not know where the German column would strike next, and they still had no idea of the enemy's strength. While the British were pondering this and other questions, there came news of the siege of Abercorn.

Stennett's column was thirty miles away when word of the German presence was brought to him. Had his column been mounted it would have made a gallant dash to relieve Abercorn, but mounted it was not. The country was treacherous and miserable to move over in teeming rain. Stennett nevertheless forced the pace, marching his troops through the night, and managed to cover the thirty miles in the next twenty-four hours. He arrived in Abercorn on 9th September, just in the nick of time. The sudden appearance and deployment of Stennett's battalion-strength column were enough to convince von Falkenstein that Abercorn was an unhealthy place and he tactfully retired.

A few days later, Sillitoe's brigade of irregulars trudged into the outpost with their precious screw gun, footsore but happy. Sillitoe had covered the 520 miles in thirty days—a magnificent achievement.

Other reinforcements were trickling north to strengthen the border, including a battalion of askari rifles, despatched from the Belgian Congo. In a very short time Lettaw-Vorbeck's southern prong had its tip blunted, and there resulted a lull which allowed the British and their allies to get themselves organised along the Tanganyika border. But if they thought the action was over they were mistaken. There was still German domination of Lake Tanganyika to be reckoned with.

The armed steamer *Hedwig von Wissmann* had done a creditable job of knocking out of action all other craft on the lake, and from then on had acted in a thoroughly objectionable manner by raiding the enemy shores at will. Lake Tanganyika, it should be noted, is a huge body of water some four hundred miles long and forty miles wide; over this great lake the *Hedwig von Wissmann* roamed at liberty like a prowling lion. Shortly after von Falkenstein's repulse at Abercorn, the *Hedwig von Wissmann* put in an appearance at the south end of the lake.

Orders were given for the screw gun to be brought up there, but Sillitoe did not have the satisfaction of seeing it used against the *Hedwig von Wissmann*, although he was sent to the lakeshore from Abercorn to investigate a report that the ship was in the vicinity. On that mission, he met up with an enemy force and exchanged fire, but left the area before the gun could be put into action. Promoted to captain, he took over a newly-formed company of Askari Rifles and moved inland along the border to form part of the defensive line.

For the next few weeks the attackers and defenders scurried about the south-east corner of Tanganyika and adjacent territory of Northern Rhodesia in a huge game of hide-and-seek. Effectively a stalemate, it continued well into the new year, during which period a number of changes of fortune occurred to affect the campaign in general, and Sillitoe in particular.

Command of the southern forces opposing the Germans was taken over by General Northey, who took steps to build up his forces and supplies for a large-scale offensive. Two other important events took place. First, the *Königsberg*, which had enjoyed a spectacular career for a short period following the opening of hostilities, was forced to retire up the Rufiji River delta to carry out engine repairs. Discovered by a hunting British naval squadron, she was attacked there and knocked out of action. Despite this setback, the *Königsberg's* commander, Admiral Max Looff, succeeded in transferring the cruiser's armaments ashore for use by the German land forces, which action was to provide the Germans with a superior arsenal of artillery throughout the East African campaign. The second important development was the successful transportation of two armed motor-boats from Cape Town following their shipment from England, over the Mitumba Mountains, down the Lualaba River, and thence by railway and another river journey to Kalemie on the Belgian side of Lake Tanganyika.

The plan for this extraordinary exercise was conceived and mapped out by a big-game hunter, John R. Lee. However, the expedition was under the command of Commander Spicer-Simpson who, although possessed of an unusually strong streak of vanity which detracted from his leadership qualities, not only brought the tiny boats to the lake in seaworthy condition but also achieved the objectives set out by his superiors.* These were, first, to search for and destroy the *Hedwig von Wissmann* and any other German vessels and thereby take control of Lake Tanganyika and, secondly, to render assistance to General Northey's forces in any northward advance into German territory. Spicer-Simpson captured a small German vessel, the *Kingani*, in his first engagement on the lake and sank the *Hedwig von Wissmann* in the second battle, thereby winning control of the lake for the British and Belgian forces. The case of the *Graf von Götzen*, earlier mentioned as being under construction at Kigoma, is an interesting one. Throughout the spring and summer of 1915 the *Graf von Götzen* lay in the slipway at Kigoma under construction. Fitted out with armament from the *Königsberg*, she was launched and ventured across Lake Tanganyika on 25th January 1916, steaming past Spicer-Simpson's flotilla base at Kalemie. This huge landlocked warship had control of Lake Tanganyika for the taking. For some reason which has never been explained, the *Graf von Götzen* returned to Kigoma where she remained, her *Königsberg*

---

* An account of this remarkable achievement is given by Peter Shankland in *The Phantom Flotilla*, Collins, London, 1968.

guns replaced by wooden dummies, until she was scuttled by the retreating German forces some months later. In any case, from January 1916 on, Spicer-Simpson's tiny warships were able to plough the lake at will.

Northey was now able to launch a major offensive along the lakeshore into Tanganyika without fear of having his communications cut in the rear by enemy troops landed from the lake. Sillitoe and his askaris took part in Northey's northward advance. It was a remote kind of war that they fought, and it was impossible to appreciate the overall strategy when moving through thick woodland vegetation or lying in the stygian darkness listening to the sounds of the bush. Sillitoe's detachment moved out of the fighting area for a rest and back in again and out again so many times that he lost count. Far more than any bullets of the enemy, disease and fever took a great toll of the combatants, friend and foe alike. In 1916, after nearly two years of active campaigning, Sillitoe went down with enteric fever, was removed from the front and sent to Johannesburg for treatment.

There, lying in bed at the military hospital, he became extremely depressed. The confinement and lack of activity were irksome. It was not as though he suffered the wounds of war. To be laid low by disease was more than he could bear. The only consolation of his forced stay in Johannesburg was that Dollie's letters arrived sooner—the transports were slow enough, but at the fighting front, where he was constantly on the move, letters could take months to get to him.

She gave lively accounts in her letters of what she called 'darkest domestica' but, underlying this unfailing good spirit, was the tragic loss of her brother Cecil. He had obtained a commission in the King's Own Yorkshire Light Infantry only to be blown to pieces almost as soon as he stepped ashore in France. She couldn't get over this and no one, not even Tod, could console her. They had been as close as brother and sister could be and nothing could make up for the grief she felt. But in all else Dollie was effervescent. Her letters revealed her as a sensible girl who was in every way as shrewd and sound as her father the J.P. Tod cursed the war for intervening in his private affairs. They had had such high hopes of getting married in 1914. 'Never mind', he wrote from his hospital bed, 'the way things are going out here, the war will be over in a couple of months.'

The war changed many things. It altered the face of places

Sillitoe thought unchangeable, including Livingstone. Stopping there for a few days on his way north following his recovery and convalescence, he found the town completely different from the place he had left only two years before. In late 1916 he could see that new buildings had sprung up, the army had established stores depots, and the streets were thronged with military personnel on leave. Gone was the old sedate atmosphere of Edwardian reserve. There was a licentious gaiety about the place with newcomers; barkeepers and prostitutes were doing a roaring trade. In this desert, the Stennett house stood like an oasis of tranquillity, and he visited Mrs Stennett for tea before continuing his journey.

Military operations being by their nature destructive, it was only right that they bestowed some benefits on the undeveloped land. An improved communications system was one. When Captain Sillitoe travelled north to report for duty, hopefully to resume command of his askari company, he did so along a new, serviceable road. The journey from Broken Hill to Abercorn (and from there to Zomba) was altogether different from the last time, when he had foot-slogged the whole way. Signs of activity along the route were unmistakable. Convoys of empty trucks, with ambulances and wrecked equipment in tow, ploughed through the dust, and there were encampments, workshops and rest areas dotted along the way. Tod was getting the smell of battle in his nostrils again; but war, like the tide, waits for no man, and the situation had by now changed considerably.

During his absence, the British troops under Colonel Murray had, on 15th June, left Bismarckburg to pursue the retreating Germans. British seaplanes had a few days earlier attacked the *Graf von Götzen* at Kigoma, claimed a direct hit and reported her out of action. Towards the end of the following month General Tombeur, who commanded the Belgian arm of the allied forces, captured Kigoma to discover the *Graf von Götzen* scuttled off the harbour entrance. Before their retreat, German blue-jackets had greased her machinery (they clearly intended to return) and pulled the plug.

The steady build up of the allied forces, supplies and equipment throughout the last half of 1915 and first half of 1916, and the constant drain of Lettaw-Vorbeck's resources which he could not get replenished, gave the allies the upper hand. The enemy, by late 1916, was confined to the eastern half of its former territories, all the time being compressed into a smaller and smaller area by the weight of superior forces. Lettaw-Vorbeck had made —perhaps unavoidably—the classical German error of fighting on a multiplicity of fronts and paid the price for doing so.

Chapter Five

Political Officer

Nothing depresses an active man more than a protracted period of inactivity. Long weeks of illness and convalescence had naturally sharpened Sillitoe's appetite for action. He reported to Northey's headquarters at Zomba, the capital of Nyasaland, relishing the idea of meeting his company of askaris again, only to be bitterly disappointed. The war—or what was left of it in East Africa—had passed him by.

He was not, however, condemned to further idleness. The conquest of so much Tanganyikan territory presented Northey's staff officers with a number of administrative problems and, among these, that of finding competent officers who were knowledgeable in African affairs was of the utmost importance. With Sillitoe's policing experience and fluent command of at least three difficult African languages, plus a smattering of Swahili, no one in their right mind was about to squander him at the fighting front. In any case, by this time, the war had moved far into the eastern half of the territory and there was not the same urgent need for front-line men as at the beginning. He was assigned half a dozen askaris to act as constables and ordered to report with them to Bismarckburg, the capital of a province of the same name.

To his dismay, the African 'constables' proved to be askaris in name only. Not only did they not have the foggiest notion of police work, there wasn't one among the lot who knew one end of a rifle from the other. Captain Sillitoe, so recently in charge of a crack infantry company, was now reduced to remaining in Zomba for a few days, trying to lick his policemen into shape before taking them to Bismarckburg.

The provincial capital, much the worse for wear from the

recent fighting, was swarming with army supply officers and military personnel when he arrived. The harassed town administrator was striving hard to sort out the chaos. No one cared —nor had the time to spare if they did care—for the interests of the bewildered natives whose lives had been disrupted by the passing flame of war. Sillitoe and his small police force were welcome additions to the administrator's forces. They did useful work in helping restore order, but Sillitoe had hardly had time to settle into a proper routine before he was told to pack his bags and move with his askaris to Ilunde, a tiny hamlet in a remote district some 150 miles south of Tabora.

To this day Ilunde and its surrounding district has remained a backwater. It is located plumb in the centre of a hilly, forested country in which a number of rivers have their source, and from which they flow in all directions of the compass before eventually turning east to finish up in Lake Tanganyika. It is unhealthy country, infested with tsetse-fly and mosquito, a God-forsaken place where forest and dry grassland, searing heat and torrential rains conspire to make life abysmally difficult. Grass fires, set alight by the scorching sun, sweep across the landscape and, amidst this torture to man and beast, the inhabitants eke out their primitive existence. Even today there is no direct route from Ilunde to Tabora; one must travel either east or west for many miles along dusty dirt roads, then strike north. In 1917, the communications were even more primitive; mail was brought and despatched by native runner, the journey took five or six days; supplies were brought in on the heads of the bearers; and for medical help he relied on his own good sense or the local witch-doctor. Yet none of these drawbacks prevented him from getting himself organised and making the best of a bad job—it was not as though he were a stranger to isolation.

Upon his arrival, Sillitoe announced his presence in the district by despatching his askaris to the headmen in the surrounding village. Then, with methodical thoroughness, he set out himself, with a couple of askari escorts, to pay his respects, assuring each chieftain in turn that his presence meant peace and the rule of law. In a short time he became a familiar sight, inspiring confidence and, perhaps, grudging admiration, for he would not deign to carry a gun; he left that to his askaris. That confidence was to be tested soon enough.

He had known from the beginning that small bands of German-trained askaris were roaming in the district, carrying on a half-hearted guerilla warfare, but bent more on imposing their own brigandish authority over the locals than on maintaining a military posture. Elusive as wild cats stealing through the forest, but equipped with modern small-arms, these bands raided villages at will for their food and other supplies. Sillitoe was undeterred by their presence and considered his own influence and leadership in the district a far more potent weapon than any force of arms. His ability to inspire the confidence of the indigenous tribesmen in himself stemmed more from his personality, his police training and experience with the BSAP than in behaving as a military-style commander. His policeman-style of leadership depended on 'public' co-operation (in the sense that the local tribesmen constituted his public). He won this confidence by the manner in which he approached and dealt with village headmen and tribal chiefs—a technique developed by the BSAP and NRP in which troopers and officers were taught to respect social more and customs of the subject peoples. Arriving at a kraal, he would ask for the headman and exchange lengthy greetings without which no native would begin a conversation; he would then enquire as to the welfare of the people in the kraal or village, discuss the state of the crops and the condition of the cattle. Accepting the hospitality which followed (generally a drawn-out affair), there would be ample time to discuss questions of mutual concern and interest. Questions of local government and communication between Sillitoe the administrator and the headman would be settled—an exercise calling for tact and diplomacy. A promise to provide information and to exchange messages by means of runners would then be obtained, by which means Sillitoe would assure himself knowledge of what was happening in a particular village and its surrounding area. The use of runners was the common means of communication: they brought Sillitoe mail and supplies from his headquarters in Tabora, carried messages to the outlying communities, and brought in information useful to the administration of the district. Response from headmen to this system varied from village to village, naturally, and while the system took weeks to develop, Sillitoe did provide himself with a reliable information-gathering network. His askaris, the headmen and the runners soon became his eyes and ears so that he did, in effect, organise an intelligence network as an important tool for the sound administration of his district.

He had not been in Ilunde more than a few weeks before word was brought to him of a hostile presence—an armed band of askaris, twenty strong, led by two Germans, and intent on wiping out his police post. Relying on the inquisitive nature of the local tribesmen, Sillitoe had a large fire built. It blazed like a beacon, and, true to his expectations, the villagers in the vicinity flocked to it like moths attracted by a candle. In addition, he sent runners to summon the chiefs and their able-bodied men, then set himself to wait patiently in the crackling light of the fire. Not until a sizeable crowd had congregated did he speak, and then it was briefly and to the point.

'The Germans know you have been friendly towards me,' he told the gathering. 'If they do not kill you they will certainly steal your food and burn your villages. Do you want me as your friend, or do you want the Germans to come back?'

While the chiefs held council he moved among them offering his advice, leaning nonchalantly on his walking stick or poking it into the ground; it was an effective demonstration of his calmness and imperturbability. The chiefs were not long in coming to a decision. The bwana was right—he *was* preferable to the alternative. They bade him lead them to the foe.

'Then arm yourselves,' he told the assembly, 'and let us be on our way.'

Scouts were sent ahead to reconnoitre, while Sillitoe followed at a leisurely pace leading the main force, 'armed with hunting spears', he records, 'and some comically ancient muskets dating from around 1800 which would not in any circumstance fire'.

He was fortunate. One of his scouts was captured by the approaching enemy and the leaders, hearing from their captive's lips that three hundred armed men were coming to do battle, promptly fled the field with their followers and disappeared for good. It was a happy, bloodless victory for Ilunde's administrator. By this bold action he took on a new dimension in the eyes of the natives, and from then on he was a hero to be welcomed wherever he went. His rule of law was firmly established, and the remaining nine months of his stay at Ilunde were relatively peaceful.

This did not mean he remained idle: there was still work to be done. Whether he was instructed by his superiors to take a census of his district or did so on his own volition is uncertain, but the fact is, he did take one, going about the task in his usual methodical fashion. Writing later of his work as a chief constable in various cities, writers have praised Sillitoe for 'applying methods developed in Africa' in dealing with city gangs. No one, it seems, bothered to enquire or explain exactly what those methods were, but it is now abundantly clear that his 'methods' were centred simply on a well-organised system of gathering and collating information. This is evident in everything he did, whether as Chief Constable of Glasgow, Director General of MI5 or head of the Diamond Security Organisation.

His census-taking operation, whilst it was a formidable task, was not as difficult as it would first appear—although one might expect it to be a tedious one. Each village was a self-contained social unit, and there were no odd families living in the bush to be accounted for. Having plotted each community on what must have been a pretty blank map of his district, he set out to visit them all, counting his inhabitants as he went. When the census was finished he was able to report to his superiors in Tabora that there were some 20,000 people in the Ilunde district in mid-1918.

In many ways Sillitoe was a loner, wandering as he did over the face of east and central Africa for years on end. Constantly on the move, he made very few friends, yet the lack of company of his own kind made him very self-sufficient. He had been in Africa now for ten years, except for one short break in England, and had spent most of that time in lonely outposts. Relieved by another officer at Ilunde, he moved for a short period to Tabora, and from there to Dodoma, where he was plunged into a famine-relief operation. It was a period of feverish activity when he drove day after day to bring supplies of food to the famine-stricken natives. Although at this time he was serving as a political officer, he had no official Colonial Office status. He planned to rejoin the NRP to pick up the threads of his career, but to do so he had to return to the NRP headquarters at Livingstone. He might have got back to Livingstone earlier but for the famine. As it was, for some time after the cessation of hostilities he remained there, until the area had returned to some degree of normality.

Dollie was getting impatient, understandably enough. The war was over and she felt she had waited long enough. Tod told her that he first had to return to Livingstone to see if he could pick up the threads of his NRP career. Because he was familiar with the exploits of Spicer-Simpson and had the time to spare, Sillitoe chose to return to Livingstone by a leisurely and indirect route. This was by way of Kigoma, the terminal point on the Tanganyika central railway, across the Lake to Kalemie in the Belgian Congo where Spicer-Simpson had based his midget warships, and then travelling along the route the commander used to bring the two craft from Elizabethville to Kalemie.

During the whole of his four-week journey back to Livingstone it must never have crossed Sillitoe's mind that he would not be welcomed by his brother officers with open arms. As it was, by his own account, he was received with marked coldness. Having fought as well as the best of them, having foot-slogged and roughed it through four years of war, he felt the snub keenly. Their apparent indifference angered and dismayed him, but it is more than likely that their 'coldness' was to a great extent the product of his imagination. He was in any case quick to take offence when he thought he was being snubbed so, without questioning what the future might hold, he resigned his commission and cabled Dollie that he was coming home. She was overjoyed at the news. They had not seen one another for seven years, and she was beginning to feel that she was doomed to become an old maid.

During a lively correspondence they had carried on a protracted argument as to whether Tod should remain in England after they were married or continue making a career in Africa. Tod had insisted they return to Africa and she had been equally adamant they remain in England. For one of his experience, she had argued, there was every opportunity to join some home police force. It would enable them to live well and in comfort. Nothing, she added, would induce her to face horrible years in the African jungle with creepy-crawly things pestering her night and day. 'But it's simply not what you imagine it to be, darling,' he replied, and told her that she had been reading too many books. With his cable in her hands, Dollie felt an immense burden had been lifted off her shoulders. He simply said he had resigned his commission and was on his way, and made no mention of a return to Africa.

Plans for the wedding were quickly begun and Dollie, in a buoyant state of mind, journeyed to London to meet him at Waterloo Station. (Her London suitor, incidentally, had been turned down so many times that he had finally abandoned hope and married another girl.)

Before returning to Dollie's parents' home at Elloughton, the couple visited Percy's mother at Tulse Hill. His father by this time was in an old people's home in Monkseaton, Northumberland, where he was to spend the rest of his days.

At Elloughton, in contrast with the cool reception John Watson had given him when they first met, he now made much of his future son-in-law. At the Constitutional Club—of which Watson was the chairman—Percy was wined and dined and introduced as a war hero to friends and acquaintances in the city of Hull. Dollie's father was also a leader of the Hull Unionist Party and therefore had important connections to whom to introduce his daughter's fiancé.

Of the numerous receptions and activities preceding the wedding, none was more important to Watson than the garden party held in Dollie's honour by the staff and residents of Lee's Rest Homes. This institution, designed by his architectural firm, was the project to which he owed his MBE. He was also chairman of the Lee's Rest Home trustees and Dollie had devoted much of her time to the comfort of the residents. John Watson was flattered by the reception in honour of his daughter; it appealed to his own sense of importance, particularly since a number of important guests would attend.

The garden party was held a week before the wedding. The gardeners had worked hard, and in the warm sunny weather (as if ordered for the occasion) the gardens looked charming. The flowerbeds were in full bloom, shrubs were trimmed to perfection and a large display of flags and bunting was put out to add colour.

It was a gay, gentle affair, with residents and guests mingling on the lawn in summer dresses and wide-brimmed hats. Ostrich feathers were still very much in fashion; gentlemen attended in top hats, morning dress and spats. There was croquet on the lawn, a bowling tournament, prizes, and gracious smiles to add to the warmth. Following afternoon tea there was an indoor concert; the happy couple took part, Percy singing and Dollie accompanying him on the piano. During an appropriate interval, Dollie was presented with a silver tray, 'In appreciation of helpful consideration in carrying out the provisions of the trust,' as it was later reported in one newspaper.

The round of parties, receptions and dinners at which the Watsons introduced their daughter's dashing young captain to their friends culminated with the wedding ceremony and reception at Elloughton on Wednesday, 23rd June 1920. The wedding was held in St Mary's Church. Percy's brother Hubert officiated, and his sister Bertha was one of the bridesmaids. Dollie wore a wedding gown of ivory charmant with a girdle of gold-brocaded chiffon, weighted with gold tassels. The trails of chiffon, hemmed with a wide band of gold cloth, hung from her shoulders, and a wreath of gold leaves held her embroidered Brussels lace veil in place. The bridesmaids were decked out in tulle and crêpe-de-chine and georgette, with green leaves and yellow roses. Mrs Watson, reflecting her own generation's tastes, carried a bouquet of cream-coloured stockinette embroidered in black, and wore a large hat of black lace with paradise plumes.

It was the wedding of the season. In the warm sun on the Watson's shaved Lynton lawn, the bridal party was photographed standing on the skin of the lion Percy had shot at Matetsi in 1909. The house was festooned with Matabele shields and spears and African artefacts; even the bridesmaids' presents were of distinctive African flavour. Each was presented with a lion's claw brooch set in gold—trophies from the Matetsi lion, of course.

Following the reception, the couple spent their honeymoon in the south of England. They then sailed almost immediately for Dar-es-Salaam, where Percy had succeeded without the least difficulty in getting an appointment as a political officer. Dollie had seen that it was no use trying to argue him out of returning to Africa. He was adamant that it was the only life he knew, and if they were to work out a future it would at least have to start there. His father-in-law had offered him a position in the firm, but that would have meant taking up an entirely new way of life, which was not at all to Percy's liking. He was basically a policeman and a policeman he decided to remain. Perhaps there was a future in the Colonial Service, but that was not much different from being a full-time policeman. In any case, the thought of settling down to a dreary office routine in England was enough to make him shudder.

From the moment they arrived in Dar-es-Salaam things seemed to go wrong. Dollie loathed the place and simply couldn't reconcile herself to the 'creepy-crawly things' she used to write Tod about. But that was not all; it was an unsophisticated community in which one was expected to tolerate the most primitive living conditions, and Dollie decided that she was not cut out to be a pioneer. When she discovered she was pregnant, it was with some relief to find Tod in agreement that she return to England, alone, to have the baby. This arrangement left Sillitoe free to be moved yet again to remote districts. It was as though he had never been away.

Considering their protracted courtship, his demonstrated self-sufficiency and obvious willingness to accept another lengthy separation, we have some measure of the sacrifice he would accept in the interest of his career. That he would permit Dollie, in her pregnant state, to make a long journey to England alone, knowing they would not meet again for at least a year is again a measure of a fair degree of selfishness on his part.

In the post-war division of the former German territories, the British were to take over the district of Uha in Kigoma Province from the Belgians, under whose control it had been since the overthrow of the German suzerainty. Sillitoe was ordered to Kasulo, sixty miles north-east of Kigoma, to officiate in the take-over. It so happened about this time that Mwami, the ruling tribal king of the district, had recently died, leaving as his successor his closest relative, Kenyoni, a mere child. The tribal government was left in the hands of a Regent called Senura, but the Belgian Commissioner sadly neglected to give Sillitoe the information. Instead, the person he presented to the incoming British Commissioner was an older half-brother of Kenyoni who styled himself 'King Ntare'.

The day after the hand-over, the Belgians marched out of the district with their two platoons of well-disciplined askaris, leaving the field to Sillitoe. He installed himself and his six askari policemen in the local Boma (stone fort), and hastily reviewed what was rapidly revealing itself as a very complex situation. His preliminary enquiries made him aware of the existence of Kenyoni, and he further discovered that King Ntare was not the rightful successor to the throne, because he was not of pure Tusi stock. The law of succession was that kingship went to the nearest pure-bred relative of the deceased monarch.

Sillitoe made enquiries about Kenyoni, and discovered that he was in hiding with a priest, Father Drost, some forty miles away, fearful of his half-brother Ntare. He sent word for Ntare to visit him. The usurper realised that his kingship was being questioned, and countered by sending some of his followers to loot a village near Kasulo and carry off some women. Sillitoe was furious at such flagrant abuse of his authority and sent a message demanding an explanation. All he got from Ntare was an insolent reply telling him to mind his own business; tribal affairs were not his concern. It was a situation which could not go on indefinitely.

And indeed, a few days later Ntare and a great concourse of his warrior followers descended on the Boma in the first light of dawn, sunlight glinting on their spears and their voices swelling in volume like the approaching roar of a tidal wave as they swept down the foothills to defy the white commissioner. Hearing the tumult, Sillitoe hurried out and posted his men at the Boma's only entrance, prepared, if necessary, to meet the mob like some latter-day General Gordon. Miraculously, the tidal wave of warriors checked its course. The bristling array, brandishing weapons and jostling for front positions, came to a stop at a respectful distance from the Boma entrance then parted to give passage for the leader to come from the rear, accompanied by a retinue of warrior attendants. These were the men who had made war on the German railway builders. Sillitoe asked the rebel leader to be seated, but Ntare replied that he had not come to take orders. Nevertheless, he did sit down on the chair provided, surrounded by his host of followers.

If the people would not obey him, he said, and discard the youth Kenyoni, he would continue to burn villages and show his wrath. In reply, Sillitoe demanded the production of the leaders who burnt the village. There was a moment's silence. Then on a nod from the king, three men stepped confidently forward. Their manner was arrogant; what could a single white man do in the presence of the king?

Upon being questioned, they said they had done what the king ordered and that, in their opinion, was sufficient justification for their actions. Sillitoe called a couple of his askaris forward and ordered a chair to be brought. The offenders were then held over the chair one at a time and given six strokes of the cane across the backside for breaking the law. Ntare watched the proceedings in open-mouthed amazement. One word from him and Sillitoe's party would have been wiped out in ten minutes but, though the atmosphere was tense and a murmur of dissent rippled through the ranks of Ntare's warriors, no one made a move to stop the punishment. The offenders took their places back in the ranks, not having uttered a whimper of pain for fear of losing face among their compatriots. There was another long silence as king and commissioner faced one another in a contest of wills.

Suddenly, as Sillitoe described the incident later, he was

possessed by inspiration to say to the assembled multitude in a loud voice, 'The Belgians have informed me that you men refused to pay your hut and poll tax. Every man who has not paid, step forward.'

Then an astonishing thing happened. Everyone turned and fled. To overwhelm the commissioner was one thing; to be reminded of their taxes was another. Ntare was left sitting in his chair, a solitary, dejected African King Canute. Sillitoe signalled his askaris to surround the usurper and place him under arrest. For a couple of days he was kept prisoner in the fort while Sillitoe considered the best course of action, and Ntare's followers, presumably, laid plans for their king's release, by force if necessary. Sooner or later Sillitoe would have to despatch the usurper to Kigoma for trial. The natural route to the provincial capital led by way of Ntare's own villages. The party was almost certain to be ambushed. Sillitoe therefore outwitted Ntare's followers by having him taken to Kigoma by a more circuitous route. At the provincial capital, Ntare was sentenced to a term of imprisonment which permitted the true king, Kenyoni, to assume his rightful inheritance.

Sillitoe's troubles were far from over. Witch doctors and native superstitions were a constant source of difficulty to him. Both played an important part in tribal society, and one of the cases which he investigated had tragic consequences.

One of the tribesmen in the area consulted the village witch doctor on a most serious matter. He had two wives but, for some unaccountable reason, both children of the second wife had mysteriously died. What ought he to do? To the witch doctor it was quite clear that the children had been bewitched by the first wife, but he was cunning enough to refuse to tell the supplicant what to do. All he would say was, 'You know what the custom of the tribe is.' The man was in a quandary. He consulted the chief, who gave the same reply. 'You have been told. You know what the custom of the tribe is.' With unquestioning obedience to the law of the tribe, the distracted man took his first wife and her eight-year-old son into the forest and instructed the son to kill his mother with a hatchet. Then he killed the boy to prevent the devil passing from the mother to the son. Sillitoe was appalled when he finally unearthed the truth and swiftly removed both the witch doctor and chief to Kigoma for trial. The witch doctor was convicted and hanged, the chief jailed for life.

Sillitoe himself was not immune to the witch doctors. Some time after King Ntare's arrest, a witch doctor friendly to the usurper's cause put a curse on the commissioner. Sillitoe records that the crafty man had detected that he was suffering from the early effects of rheumatic fever. His knee began to swell and with each passing day the swelling grew until the pain was excruciating. He put out a call for a witch doctor who could effect a cure and offered a reward to anyone who could ease the pain.

Witch doctors friendly to the white commissioner flocked to Kasulo Boma from miles around with their potions and herbs; Father Drost, the priest with whom Kenyoni had sought refuge, heard of Sillitoe's plight through the bush telegraph and trudged the forty miles with a supply of aspirins; but salvation finally came in the person of a wizened old witch doctor whose answer was emergency surgery. He made an incision in the affected knee and cupped a heated cow's horn over the wound to draw out the evil spirit. Repeated applications of the cow horn over the next few days were sufficient to ease the pain enough for Sillitoe to be moved from his remote outpost to Kigoma.

A little while before undertaking this journey on a stretcher, a cable arrived from Dollie telling him of the birth of their baby, Audrey, but as a result of the fever and his weakened condition, Sillitoe was unable to send a reply until he reached Kigoma. The thousand-mile rail journey from Kigoma to Dar-es-Salaam and from there to Tanga took more out of him. He was in as low a state as he had ever been. At Tanga there were sulphur springs which had not been in use since being abandoned by the Germans. After these had been cleared of the encroaching bush, he spent the next ten weeks bathing in the waters, which proved to be a great help. Even so, there was no disguising his weakened state from Dollie. She had a woman's intuition about Africa, and from the letters she was receiving she deduced that her worst fears had been realised. But with a new-born baby on her hands, there was little she could do.

From Tanga, Percy was moved for his convalescence to Moshi, a small place at the foot of Mount Kilimanjaro where the air was cool and dry. At Moshi he seriously reviewed his situation, as he later conceded, from Dollie's viewpoint, for a change. Since going to Africa thirteen years earlier, he had fallen victim to more than his fair share of tropical diseases. He had contracted malaria, typhoid, blackwater fever, each of half a dozen varieties of dysentery, and now rheumatic fever. Even he realised that Africa was ruining his health. Only an uncommonly perverse and stubborn streak in his nature prevented him from quitting. According to his son, Richard, the nagging question of what line of work he might follow if he did leave Africa remained uppermost in his mind. As a senior colonial administrator, his career and future in Tanganyika were assured. Back in England the prospects would be far less rosy. But worrying about this problem did nothing to improve his condition and, instead of improving, his health gradually deteriorated. Dollie became so concerned with the reports and the general tone of his letters that in early 1922 she left the baby in her mother's care and booked passage to Tanga.

By this time Percy was back in Tanga, too. When Dollie arrived she was distressed beyond measure to find him in a much worse state than she had believed possible. She had a wreck of a man on her hands. She insisted that for once he submit to her will. She brooked no objections from him about how it would affect his future, and immediately set about nursing him back to sufficient health to make the return journey to England.

To crusty old John Watson's credit, he was equally concerned, and used what influence he could to be of help. When he heard that the position of Chief Constable of Hull was about to be vacated, he despatched a cable suggesting that his son-in-law apply for the job. Then he set about using his influence on the city's watch committee to secure the position for Percy. Watson's news was just what Percy needed to spur him to action. He cabled his application and made hasty plans for his and Dollie's passage. They had to make a mad dash for England to be home in time for the interview. They sailed from Tanga for Mombasa by dhow and there caught a ship bound for England.

The prospect of beginning a new life was indeed exciting. It renewed hope and revived Sillitoe's spirits. Dollie was wonderfully happy, for she had achieved the impossible in tearing Tod away from the infernal gloom and doom that was Africa.

Chapter Six

Rock Bottom

The return of the Sillitoes to England in the summer of 1922 coincided with the opening phase of an economic depression and a period of social unrest destined to last until well into the next decade. The England of 1922 was vastly different from the Edwardian England Sillitoe had left in 1908; and, indeed, from the immediate pre-war year, 1913-14. The Great War had changed everything. Styles, manners and social patterns were altered beyond recognition; nor would the former relationships between the classes ever again be what they were before the war. There were still those who strove to put the clock back, but they were like drowning cavalrymen clutching their sabres for support. There was a new permissiveness which the older generation could not or would not understand; working people found a national voice by switching their political allegiance to the left; and—of considerable importance to men like Sillitoe—those statistics relating to civil and criminal offences reflected a remarkable transformation in the quality of life of ordinary people.

In 1908, for instance, some 27,000 persons were committed to prison for the offence of 'begging and sleeping out'; for the same offence in 1912 (a prosperous year, even by today's standards) some 16,000 persons were committed; in 1920 the figure was down to a mere 2,500. There was an equally dramatic reduction in the pattern of 'drunkenness and assault' convictions. The figure was a staggering 62,000 in 1908, whereas in the last year of the war the number was down to 1,670. It is true that public houses had restricted opening hours during the war, and the beer was watered down, but these facts do not wholly explain the drastic reduction in convictions. After the publicans and breweries agitated for longer opening hours—and won—the figures climbed again, but only slightly. In 1913 some 15,000 prison sentences were meted out for offences of prostitution; the number committed for plying the trade in 1919 was negligible. Even between 1919 and 1921, there was a marked drop of 62 per cent in the number of 'general admissions' to prison. Statistics alone prove nothing; they do, however, indicate a change in social patterns.

So in 1922, though he was on the threshold of a brilliant career in the police, Sillitoe, like most of his fellow men, was disoriented and fearful of what the future held in store. His fears were the nation's fears in microcosm, and they were not without some foundation in fact. There had already been considerable strife and public unrest since the war, but it was nothing as compared with the hard times that were to be experienced during the next few years by all but the very rich.

The 1920s have been condemned as decadent years for long enough. Historians are only just beginning to acknowledge that, far from being decadent, the decade was one of enlightenment and human progress. A reason in great part for the dramatic reduction of convictions and committals over the preceding decade—for all offences—was the Criminal Justice Administration Act of 1914, which gave offenders time to pay their fines; hitherto many of them would have had to 'serve time'. A second major reason was that the war had opened up new employment opportunities for large segments of the labour force. For example, as late as 1914 'domestic service' employed some 1,261,000 persons—men, women and children. The war drew large numbers into war service occupations, and afterwards nothing would induce the bulk of the labour force to return to 'domestic service' employment.

Following the exchange of cables between Percy and his father-in-law concerning the Hull appointment, John Watson had not been idle. He had worked hard behind the scenes on Percy's behalf. A number of members of the Hull Watch Committee—the body responsible for finding a suitable candidate to fill the vacant position on the city's police force—had attended the wedding reception two years earlier, and Watson hoped no doubt that this would be sufficiently fresh in their minds to influence their decision. Of the 146 applicants for the post, most were not interviewed; a short-list of six remained.

In their dash for England to be in time for the interview, the

Sillitoes left Tanga by dhow for Mombasa, where they were in time to catch a home-bound ship. Once arrived in England they hurried to Elloughton, excited at the prospect of Percy winning the appointment. A few days after his appearance before the Watch Committee he learned the worst. All his father-in-law's efforts were to no avail, and it was hollow comfort to him that he was placed second in the final standing. He was bitterly disappointed, and for a long time afterwards was depressed beyond measure. Of all Sillitoe's weaknesses and failings, that of extreme sensitivity to any form of rejection was his personal millstone. Perhaps this stemmed from his competitive spirit; he simply did not like being a loser. Even if he only imagined he was being rejected, he took it very much to heart.

For many weeks following his failure to secure the Hull appointment he did little but idle away each passing day, brooding, not knowing what to do. Having applied for, and being granted, leave he was still officially a political officer of the Tanganyika colonial service. The thought of returning to Africa was uppermost in his mind, but Dollie was determined to keep him in England.

About this time the Chief Constable of Nottingham announced his retirement and the position was advertised. Dollie persuaded Percy to submit his application, although he was now utterly convinced that chief constableships were beyond his reach. There were 250 applicants for the post, and Sillitoe was pleasantly surprised to be called for an interview. When he was invited to attend a second time, his hopes soared; it was characteristic of him to work himself up to new heights of enthusiasm and excitement at the merest hint of success. But his efforts again ended in failure (he was placed second once more), and he was plunged into another abyss of despair which ended with an irrevocable resolve never again to harbour such lofty ambitions.

Since their return, the Sillitoes had been living with Dollie's parents. John Watson's house, with its six bedrooms, facing south and fronting parkland, was a pleasant place to live, and there was ample room for both the Watsons and Dollie and her husband. The village, lying between the foot of the Yorkshire Wolds and the Humber River, was a quiet and beautiful spot where one could enjoy a tranquil existence—anyone, that is, but Sillitoe. He took long walks with Dollie (they were fortunate in having a nanny for the baby, Audrey) and talked and walked and talked. They discussed, privately and with the Watsons, what other avenues were open to him. Although he was now thirty-four years of age he felt that the most obvious alternative to a police career seemed to be one in law. The basis for this conclusion was that he had a knowledge of English common law, having passed an examination in the subject when he was with the NRP. Also, during his period as a political officer in Tanganyika, he studied for, and passed, the Tanganyika Penitory Law examination. In the end, he and Dollie agreed that he should enrol as a student at Gray's Inn; if the worst came to the worst he could always return to Africa to practice. (Why he should come to this latter conclusion is not entirely clear and can only be put down to extreme pessimism, since he would presumably have had little difficulty finding a suitable position in England after three years at Gray's Inn.) John Watson generously gave him £500 as a gift to help cover his expenses, and this, together with his own savings, was sufficient to tide him and Dollie over the three years.

He enrolled at Gray's Inn, but although he studied through the autumn and winter of 1922–3 he felt that he was not cut out to become a member of the legal profession. An upholder of the law, yes; a lawyer, no. It seems that during this same period he managed to spend some time working with the Hull City police force. At that time it was common practice for people aspiring to be chief constables to become 'attached' to other chief constables in order to enlarge on that fact in their applications later for chief constable posts. Sillitoe's part-time attachment probably came about through the influence and contacts provided by John Watson. In any case, the need to do a useful job was uppermost in Sillitoe's mind and, because he could not get what he most wanted, he fretted like a war-horse prematurely put out to pasture. Without work and with no prospects in sight, he was in the doldrums.

At thirty-five, an age by which most men have clearly established for themselves a niche in life, Sillitoe was living a purposeless existence and this at the expense of Dollie's parents which, having lived so independently up to now, he must have found galling. Living with his in-laws was not, as most people find out who try it, a good thing for either the Watsons or the Sillitoes, however accommodating each might be. By all the evidence available Percy Sillitoe was at the lowest ebb of his career; indeed, he was in his own estimation at rock bottom.

Dollie was well aware of his state of mind and did what she could to lift up his spirit. When one considers that despite their having known each other for many years they had, in fact, spent very little of this time together, then one can understand it must have been as trying an experience for her as for him. Getting to know the man she married was still a relatively new experience for her. Realising that his studies were not going as well as they might have gone, knowing he still had it in the back of his mind to return to Africa, knowing he was still bent on a police career, Dollie persuaded Percy, in the spring of 1923, to go away with her for a while, and they visited his parents in Monkseaton.* There a chance acquaintance suggested that he should apply for yet another vacant chief constableship, that of Chesterfield. He must have been quite without hope of ever getting anything, with what he considered to be two positive failures behind him. It seems to have been a case of 'nothing ventured, nothing gained', however, for he went so far as to telephone the Clerk of Chesterfield Council to beg time to submit his application, because the closing day was the day after.

It is curious that in adversity Sillitoe was not the stoic one would expect a man of his nature to be. When things went well he bristled with self-confidence, he was tough and self-demanding, and very much the efficient perfectionist. When circumstances worked against him he became the most miserable of men, and that same tough self-confidence, so characteristic of him in public life, melted away like snow in a shower of rain.

Now, however, given yet another opportunity, he pursued it with new-found determination. Nevertheless, no one was more surprised than he was when they offered him the job. He recovered quickly enough, and accepted the appointment with alacrity.

---

* Sillitoe's reference in his autobiography to the Monkseaton visit is curious inasmuch as he refers to his mother's and father's house. By all accounts his father was then at Monkseaton, in some kind of public institution but his mother was still in the house at Tulse Hill. One can only suggest that at the time of their visit, his mother was visiting. Did she visit Monkseaton often enough to have friends in the district? The interest in this is that Sillitoe records that one of his mother's friends was instrumental in persuading him to apply for the appointment.

Chapter Seven

A Different Kind of Policeman

Chief Constable Kilpatrick of Chesterfield had held that office for twenty-two years. He was well respected, had served his superiors and the force diligently if not with brilliance. His retirement was a harbinger of a new age in police constabulary, not simply in Chesterfield but throughout the country. Kilpatrick was of the old school of police chiefs who were content to run their respective forces along conventional lines, accepting the traditional pattern of relationships in society, a pattern which had been established for generations. In the early 1920s, younger policemen began taking over the senior positions and Sillitoe was typical of them.

The wave of change was in all probability directly related to a new piece of government legislation passed in 1921, the Police Pension Act. The importance of this Act has not been given the recognition it deserves. Whilst its effects were far-reaching, the Police Pension Act was no unsolicited gift on the part of the national government. The mood of the police at the end of the war, in common with that of much of the labour force at large, had been one of dissatisfaction, and an alarming outburst of strikes in the police force in late 1919 had forced the government into taking some positive action.

It must be understood that the national leaders mistakenly interpreted an atmosphere of general social unrest during the immediate post-war period for a mood of revolution. It is true that a number of military units awaiting demobilisation had mutinied, and the work force was certainly in an ugly mood, but that mood was not a revolutionary one. The Police Pension Act of 1921 was designed to secure the loyalty of the police in any ensuing conflict; but the effect of it was somewhat different than that intended and, as it turned out, a beneficial one to the country as a whole.

Briefly, the Act insured a police officer against accidental and non-accidental injury while on duty, and against disablement or partial disablement and, in the event of his death, provided his widow with a pension as well as support for his children until they reached the age of sixteen. It also allowed a policeman to retire after thirty years' service on a pension of two-thirds his pay. Prior to this, the retiring police officer received a very small pension and he naturally, therefore, served as long as he could to stretch out his 'high-income' earning years. The effect of this was a build up of an increasingly aged force leaving little room below for fresh, young recruits. The Act gave longer-serving policemen an unparalleled opportunity to retire with some measure of financial security. The importance of this new legislation came quickly to be recognised by the governing bodies—the county and borough councils—which seized the opportunity of infusing their police departments with new blood. There was no conscious or concerted effort to do so; there was simply a nationwide reaction to the new legislation.

On 2nd May 1923 the combined police force and fire brigade—in Chesterfield the chief constable managed the fire brigade as well as the police—assembled on parade outside the police station and court building for the change of chief constables. It was a blustery day, with great gusts of wind sweeping in from the surrounding Derbyshire hills. The mayor, aldermen and various members of the Watch Committee were present with the retiring and incoming chiefs. Along the ranks of the assembled firemen and constables many an eye flickered beneath stiff helmets in an effort to assess the tall newcomer standing among the dignitaries. Sillitoe, in dark suit, black topcoat and bowler hat, stood impassive and unsmiling beside the mayor, as befitted the occasion.

Chief Constable Kilpatrick opened the proceedings with a farewell address in which he spoke of loyalty and service to the borough. He told the men what they expected to hear: that they were a force second to none in the country, and he hoped, naturally, that they would give his successor the same support they had given him.

The mayor was next. He thanked Kilpatrick for 'his unfailing devotion to duty' and said that he would always be remembered with respect for the fine example he had set the men. The mayor then called for three cheers and the assembly responded with dutiful and lusty enthusiasm. In the vicinity the tall, twisted spire of St Mary's and All Saints Church looked as though it would topple over at any moment, but it had been that way for many a year, and it would take more than a gusty day and the cheering Chesterfield police force to bring it down.

Beckoned forward by the mayor to be introduced, Sillitoe moved with confidence and self-assurance. Gone was the depression resulting from his months of inactivity. Square-jawed and steely-eyed, he surveyed the men who were to be his subordinates with measured calm. 'Look at him,' the mayor told the assembly, 'and you will have no fault to find with the council for appointing a gentleman of his standing.' The impassive faces of veteran firemen and constables were outwardly not moved by the worshipful mayor's words; to them it was all in a day's work. The heavy-booted men who pounded the beat through Chesterfield's ancient streets—through Knifesmithgate and Packer's Row, along Glumangate and The Shambles (where the only remaining Tudor building in town stood)—twitched not a muscle.

When the new chief constable was invited to say a few words, he was no more enlightening than the mayor as to what the men might expect for the future, except that his brevity of style must have left some of them wondering. Having thanked the mayor for his introduction, Sillitoe told the men that he hoped they would look upon him as their friend as well as their chief when they got to know him. He knew from experience that uniformed men did not thank their superiors for long and boring speeches; it was enough that they should hear him speak, and the less said on such occasions the better.

During his first few weeks as Chesterfield's new chief constable, Sillitoe made it his business to get to know each member of the Watch Committee. Every chief constable commands a force 'second to none', but unless he has the ears of those to whom he is responsible, the wise commander knows that his stewardship is next to worthless. Unless he was able to sell his new ideas to the committee they would remain what they were—mere ideas and nothing more. He had taken over at the psychological moment; the time was ripe, and the councillors receptive to suggestions.

Within a very short time, Sillitoe had persuaded his employers to have the old building housing the court and police quarters demolished and new buildings constructed. It was a good start. He next turned his attention to improving the efficiency of both the police and fire brigade. Even at this early stage of his career Percy Sillitoe's flair for organisation, and in particular for effective communications, began to shine. His abilities as an innovator of new ideas and as a reformer, for which he later gained national recognition, began with the Chesterfield appointment. For him, it was not sufficient to exchange civilities with the man on the beat; he wanted to know what they did, and how much the constables knew about their work; he asked awkward questions, to discover what they knew about standing orders, routines and procedure. His interest in the men, in their development as policemen as well as in their amenities and working conditions, was part of his interest in reforming the police force. During the years that followed in the East Riding of Yorkshire, at Sheffield and Glasgow, he gained experience as a police reformer and developed more ambitious programmes for upgrading the performance and efficiency of the police. This interest was, however, first applied to the Chesterfield force. His introduction of strategically-placed fire alarms about Chesterfield was, so far as one can gather, an entirely new idea. He was later to extend it to police call boxes in other cities, though there is no evidence to suggest that telephones directly connected to police headquarters now general in Britain, stemmed directly from the remote fire-alarm system he first introduced.

He achieved another success when he convinced the Watch Committee to invest in a second fire pump and, to offset the cost of the investment, himself undertook the task of getting the surrounding rural authorities to pay a retaining fee for the use of the city's fire-fighting equipment.

In securing the Chesterfield appointment, Sillitoe took on a new zest for life. The £500-a-year salary—with certain additional allowances—took him well out of the ranks of the unemployed, and he more than justified the committee's selection by becoming devoted to his job. In industry he would have been known as 'a company man'. Ambitious to succeed and eager to satisfy, he spent long hours on the job. When he was not in his office he was out tramping the streets, visiting and getting to know the man on the beat. A few years later, Lord Trenchard, Commissioner of the London Metropolitan Police, was to be found adopting the same methods in his efforts to reform that force. Trenchard and

Sillitoe had much in common—as well as differences and disagreements—but it is worth noting that Sillitoe, the younger of the two, was among the first of the new generation of police chiefs to have experience in reforming a force.

While Percy concentrated on his work, Dollie was left to manage their private lives. She worked out the family budget, looked after the finances, and saw to the upbringing of the children—for a second child, Anthony, was born at Brampton on 8th January 1924. It would be giving an erroneous impression to record that Sillitoe was a 'family man' according to the generally accepted meaning of the term because, in Richard Sillitoe's view at least, he was not. He had a good relationship with his children after they grew up, but when they were small he appears to have left their upbringing very much to their mother. This is not to say that he was not conscious of the family's welfare and security. Indeed, he was unusually so; and this probably explains why he continued reading for the bar for some time after he became a chief constable, seemingly as an insurance against disaster. With increased confidence in his new role his interest dwindled, however, until, by the time he left Chesterfield, some fourteen months after his appointment, the last had been heard of his legal aspirations.

On Easter Day 1924 he met a man who was to influence him a great deal in the years to come. The otherwise placid life of the Chesterfield police force, usually punctuated by nothing more serious than drunken driving charges, petty larceny and family disputes, was interrupted by a serious assault. This took place at the Anchor Inn at nearby Whittington Moor. In a rage, a man attacked his girl friend with an axe. The young woman was taken to hospital, and her assailant into police custody. There was no question as to the prisoner's guilt, but as part of the subsequent investigation it was necessary to obtain a statement from the victim. The CID officer responsible for the investigation was repeatedly denied access to the young woman's bedside, and, piqued by what seemed to be a cavalier attitude on the part of the physician attending the woman, Sillitoe visited the hospital to see what he could do. In response to his enquiry, the doctor sent word that he was too busy to see anyone. Sillitoe, determined not to be deflected from his purpose, decided to wait and, when the doctor finally appeared, buttonholed him and asked the physician how the patient was doing.

'And who the hell are you?' the doctor irritably demanded.

'I'm nobody,' Sillitoe replied, 'just the Chief Constable.'

The two men glared at one another. Suddenly the doctor's expression relaxed.

'Oh well,' he said, 'if you're the Chief Constable I suppose you'd better come into the kitchen for a cup of tea.'

The medical man turned out to be a Scot, Dr James H. Webster, an unkempt, stocky man who cared little for outward appearances, and even less for what others thought of him. But his appearance was deceptive, for he possessed a sharp, analytical mind and went on to become one of the country's leading pathologists.

Later, when the two of them were standing by the still unconscious woman's bedside, Webster said, 'She is very badly injured and it isn't just the axe wounds, either. See, the fellow kicked her there, and this was probably a blow from his fist.' He pointed to the various wounds and bruises, explaining why one blow was delivered when she was standing and another when she was on the floor; why one type of bruise had to be from the blow of a fist and another the result of a kick. As a policeman, Sillitoe was impressed by the doctor's simple logic and explanation. He listened in silence, fascinated with all Dr Webster had to say. It was as revealing as following the honey-bird through the African woodland all over again.

The doctor and policeman met again occasionally while the two remained in Chesterfield, but afterwards their paths diverged, and were not to cross next until Sillitoe became Chief Constable of Sheffield. In the meantime the germ of an idea, implanted in Sillitoe's mind by the Scottish doctor, had begun to blossom in a practical way. He considered co-operation between the police and the medical profession an important collaboration in the fight against crime. This collaboration, known today as forensic science, was put on a firm footing when Sillitoe reached Sheffield and chance brought Sillitoe and Webster together once more. As a result, one of the country's first forensic science laboratories was established, pre-dating a similar centre at Scotland Yard by at least a year.

Another Sillitoe brainchild seems to have been born during his Chesterfield experience; a practice which is today taken very much for granted. He was often quoted later by reporters as 'using methods he developed in Africa', a rather mysterious-sounding phrase (had he, perhaps, taken a compressed course in black magic and applied it to police work?) which refers quite simply to 'daily occurrence reporting'. It is not certain that Sillitoe first introduced the system to the Chesterfield constabulary or to the East Riding or to Sheffield, but he was undoubtedly a pioneer. The procedure has become so much a part of police work today—to say nothing, at this stage, of its importance as an intelligence tool—that it is surprising how little has been written on the subject.

The way it works is straightforward. Each constable is required to put in a report at the end of each patrol, noting any unusual incident or observation which has come to his notice—say, the licence number of a car parked outside a factory at unusual hours.

A good example is of a case that occurred at Chesterfield. Three times a week—on Monday, Wednesday and Friday—a lorry was driven to Manchester for a load of wool. The driver was in the habit of parking his loaded vehicle overnight on a vacant site near his home, then making delivery the following day. Because this was a regular routine and the parked lorry a familiar sight to the beat constable, it was never entered on his occurrence report. At midnight one night, the lorry-driver's family reported him missing. Checking through the last occurrence reports, the superintendent saw that the constable covering that beat had noted that the vehicle was missing at six the same evening. The superintendent concluded that something had happened to the driver and vehicle on the road from Manchester, and a police car was despatched to look for signs of an accident. The truck was found empty with the driver unconscious in the cab. A gang of thieves—as observant as the police as to the movements and purpose of the wool truck—had hijacked the load.

The collection and collation of thousands of reports may seem pedestrian and dull, yet it was the type of information-gathering system on which Sillitoe placed great stress. He was to use it with telling effect throughout his career, and never more effectively than when he became head of MI5.

The lack of material by which one might reveal Sillitoe's personality makes those things he did and his achievements doubly important as indicators of the kind of person he was, and it would be deceptive to paint a portrait of him all sweetness and light. One is moved, for example, to reveal the tinge of hypocrisy in his nature. Perhaps he was no more hypocritical than most people, but knowing how tenuous were his religious convictions—he frankly loathed attending church and did so only when he had to for appearances' sake—his unctuous praise of the missionary movement in Africa comes across as a woeful reflection of his true feelings. This attitude is plainly evident from records of his many public lectures. Shortly after moving to Chesterfield, he became a Rotarian (would the singing of those crushingly sentimental songs by grown and ageing men be so out of keeping with his character?) and from then on delivered numerous addresses on the subject of his experiences in Africa. Whether he was addressing the Chesterfield Rotarians, the Junior Imperial League of Beverley or the Sheffield Literary and Philosophical Society, he invariably ended with words of praise for 'the splendid work being carried on' by the Universities' Mission or another. Indeed, there is a very unctuous quality about his praise of one missionary society or another, coming as it did at the tail end of otherwise fascinating lectures on totally unrelated subjects such as big game hunting, police work, the East African Campaign, tropical birds, tribal society. Why this particular observation? Because what he had to say about the 'splendid work of missionary societies' simply does not ring true. For the greater period of his stay on the 'dark continent', African missionaries comprised the biggest single identifiable group—larger, that is, than settlers, police and civil administrators combined. In fact, the combined Africa and India missionary force (I am unable to separate the Africa component) ranged from 60,000 to 65,000 between 1908 and 1914 and, as a policeman having to contend with large numbers of them interfering with tribal society, Sillitoe clearly did not hold them in high regard as a group. Why he should later single them out for special mention in his public lectures remains, therefore, a minor mystery which can only be explained in the manner I have chosen.

During the summer of 1924, having stamped his imprint on the Chesterfield force, he began casting his eyes about for fresh fields. The family was growing—their third child was on the way—and Percy felt it was time to look for a more remunerative position. For a chief constable as young as he was, as inexperienced in the British police system, as sensitive to depression when things went against him, his decision to look for a more remunerative position is highly questionable. To have served for little more than a year when he began casting about did not speak well for the confidence placed in him by the Watch Committee. On the other hand, he knew that the appointment, in common with British practice in the matter of chief constableships, was 'for life' and there was, therefore, little risk of incurring anything more than the displeasure of the Committee members had they discovered what his intentions were, for they were powerless to take action against him. Whether he was wise or unethical or ungrateful to change jobs so swiftly (in the face of his earlier experience of being without a job) is open to question. When the top job in the East Riding of Yorkshire was advertised he applied—along with fifty-one others. The salary offered was not that much higher than the Chesterfield post carried, but the chief constable's residence in Beverley was an attractive part of the offer. So far as Dollie was concerned, living in Beverley would mean being within easy travelling distance of her parents at Elloughton, and at the time this seemed a good thing. So, having appeared before the twenty-eight-member Standing Joint Committee of East Riding, he was delighted to be offered the appointment and promptly accepted.

In many ways, his departure from Chesterfield was a sad one. It had been his first experience as a policeman in England, one which enabled him to get his feet wet. He had proved his worth and ability by getting on remarkably well with the Watch Committee, with the firemen, police, court officials and, undoubtedly, his fellow Rotarians. Still, he was not out to gather moss; there were plum chief constable's appointments occurring all over the realm, as evidenced by the appointments advertised in the police journals of the period, and he had made up his mind to reach for the top.

Chapter Eight

Country Policeman

When Sillitoe took over as Chief Constable of the East Riding of Yorkshire, with his headquarters in Beverley, he came into the princely salary of £700 a year, plus a £250 travelling allowance (to include the upkeep of a motor car) and that large house that he and Dollie had found so attractive. He was told that he would not be entitled to use a police officer as a personal servant, but a constable would be made available to drive or attend to any motor car he kept for police duties.

With his appointment, too he was invited to take his place among the country gentry of the district. Lord Deramore, Lord Lieutenant of the County and Chairman of the East Riding Joint Standing Committee, told him just before he took up his new post, 'If there is work to do, Sillitoe, you will of course do it, but otherwise we shall be glad to see you in the hunting field; and if, by the way, you are out of the county for more than three weeks, you might let me know.'

If the Chesterfield appointment had been Sillitoe's basic training period in the British police system, the new one was a postgraduate exercise. Had he had a private income, as he himself observed in his memoirs, the appointment might well have been a sinecure sufficient to satisfy him until he was ready to retire, but this was not his way. Not content simply to meet with the district superintendents and senior officers during his first few weeks, he visited the remotest village to get to know the man on the rural beat.

One of the qualities that most marked Sillitoe as a leader was his evident concern for the welfare of the men under his command—for reasons of both humanitarianism and efficiency. Once appointed Chief Constable of the East Riding, a largely country district, he was swift to see the importance of these much-maligned and far-flung rural bobbies, and he immediately set out to improve their accommodation and living conditions.

The village policeman has long been the butt of ridicule, equated somehow with the village idiot and other caricatures of country life. Such a portrait is far from the truth for the rural constable, subject to the same dangers and vicissitudes, faced with having to deal with the same range and degree of crimes as those experienced in larger, more compact communities, has proved himself to be as competent as his city counterpart. In one respect he is different and that is in having to spend a great deal of his time on duty alone, and without the companionship of his fellow officers. Indeed, until the advent of cheap, high-speed transportation, the village policeman was one of the loneliest people in rural England and, to some extent, still is. He and his family were isolated from village life by the very nature of his work. In the 1920s his accommodation, provided by the authorities, was, more often than not, much the same as any farm labourer's—and his wages not much higher, but in most cases he was an outsider in the community. Before taking up his post he was warned by his superiors not to make friends, for the obvious reason that he could not be expected to remain impartial in the administration of the law if he did. If he was married, the injunction was extended to his wife. In short, he and his family were told to keep to themselves. To endure the life he chose, the village policeman had to be a pretty strong character, thrown on his own resources —rather like a lonely BSAP trooper.

Sillitoe went out and made the personal acquaintance of the rural bobbies, and they were suddenly made aware that there were men in the force above the rank of sergeant; their unvarying routine of patrolling the same area for years on end was suddenly interrupted by the august presence of their chief constable. He made them feel that they were not merely cogs in a large impersonal machine, but part of a living and vital system which would collapse without their individual efforts.

Ex-Superintendent C. E. Vernon who became Deputy Chief Constable of the East Riding, commenting years later on Sillitoe's period as Chief Constable of the East Riding, said, 'Sillitoe was only in the East Riding fourteen months, but he did more in that time than had been done in the previous twenty-five years.' He was, in fact, an innovating, vigorous chief and proved himself as original a leader as he had been in Chesterfield.

Within four weeks of his arrival Sillitoe began exerting his influence on the controlling body of his force, the Joint Standing Committee. He had made a thorough inspection of the area for which he was responsible, and formed the conclusion that a number of changes were urgently needed, and he delivered to the Committee a report with comprehensive recommendations.

High on his list of priorities was 'systematic training on proper lines of new entrants to the force'. He had found no such system, nor any officer suitable to be an instructor. That man ought to be a qualified detective, he said, but there was not one to be found in the whole of the East Riding. Even rudimentary aids to instruction were missing from the force, he told the Committee. 'All other forces have instructors to teach ju-jitsu and things like that.' One can imagine the raised eyebrows at suggestion of ju-jitsu!

He pointed out, too, that there was no one on the force who understood the theory of fingerprints or who could take photographs, and he asked for a sergeant who was qualified in those subjects to be recruited.

Another area in which he felt there was a need for immediate improvement was that of living accommodation. As has already been observed, the living quarters in which policemen were installed, especially in outlying districts, were often of indifferent quality, and Sillitoe made recommendations for the conversion of more suitable premises.

To his gratification, and the credit of the Joint Standing Committee, his proposals met with a warm welcome.

He must have been like a whirlwind in rural Yorkshire, but the crime statistics of the law-abiding East Riding testify to the impact of his reforms. In his first report, covering the period immediately after his taking over, there was a dramatic decrease in crime over the corresponding period in the previous year during which there had been '56 indictable offences with 39 persons proceeded against and 6 committed for trial'. The following January, Sir Alexander MacDonald, chairman at the Quarter Sessions, noted that there were no prisoners for trial at the session and, he said, the police ought to be congratulated for 'this welcome absence of crime'. He also thought it right to congratulate the whole county 'because it showed that they had kept their tempers in good order—and their hands out of their neighbours' pockets'.

Said ex-Superintendent Vernon, 'When Sillitoe took over, very few of the rural police houses were on the telephone. Sillitoe altered that and saw that the houses were improved. He was a hard taskmaster and expected them to work hard. He was out to get the best from his men, and that meant he got the best from the public as well.'

A government inspector visited the area and reported to him the force was well below the authorised strength; that a further seventeen constables and one sergeant were required immediately to police the district adequately, and as a result his men were doing more duty hours than they were required to do under police regulations. In a trice, Sillitoe was back again to the committee to press the case of his policemen. He also took the opportunity to ask for the appointment of a policewoman for duty at the seaside resort of Bridlington where, in common with the experience at many coastal resorts, the police had to deal with the incidence of sexual offences, such as indecent exposure, during the summer period. He rightly thought that female complainants would be more willing to answer questions put by a policewoman than those of a man. A woman police officer would also be available for similar investigations where they were necessary elsewhere in the East Riding. He was very conscious of the need to have a policewoman in his force to deal with special circumstances involving women, instead of using female clerical staff as had been necessary in the past.

But when any of his policemen stepped out of line he was the first to pounce on them, and to advocate the utmost severity in dealing with them. In the summer of 1925, for instance, two of his constables were charged with theft. Sillitoe showed no mercy, and went so far as to cross-examine them himself in court before a gallery crowded with spectators. The two constables were found guilty as charged and sentenced.

Through this and similar incidents, and by his outspokenness on public issues and matters concerning the welfare of the force, Sillitoe began to exert his influence on a wider public audience.

A major opportunity to do so occurred during his first year at Beverley, for example. There was an outburst of criticism on a national scale, conducted by various motoring organisations against police prosecutions of motorists. The East Riding had its fair share of these, but, as reported by the Beverley press at the time, Sillitoe's fair treatment and courteous hearings of deputations from local motoring organisations, protesting against what they considered to be unfair treatment, was vastly different from the usual reception meted out by police officials in other parts of the country. It was not a dramatic mark he made, but it was sufficient to warrant mention in the press as 'an example of how an "understanding" police official' could deal with the burgeoning motoring problem.

For all that Sillitoe was concerned with reforms, he led on the whole a quiet life and, but for an important incident, he could have gone on indefinitely, content to initiate gradual improvements in the efficiency of the force. As it turned out, the 'incident' left an indelible mark on the force as a whole, and altered for ever after the relationship between the force and the local landed gentry—and it pushed Sillitoe into looking for another job.

Chapter Nine

Sheffield Fine Steel

Sillitoe was sworn in as chief constable of Sheffield on 1st May 1926. The situation in that city was just about as bad as it could be. His predecessor, Colonel Hall-Dalwood, had all but resigned in January to take three months' sick leave, and the day before Sillitoe arrived Hall-Dalwood made a public statement which indicated that his last years in office had been unhappy ones. One can only sympathise with the authorities who had to deal with him and who, eventually, were compelled to find a replacement. That he was extremely sick and probably suffering from some mental illness in which he thought that everyone in authority was against him is evident from his farewell statement, made at the presentation given in his honour, and from the reaction of leading city councillors. He said:

> 'It has been my misfortune to become the victim of some insidious influence from outside, which has for years been working against me. At times during the war and since, my anxieties have been considerably increased by this disquieting and horrible element, which rendered one's position intolerable.'

This dark and sinister statement, full of innuendo but containing little of substance, left those present utterly dismayed. Hall-Dalwood added to the innuendo when he went on to defend the force against charges that many officers were over-drinking and neglecting their duty when, in fact, there is no public record that such charges were ever made by anyone. The following day, when Sillitoe took his oath, Sir William Clegg, leader of the Citizen's Party then in power in the City Council, repudiated the former chief's statement, saying that 'If there was any truth in it the facts should have been communicated to those in authority'. The events which led to Hall-Dalwood's resignation still remain obscure, but as the task of choosing his replacement was conducted with 'unusual secrecy' as reported in the *Sheffield Mail* at the time (the position not being publicly advertised) and because Home Office assent was required for the new appointment, one is led to conclude that Sillitoe's predecessor was forced out of office by ill-health, or as a result of an irreconcilable disagreement with the Watch Committee for which no other solution could be found.

Whether or not there *was* any truth in such allegations, there is no doubt that morale was at a very low ebb in the Sheffield police force when Sillitoe took over, and a lot of the blame for that must be attributed to the lack of vigorous leadership.

That lack may also have been responsible for the biggest single problem that Sillitoe inherited. For the last few years of Hall-Dalwood's term of office the city had been firmly in the grip of gang warfare and the police seemed powerless to put a stop to the terror.

The gangs feuded and fought, not only with each other but with shopkeepers, publicans, innocent bystanders and the police, and when they were not doing that, they were engaged in extensive, violent and bare-face crime. Sheffield had become a city where taxi drivers could be menaced while they were lined up at their ranks, a city where thugs could chase surprised victims through the main square or crowded thoroughfares with impunity. The City Recorder publicly referred to this 'intolerable state of affairs which must be supressed' and a coroner said that the city was gaining an unenviable notoriety for crimes of gang violence.

And to compound the troubles which faced Sillitoe when he arrived, the General Strike began the following Monday morning.

Sillitoe's first weekend was spent attending hurried conferences at which he was briefed on the likely effects a General Strike would have, and making plans to cope with any emergency and the expected confrontation. He needed all the help he could get: as one of the leading cities of the industrial Midlands, Sheffield was an important centre of trade unionism; it was also suffering particularly badly from unemployment that then racked the country. During the month of the strike, and not counting those actually on strike, there were 60,000 unemployed in the city.

He found himself confronted by chaos and disorder of massive proportions. Though, as the city's senior police officer, he bore the primary responsibility for maintaining law and order, his knowledge of the city and its geography was at best only slight. He was in the position of an army commander called upon to place his forces strategically over unfamiliar terrain. He had visited Sheffield a few times while he was chief constable of Chesterfield, but these visits provided him with little more than a passing acquaintance.

His total force numbered seven hundred officers and men, although before the week was out he was able to swell their ranks with three hundred 'special' constables, recruited from the ranks of the strikers themselves. Today such recruits would be denounced for 'scabbing'; in 1926 the use of strikers to control strikers went almost unnoticed. Sillitoe deployed his few mounted police at points where the dissident workers gathered to demonstrate, but he relied on the beat constables as his main deterrent against trouble. He insisted in his instructions to the division superintendents that the police intervene only if and when the strikers resorted to physical violence. But this came soon enough. University students and other government supporters were employed to operate the public transportation system and other essential services. The strikers expressed their resentment of these tactics in a practical way by smashing tram windows, hauling the drivers out of their cabs and turning over a number of vehicles. Tempers flared. The police intervened, first without weapons and then with drawn batons. The strikers retaliated with bricks, fists and anything else they could lay hand to.

One of his main antagonists during the strike was a Labour member of the city council, Frank Thraves, who was also local secretary of the Transport and General Workers' Union (the Passenger Transport Branch). He frequently visited Sillitoe's office to complain of police brutality. Sillitoe, needless to say, was equally vociferous in defending the actions and behaviour of his men. The contrast between Thraves and Sillitoe was striking, for they were both seasoned fighters in their own way. Thraves, a short, stocky man with a walrus moustache, was the product of a working-class background, tough and uncompromisingly outspoken. He had fought his way through the ranks of organised labour to represent his own district on the city council. His small stature in no way detracted from his fighting abilities, and although he looked a bantamweight beside the towering Sillitoe he stood in awe of no man. Least of all would he be put down when it came to matters of rights and principles.

They had first met when Sillitoe was being considered for the appointment, and at that time they seem to have got on reasonably well with one another, but directly the General Strike broke out the two clashed head on. At the first hint of trouble Thraves is reported to have stormed into Sillitoe's office, his opening words, 'If you'd kept your bloody policemen off the streets there would have been no trouble!'

Suppressing an impulse to give the councillor a cutting reply, Sillitoe called in the sergeant posted outside his office.

'Please bring Councillor Thraves a cup of tea,' he said and, as the sergeant was leaving, added, in just the right tone of voice not to give offence, 'and put plenty of sugar in it, will you?' It was enough to throw his visitor off balance. Thraves at first refused to be deflected from his purpose by the diversionary tactic, but soon calmed down and they were able to discuss the situation objectively. Later, when they got to know one another better, Thraves became one of Sillitoe's strongest allies—and a vigorous supporter when it came to the improvement of police working conditions.

As chief constable of Sheffield and Glasgow for the greater part of his police career, Sillitoe was to have considerable contact with labour leaders such as Thraves, strikers, industrial workers and municipal councillors of every political hue, and from these contacts he developed first, a sympathy towards the ordinary working man, and, in time, a moderate socialist tendency. Outwardly, however, he was apolitical, and there is no evidence that he ever betrayed his political leanings in public; he firmly believed that in such matters a policeman should be scrupulously impartial. He considered himself a 'working man' and often spoke of the 'essential goodness of the working man', and of his being 'the salt of the earth'.

Coping with an emergency of such huge proportions from his first day in office meant that until the strike was over Sillitoe had little time to spare to tackle the enormous problems besetting the Sheffield police. Shortly after the General Strike ended, however, municipal elections were held and the Labour Party won a resounding victory. Frank Thraves had no difficulty being returned to office, and became a member of the Watch Committee.

In that position he was of enormous help to the new chief constable, and worked as hard for the police as ever he had worked for the Transport and General Workers' Union.

He was certainly in agreement with the sweeping reforms which Sillitoe launched, now that he was able to give them the proper time and attention.

They began, as at Chesterfield, with a purge of the force's upper echelon. It was an unpopular action on Sillitoe's part, to call for the retirement of so many senior officers under the Police Pensions Act, and hardly calculated to win him friends among those who had effectively ran the force for so long, but he was adamant about it. The trouble was that like so many forces (including the London Metropolitan Police, which was to feel the weight of Lord Trenchard's hand a few years later), the Sheffield police were suffering from a problem whose only solution was to cut it out. Morale was just about as low as it could be. Officers worked in a brackish atmosphere of stagnation, for promotion was more often than not bestowed on the principle of whom, rather than what, one knew.

Moreover, the conditions under which single officers lived—in those communal dwellings called 'section houses'—were appalling; recreational facilities were non-existent and welfare was just a word in the dictionary.

Sillitoe argued that men who were expected to work efficiently under such indifferent conditions of service were unlikely to give their best. In striving to improve the quality of their lives, to give them stature and dignity and self-respect, Sillitoe was fiercely loyal to his men.

Having removed from the force many senior officers, he replaced them with younger men of his own choosing—but he went further. For greater efficiency, for a more compact force, he reduced the number of divisions in the city from seven to four, thereby improving the communications network and releasing certain officers for specialist duties.

It will be remembered that communication was a big item on Sillitoe's list of priorities. It was he who introduced in Sheffield the police call-box system which has since become so common an installation throughout the country. He has in fact been mistakenly credited with being the originator of the police call-box, which enables a constable on the beat to telephone direct to his division headquarters. It was first introduced by a contemporary of Sillitoe, Chief Constable F. J. Crowley of Newcastle-upon-Tyne, and Sillitoe first came across the idea during a visit to that part of the country. He probably got the credit for them as a result of a visit to Sheffield by Sir George Abliss, Deputy Superintendent of the Metropolitan Police, who introduced them to London, where they subsequently became known as 'Sillitoe's boxes'.

He now turned his attention to the police section houses. In these lived the single constables, fending for themselves as regards the preparation of meals, cleaning and so on. Sillitoe quickly improved living conditions. Again with the help of Thraves to argue his case, he got permission from the Watch Committee to engage a cook and housekeeper. Next he invested in a steam press for the maintenance and upkeep of uniforms, manning the equipment with an elderly constable who was near retirement. When news of the investment was made public—and as with most things with which he was involved this was pretty quickly—he was promptly decried for being unnecessarily extravagant. This uninformed criticism he countered by pointing out that it was simply a question of economics; the savings realised by proper care of uniforms would more than pay the cost of the steam press installation.

Whatever the public and local press thought of Sillitoe, there was general agreement that the city had not been the same since he arrived. There was always something in the *Sheffield Herald* or the *Sheffield Star* to remind readers that a man of action was in their midst. He was praised, he was attacked and ridiculed, but he was always treated as a force to be reckoned with. Whether appearing at public functions, banquets, boy scout parades, motorcycle rallies or civic gatherings, Sillitoe demonstrated by his dominating presence that the police were an integral part of the city's life. He was never shy to express an opinion when invited to by reporters, nor unwilling to speak out on national issues affecting the police.

For instance, when the cost of administering the burgeoning motor traffic problem flowered into a national issue, Sillitoe was ready with his own logical and reasoned argument as to what should be done about it. He knew from the published statistics of traffic accidents (accounting for more than 70 per cent of all reported accidents in 1927–8) that traffic control was an enormous drain on police resources, a subject at that time much occupying the attention of the municipal governments. There was, first, the question of available manpower and, secondly, the source from which funds were to be taken to pay for the service. Sillitoe was of the opinion that these should come out of the 'road fund' and not out of the rates, the difference being that the former was administered and provided for by the Chancellor of the Exchequer, whilst the latter were funded from municipal sources. Sir Arthur Griffith-Boscawen, the Home Secretary at that time, agreed with Sillitoe as to the source of operating funds, but advocated the creation of an auxiliary police force. Sillitoe was utterly opposed to this latter suggestion, expressing a strong feeling against the invention of 'a new or inferior kind of policeman who would attempt to regulate traffic without the experience and without the powers of other members of the police force'. Resolution of the 'traffic control' problem took a great many more years to be settled, but it was typical of the type of question on which he spoke out, and which served to bring him into the national limelight.

In 1927 Sillitoe again met Dr James M. Webster, the irascible Scottish surgeon whose acquaintance he had first made at Chesterfield. Prior to Sillitoe's appointment the Sheffield force did not have a full-time medical doctor on its staff. The Watch Committee accepted his suggestion that a 'police surgeon' should be appointed and, following an advertisement, Webster was among the applicants. From the moment Sillitoe realised he was applying, no one else stood a chance. From then on the problem of catering to the health and medical needs of the police was largely solved.

Sillitoe now turned his attention to police welfare, recreation, the formation of an Old Comrades' Association, police education and a recruiting campaign. In fact, there was almost nothing he overlooked in the way of improving the working conditions of his subordinates. Sometimes his concern for their welfare got him into trouble—as in the case of his stern injunction against rough play on the soccer field. Injuries sustained by police players on the sports field became so prevalent, and put so many men out of action, that Sillitoe threatened to prohibit the game altogether, and to confine his sports enthusiasts to some less dangerous game such as field hockey. Although the warning was contained in a confidential memorandum, the facts were 'leaked' to the press, as a result of which the Sheffield police became, within a few hours, the laughing stock of the country. 'Police wrapped in cotton wool,' the critics jibed; even other police forces laughed their Sheffield brethren to scorn. The chief constable of Leeds facetiously remarked that he did not propose to ban fishing merely on the grounds that his constables might get their feet wet. For a while Sillitoe ignored the criticism, and maintained a lofty silence. He felt obliged to explain his attitude to no one but the police themselves, and waited for the opportunity to do so; this came at the next meeting of the city's Police Athletic Association.

The thing that struck him, he told the assembly, was not what the press had to say on the subject, but the lack of taste when members of other forces—a pointed reference to the Leeds police chief and other senior officers who had joined in the laughter—went barking up trees and jibing at their own colleagues. He said he would be very sorry for any member of his own force whom he discovered criticising any other force in the public press. He continued, 'I say what I have to state in no bitterness whatever. It is an explanation which I think was demanded. I never would conduct and never had any intention of conducting a controversy in the press about it.'

Sillitoe's reaction to criticism from any other quarter than the police themselves was entirely different. A few weeks after the controversy created by Sillitoe's soccer injunction had died down, a boxing promoter, Jimmy Lambert of the National Sporting Club, arranged a much-publicised bout between two well-known boxers—Johnny Cuthbert and Francois Sybille—in the city. Twelve police officers were engaged to control the large crowd expected to attend the fight. True to the promoter's expectations, there was a large attendance, but for some reason not satisfactorily explained the crowd got out of hand. A crush at the box office resulted in a bit of a pandemonium, flaring tempers and some injuries. The press, seeking its usual two-pennyworth of sensationalism, did its utmost to promote another fight, this time pitting the promoter against the police. Spurred on by the press, Lambert accused the police of concentrating on finding themselves good positions in the hall to view the fight, and of ignoring their primary duty of crowd control for which they had been engaged. He made a public apology for the inconvenience this had caused and blamed the police as entirely responsible.

When Sillitoe read the press reports he was furious. Following his interview with the superintendent in charge of police arrangements at the boxing contest, he made a reply which was issued in the form of a press release and published. He said:

> 'The apology of Mr Lambert to the public of Sheffield for the inconvenience caused at the contest between Cuthbert and Sybille, if somewhat belated, is certainly completely spoiled (if he is reported correctly) by his unsporting effort to put the blame upon the police.
>
> The facts are that it was advertised that the doors would be opened at 6 p.m., and the necessary number of police were both inside the hall and outside also, regulating the queues which were waiting for the doors to be opened.
>
> It was at 6.20 p.m. that my superintendent, finding that the crowd outside was becoming impatient, went into the hall and requested Mr Lambert to let the public in, of which request no notice was taken.
>
> It was not until 6.45 p.m. that Mr Lambert had the doors opened, after this had been insisted upon by the superintendent, with consequential struggling and jostling that occurred.
>
> This is the first occasion which I have known where there has been difficulty in getting into the hall, even when there have been much larger crowds, but no doubt Mr Lambert, now having learnt from practical experience that the Sheffield public does not appreciate this sort of thing, will do better next time.'

The sporting scene seems to have occupied a large part of Sillitoe's energies in one way or another throughout his period in office in Sheffield. Quite apart from the boxing dispute with Lambert and his injunction against rough play on the sports field, he gave encouragement to recreational activities and showed a keen interest in anything to do with sport.

He went further in helping to provide his force with the first police recreation grounds in England. It was an outstanding accomplishment considering the fact that open spaces in the city limits were, predictably, at a premium. With the help of his councillor friend, Thraves, and with considerable determination and diplomatic persuasion, he succeeded in purchasing a few acres of ground known as the Niagara Ground at Wadsley Bridge from the Duchess of Norfolk for the sum of £4,000. It was an achievement for which the Police Athletic Association has ever since been grateful. The first nationwide police games were held at Wadsley Bridge, and the ground was quickly equipped with facilities envied by every other force in the country. But Sillitoe's most celebrated involvement with sport concerned the football lotteries, forerunners of today's football pools, then being run by many Sunday newspapers. It was the practice of these to print lists of forthcoming matches in coupon form, and to invite readers to forecast the results, large sums of money being offered to the reader(s) who supplied the winning combination. Because readers were only permitted one forecast per coupon, they would buy many copies of a newspaper to increase their chances of winning. The effect, naturally, was to increase the newspapers' circulations.

Sillitoe's eye was caught by an article in a legal journal, in which the legalities of these lotteries was questioned. Having discussed the pros and cons with the editor of a well-known legal handbook, Sillitoe decided to test the ruling of the 1920 Ready-Money Football Betting Act by prosecuting a local newspaper, the *Sheffield Daily Telegraph*. In a conversation with the newspaper's owner, Sir Charles Clifford, he emphasised that it was to be a test case and, in a sporting spirit no doubt, Clifford accepted the challenge. The case was argued before a city magistrate, a conviction obtained and a nominal fine imposed. But suddenly the case took on a more serious aspect since, it dawned on everyone, every newspaper in the country was affected by the decision. The *Sheffield Daily Telegraph* launched an appeal, which was taken to the King's Bench, only to be rejected; the outcome was a voluntary decision by the Sunday newspapers to stop publishing football coupons, a decision which left a vacuum, and this was quickly filled by the football pools operators who have Sillitoe to thank for their existence.

Sillitoe had made his point, not with pernicious intent but simply as a police officer upholding the laws of the land. With the publicity this prosecution brought, together with his successful campaign against the street gangs (discussed in the next chapter), he became a national figure, and from this time on could no longer be considered a rising young chief constable. By 1928-9 he had earned his place among the more experienced and competent chief constables of the country. His opinions and views on law enforcement were both sought by his contemporaries and reported in the national press. It was no longer necessary for him to wish himself in a position of prominence—that was now his, and it was very much to his liking.

Yet one must also note that this boldness, this prestige and prominence, brought about (by imperceptible degrees, of course) a definable change in his personality. He became more autocratic, more remote, a harsher disciplinarian to those he commanded. He was still approachable, but much more the steely-eyed chief than he had been when he commanded the Chesterfield and East Riding constabularies.

Soon after the appointment of Dr Webster as the city's police surgeon, he and Sillitoe collaborated in establishing a forensic science laboratory. Soon it was serving the needs of the surrounding counties as well as those of the city police. In this, as with many progressive ideas, Sillitoe has due credit, not so much as an originator as because of the alacrity with which he picked up, developed and put into practice new notions in police work. Medical jurisprudence, pathology and related studies had of course been known for centuries. Such pioneers as Sir Bernard Spilsbury and Roche Lynch were already well-established authorities. Captain Athelstan Popkess, Chief Constable of Nottingham had a forensic science centre established in that city some years before Sillitoe set up his centre at Sheffield, and in 1928 Derby County Constabulary already had a police scientist, Superintendent Else, on the staff, specialising in the analysis of materials such as animal and vegetable fibres. Sillitoe was aware of the work of Else and Popkess while he was at Sheffield, and in all probability inspected the establishments of these two officers. However, forensic laboratories among the police forces of the country were almost unheard of, and the two already mentioned were very small and modestly equipped centres. So it may be justly claimed that Percy Sillitoe was a pioneer in the field with Webster, certainly he had the foresight and influence to provide the Sheffield police with forensic scientific facilities of the best kind. As a result, Sillitoe and Webster were invited to the Home Office to explain their work and to deliver a report to Sir Arthur Dixon, Assistant Under-Secretary of State. A short time after receipt of the Sillitoe–Webster Report, similar facilities were established at Hendon for use by Scotland Yard and police forces in the southern counties. In addition to the forensic science centre, Sillitoe provided the city police with a photographic laboratory and fingerprint section. The science of finger printing was in its infancy still, and lacked a classification system well enough developed to identify criminals. Sillitoe made enormous strides with his new laboratory so that, within a period of two years the laboratory staff, under Webster's guidance, was able to increase the range of its investigations to cover a wide field of forensic analysis. This included the examination of clothing in alleged sexual cases; urine tests in drunk driving cases; blows, wounds and poisons connected with crimes of violence. The divisional police were soon disciplined to leave the scene of any crime undisturbed until Webster's experts, the fingerprint specialists and police photographer had had the opportunity to do their work at the scene.

As a police chief, Sillitoe's success in Sheffield lay in transforming his command into one remarkable for its efficiency, level of morale and prestige. The force, under his leadership, became an instrument of steel, a burnished sword of retribution which he used to deal with the gangs which plagued the city.

Chapter Ten

Sillitoe's Gauntlet

Writing a report of Sillitoe's impact on the city of Sheffield during his first year as its chief constable, the *Pictorial Weekly* of 25th June 1927 said:

> That there was a general increase in crime during 1926 as compared with 1925 was regrettable, but the sudden drop during the first few months of this year held portent that 1927 will stand out as a record of crime freedom for Sheffield. The credit is due to the police, and also to some degree to the salutary sentences which have been inflicted at the Assizes on lawbreakers in Sheffield.

This was the East Riding report all over again, but behind the *Pictorial's* bald statement lay an intensive period of work during which Sillitoe made a supreme effort to rejuvenate the Sheffield police force. What with coping with the General Strike and its after-effects, and the need to put his own house in order, it is surprising he managed to make any dent at all in the hard crust of lawlessness. But beneath that crust lay the cancerous criminal element, and to carry out the necessary surgery he needed a sharp scalpel; events have proved that he was right to provide that instrument by devoting the major part of his first effort to reorganisation and improving the working conditions of the force. Whether he was dealing with the Watch Committee or a sometimes critical press, he had no doubts about this side of his work, and before the close of 1926 he had gathered about him a dedicated group of men who came to share his determination to make Sheffield a safe and decent place to live in. By his efforts on their behalf, Sillitoe clearly demonstrated his concern for the efficiency of the force. In return, he expected the police to do the job which had to be done.

It is not to be supposed that, because his main preoccupation had been with revitalising the force, lawlessness and criminality had been permitted to go unchecked. Crimes were still investigated, offenders were still hauled before the magistrates or sent to the assizes, and the day-to-day activities of the law-enforcement officers continued. However, it is fair to state that the general action of the police throughout 1926 was one of coping with, rather than preventing or curing the violence which, spurred on undoubtedly by the social unrest and labour disputes of the previous year, had been steadily worsening. In the same article already referred to the *Pictorial Weekly* also reported:

> Without doubt Captain Sillitoe of Sheffield is the doyen of England's higher police officers. One has only to see his work and to notice the results he has achieved during the comparatively short period he has been chief constable of Sheffield to realise the concentrated energy and resourcefulness of the man who has thrown down the gauntlet to the criminals of this city, who no one will deny are among some of the most vicious in the country.

These English gangsters are not to be confused with American gangsters of the Al Capone stamp who operated in highly-organised crime rings. English gangsters were more of the street-gang variety, young hooligans and their girls who swaggered their way about the poorer districts, evolved their own elitist order and, no less reprehensible than their American counterparts, earned the lasting condemnation of law-abiding citizens. The Sheffield 'gangsters' of the late 1920s were about on a par with the 'Northern Scuttlers' of the late nineteenth century, the teddy boys of the 1950s and, more recently, the skinheads. They were the outgrowth of troubled times and mass unemployment, young men who, to escape the boredom of their lustreless lives, baited their fellows, defended territory and settled territorial disputes with fists and knives, and engaged in bloody battles, street by street, district by district and gang by gang.

The real problem came when they not only succeeded in terrorising ordinary citizens and innocent passers-by, but seemed able to take on the police with impunity. Even the magistrates seemed to treat them with deferential care, for they issued 'stern' warnings and hardly anything more, to the consternation of the exasperated police officers who had hauled the offenders before the bench.

Ex-Sergeant Robinson, who was one of the officers experienced in dealing with the 'razor gangsters' before Sillitoe became chief constable of Sheffield, recalls that it all started way back in 1922 with a gang murder in the Attercliffe district of the city. As he puts it, 'The Plommer job brought everything to a head.' Aside from the isolated attempts of individual policemen such as Robinson to arrest hooligans and to curb their activities, little was done officially to arrest the increasing violence and lawlessness of the gangs, and with the onset of the General Strike the situation went from bad to worse. Robinson was himself the victim of a vicious attack by four thugs who set upon him in broad daylight as he was entering a shop, and maimed him so severely with coshes and razor slashes that he finished up in hospital.

Throughout the summer of 1926 the inter-gang warfare stepped up alarmingly. The proliferation of incidents put rival gangsters into hospital, and policemen too. The main weapons were knives and razors, Robinson recalls. One man suffered seventeen stab wounds. 'I knew him well,' says Robinson, 'and he was a hell of a one with a knife.' On another occasion two constables, Dawson and McPherson, were set upon by half a dozen razor-wielding youths after cautioning them against swearing. Dawson, badly slashed about the head, neck and face, was rushed to hospital for emergency treatment.

The situation was intolerable and Sillitoe was determined to put a stop to it. The daily reports coming across his desk testified to the degree of terror being waged by the gangs; by the autumn of 1926 the situation had deteriorated to the point where even his policemen were being attacked at the slightest provocation. His first six months as chief constable made him familiar with viciousness and brutality, but the scale it had reached at this time exceeded anything that had gone before. At the first opportunity —it occurred in court, during a gang case early the next year— he appealed to the magistrates to help him put a stop to assaults against the police. He chose the occasion with care, ensuring that what he had to say would be given the widest publicity, and publicly censured the magistrates for showing undue leniency. One of the major reasons for the increasing viciousness, he maintained was that the city magistrates were not tough enough when cases were brought before them. He bluntly stated that he knew some of the magistrates themselves were afraid of reprisals from the gangs. 'The Park, Crofts and Norfolk Bridge,' he said with rising anger, 'are as rough and lawless as any (areas) to be found in England,' and one of the biggest causes of trouble were the large open-air 'tossing casinos' held in the Park district. By castigating the magistrates in this manner and focusing attention on the troubled areas, Sillitoe sought to draw the police and magisterial body closer together in a common bond to deal with the gangs.

The game of pitch and toss was played with five half-crowns. There was betting on the number of heads and tails which would come up at each toss, and it was carried out on such a grand scale that it paid to employ lookouts to keep watch for the police. So lucrative was the game, indeed, that rival gangs fought for control of it. With flashing razors and thudding coshes they waged pitched battles in the open spaces, and if the police appeared in force the combatants united to drive off the common enemy. Gang terror was not restricted to the open areas but extended into every facet of the city's life—recreation halls, social clubs, dance halls and public houses. Says Robinson, 'It had got to the point where as soon as the gangs walked into a pub everyone else went out. They would demand cigs from the landlord and God help him if they were refused. If you were drinking in the same bar and pulled out a wallet full of money you got a real going-over—and you woke up minus your wallet. They terrified the landlords and no one dared stand up to them—until we came on the scene.' The gangs grew fearless of the police; if they were hauled to court there was usually a lack of witnesses for the prosecution. Nevertheless, although the magistrates resented Sillitoe's attack they had to concede that his charges of laxity on their part had some foundation in fact, and they began dealing out stiffer sentences. In early 1927, the new spirit of co-operation between the magistrates and the police marked the beginning of Sillitoe's all-out campaign to rid Sheffield of the gangs.

To go back a year or so before Sillitoe's arrival, some moves had been made by the police to resist the gangs by organising punitive measures but, by Sergeant Robinson's account, 'the police under Colonel Hall-Dalwood had been pretty tolerant with the cloth-capped gangsters'. In fact Robinson himself, together with a handful of his colleagues, operating with the knowledge and backing of his division superintendent, had made something of a name for themselves in dealing out their own brand of justice to the gangs. Disdaining the use of their batons, Robinson and his companions met knives, coshes and other gang weapons with their fists. It was a tough way to go about dealing with the hooligans, and occasionally the police came off the worst. Even so, the handful of police officers under Robinson gained a reputation for being a no-nonsense squad, so that the area at least in which they operated became relatively peaceful and law-abiding. But their efforts were of little account in the face of the prevailing apathy of the city council, the magisterial body and Hall-Dalwood's police administration.

When Sillitoe began his clean-up campaign he called Robinson into his office. He said, 'I have not met you before, but I've read a lot about you and what you have done. I want to congratulate you on your work and what your men are doing.' Sergeant Robinson was a big man with broad shoulders and a tough face, which convinced Sillitoe that he had the man he was looking for. During the long discussion which followed, Robinson told his chief constable of his experiences and discovered in Sillitoe a like-minded and sympathetic listener.

The talk with Robinson convinced Sillitoe where the solution to the gang problem lay. He called in his superintendents and told them with his characteristic bluntness: 'We're going to meet force with greater force. Pick me out your biggest, toughest men.' A dozen men were selected—among them the veterans of Robinson's hardy gang-busting skirmishers—and given training in ju-jitsu and rough-housing. 'Hit first and question afterwards,' Sillitoe instructed them. Following a two-week intensive course in 'street fighting' they were split into pairs for patrol duty and sent out, literally, to do battle. Stern measures? Perhaps, but drastic ill sometimes calls for drastic cures. In the words of one reporter of this period, 'Sheffield was rapidly becoming a little Chicago. For many people the law was that of the jungle—the strong rules, the weak gave in.'

Two of the teams in Sillitoe's flying squad—as they came to be called by the gangsters themselves—deserve special mention because of the impression they created in the crusade which followed. These were Robinson and a strapping Irishman called Geraghty, and Loxley and Lunn. The latter pair, who had been working together under Robinson for some time, had their own score to settle with the gangs. The previous autumn they had been sued for assault, along with another constable, Farrelly, by a bookmaker's clerk. Even though the grand jury had found there was 'no true bill' against the officers, and the clerk had been sentenced to a term in jail for assaulting Lunn, the two officers were anxious to teach the gangster companions of the bookmaker's clerk a lesson. This was because Loxley and Lunn, overwhelmed by numbers, had taken a heavy beating.

There were many gangs in the city—the Park gang, the Crofts gang and so on—but by 1927 they had coalesced into two major groups known by the names of their respective leaders—Mooney and Garvin. Sillitoe had these two brought to his office separately, and told each of them what the new police policy would be. It remained to be seen whether or not they heeded his warning.

Next he let it be known among the publicans and shopkeepers, visiting and talking with many himself, that unless they co-operated in resisting the gangs the whole campaign would be doomed to failure. With his police districts reorganised, with his new police boxes and the improved communication system they afforded, help would never be more than a few minutes away, he told the small businessmen. It was a masterpiece of planning.

The patrols, in plain clothes, took up their stations in those public houses where gang members most frequently caused trouble. They usually turned up in small groups of not less than four and rarely more than six; then the two-men patrols swung into action. Robinson and Geraghty, Loxley and Lunn, began to make a name for themselves among their fellow officers, and often combined forces to deal with larger groups which the gangs took to sending on to the 'battlefield'.

Sergeant Robinson: 'I remember best of all the memories of those troubled years the night we as good as challenged one of the mobs. We heard that they were planning to get us because we had turned them out of a pub the night before. I decided not to wait for them to come to us and I took Loxley and Lunn to a pub in West Bar. Sure enough they were there, about a dozen of them. I knew we would be in trouble, so I told them I was going to search them. We found razors and coshes on them, but they knew we were out to settle it once and for all. Then the fun started. It was quite a set-to and I shall never forget it. It was the only way to settle them, and we three showed the twelve of them what for. That's how we stopped it. We kept after them all the time. I told them that three or more was a crowd and I wouldn't let them get together in the bars. If I found them together my boys split them up. We harried them until we wore them down.'

With Sillitoe's patrols in action the gangs began to take notice. A steady stream of offenders were brought before the magistrates, who, heeding the new chief constable's strictures, began dealing with the offenders as severely as the law allowed. The sentences they imposed gave rise to the *Pictorial Weekly's* 1927 report of 'salutary sentences'.

On one occasion a gangster attacked Loxley with a razor. He was arrested and charged. In court the following day the accused's solicitor asked that the charge be amended from 'assaulting a police officer' to 'attempted suicide', provoking a gale of laughter from court officials and spectators alike—among them a large number of 'friends of the accused'.

Speaking of the leadership Sillitoe gave in combating the gangs, Robinson said, 'He was a damn fine chief, was the captain' —Sillitoe was popularly known as 'the captain' to his subordinates—'and there is no doubt about that.' The chief constable kept his word by giving the flying squad all the support they needed, condoning their methods as the only way to put the gangs out of business. Such methods would not be tolerated today, but the temper of the times demanded drastic action and Sillitoe was the type of man who was willing to take the risk of incurring public censure. There were, inevitably, complaints of police brutality, but he sailed on in the knowledge that he had the backing of the decent citizens who made up the juries. Gradually the police got on top of the gang problem for which, justifiably, Sillitoe received due credit.

From this time on, he was increasingly in the public limelight. First the local papers and then the national press saw fit to praise him with bannered headlines such as THE MAN WHO SMASHED THE RAZOR GANGS, THE GANG BUSTER OF SHEFFIELD. Other cities with similar problems began to take notice and sought his advice. He was seriously considered for the senior police appointments at Hull, Manchester and Derby, and he was offered the chief constable's post with the Hampshire Constabulary, but the Sheffield Watch Committee, under Thraves' chairmanship, persuaded him to remain in Sheffield. He had succeeded in making a name for himself to the extent that for the first time he was invited to command other forces, rather than having to apply for such appointments—which, during a period when the number of qualified people exceeded the positions available, was in itself a major achievement.

As to the methods adopted by the flying squad under Robinson, Sillitoe expressed his justification of his policy when he said that the only way to deal with the gangster mentality was to show that you are not afraid. He once wrote: 'The element of a beast in a man, whether it comes from an unhappy and impoverished background or from his own undisciplined lustful appetites, will respond exactly as a wild beast of the jungle responds—to nothing but greater force and greater firmness of purpose.'

Sergeant Robinson was one of those who later went with Sillitoe to Glasgow, so he crops up again in Sillitoe's career, but it is worth noting here that when the sergeant retired he took with him the wooden staff he used to deal with the gangsters on the streets of Sheffield. During an interview with the *Sheffield Telegraph* in 1962 Robinson said that, although he was proud of the part he had played in bringing an end to those troubled years, he was glad that the streets of the city no longer resounded with the screams and curses of out-of-work toughs in conflict with policemen.

The gang warfare, corruption and gambling which went on with diminishing intensity until 1929 was not without its aftermath. As if to mock Sillitoe for his efforts on behalf of his subordinates, a number of Sheffield policemen were discovered to be receiving bribes from local gamblers and bookmakers in Sheffield's Brightside district. The disclosure came as high explosive to a public that had hitherto regarded the British bobby as incorruptible. Suddenly its faith was shattered and Sillitoe took the full force of the public reaction. The bribery cases were tried at the Leeds Assizes and the presiding judge, Mr Justice Humphreys, made some pointed remarks about the Brightside division during his summing up, clearly indicating that greater blame lay with those (the police) who received the bribes than those who gave them. Also, he indicated that the bribe-taking appeared to be more widespread than was brought to light in court by the facts. As a result, an enquiry was conducted by the Watch Committee. Following its deliberations, fifteen policemen were dismissed from the force and a further seven fined for dereliction of duty.

Throughout the court proceedings and Committee sessions

Sillitoe remained outwardly calm, but he was disgusted and furious with what eventually came to light. Privately he expressed a revulsion, and little desire to show mercy; he was as harsh against those who betrayed his code of ethics as he was ready to leap to the defence of loyal men. Not always the apple of the public eye—he had often been the butt of ridicule and criticism—he had yet to support and defend the honest majority from those dishonest ones among them. In response to repeated requests to make a statement to the press, he reluctantly issued a guarded statement, saying: 'I am not concerned with the ethics of betting generally. The matter is one on which opinions vary, and my opinion either way does not matter one iota,' but he abhorred the weakness of police officers who succumbed to bribery in any form and refused to seek any 'understanding which might defend the guilty ones'. He spoke of the degradation and ruination of a number of young men. All he asked of the public was some understanding for the overwhelming majority of the force for which, to improve efficiency 'the expenditure of public money will have been in vain unless something constructive emerges from the recent judicial hearings'.

Concurrently with this public statement he issued a sharp and pointed directive through the divisional superintendents, forbidding the acceptance by policemen of any moneys, gifts or 'considerations for services rendered' in any form. Traditionally, there had been a public habit in years past of tipping certain policemen on Boxing Day, along with the newspaper boys, butchers, bakers, milkmen and other tradespeople. He found the practice demeaning and said so in his directive. If a policeman had to accept a tip to avoid giving offence, he directed, they were to issue a receipt and turn the money over to the Police Benefit Fund.

Sheffield was not the only force to experience corruption in those years. In London in 1927, a Sergeant Goddard of the Metropolitan Police had been convicted of accepting bribes from night-club operators; some time later, the case of Money and Savidge (Sir Leo Money and Miss Irene Savidge were charged with indecent behaviour in Hyde Park) was given wide publicity because of the presiding magistrate's criticism of the police and the unreliability of police witnesses. Alarmed at the public's diminishing regard for the police, and pressured by a crusading press, the government appointed a Select Committee to enquire into allegations that the police had coerced Miss Savidge into making a false statement.

Lord Byng's appointment as Commissioner of the Metropolitan Police in late 1927 did nothing to stem the tide of public criticism because, by this time, public confidence was so lacking that not even a commissioner of Byng's stature was enough to restore it; something more was needed. The Select Committee was followed by a Royal Commission set up to investigate police powers and procedure; its report was published in 1928. The conclusions (which dealt with police training, conditions of service, recruitment and organisation), while directed at the Metropolitan Police, not unnaturally applied to the more than 340 forces constituting the country's total constabulary. The report, in which it was pointed out that the police system was unchanged since its inception by Sir Robert Peel, was widely resented in police circles for its frank criticism of what the commissioners considered to be an anachronistic police structure. One passage in particular had far-reaching effects after Lord Trenchard had taken over from Byng as Commissioner of the Metropolitan Police. This passage concerned the Royal Commission's opinion on the best source of recruits for higher police posts, and was to lead to a strong disagreement between Sillitoe and Trenchard. In the Commission's report it was stated:

> We wish to emphasise that long experience and good service in the lower ranks of the force are not the only, not even the most important qualifications for the higher posts, which ought to be filled in all cases by men who, besides being themselves upright and fairminded, are capable of impressing their own standards on their subordinates. We should therefore regard as inimical to the public interest any system which limited appointments to the higher posts to those who had entered the police as constables; and we are of the opinion that such posts be filled by the best men available, irrespective of the source whence they are drawn.

One of the results of Trenchard's appointment in 1931, assisted in large part by the influence of the Royal Commission's recommendations on the Home Office, was the opening of Hendon Police College. Sillitoe was utterly opposed to the creation of an 'officer class' in the police system, and to the use of Hendon College as a means by which college and university graduates might bypass service in the lower ranks. No matter how worthy or how academically qualified a man might be, he argued, there was no substitute for experience on the beat. He was not against the recruitment of graduates into the police—far from it, he welcomed those who had benefited from higher education—so long as they entered as police constables like any other recruit. Police service, he argued, was not to be compared with the armed services, and it was 'inimical to the public interest' that it should support a caste or class system within its ranks. Sillitoe was supported in this view by the great body of senior police chiefs (even though the majority at that time had held commissions in the armed services), the Police Federation and the public at large.

Sillitoe was already a figure of national prominence when the slaying of an Essex policeman, PC George Gutteridge, took place on 26th September 1927. The dramatic lead which Sillitoe gave to Scotland Yard, and which led directly to the solving of the murder, brought him once more into the limelight.

PC Gutteridge was with Essex County Constabulary, and stationed at Stapleford Abbotts near Chipping Ongar. On the morning of 26th September 1927, he met with a fellow policeman, PC Taylor, at a 'conference point' at 3 a.m. on a country road. They exchanged notes, conversed for a short while and then parted. Taylor, who had just finished a tour of duty, went home and to bed. Two and a half hours later Gutteridge was found shot to death within half a mile of where they had met. Within an hour, Inspector Crockford of the Romford CID arrived to examine the body. The dead man still had a pencil clutched in his hand, and his open pocket book and helmet were found a few feet away. He had four bullet wounds in the head, two of which had been fired into the eyes. Crockford deduced that when the constable was first shot he had probably been using the headlights of a car to write by. This was substantiated by the fact that there were fresh tyre marks on the roadway and that his flashlight was in his pocket.

News of the murder sent a shudder of revulsion through the country, and a nationwide hunt for the killer began. A doctor's car reported stolen in Billericay, Essex, some hours earlier, was found at 7.30 that morning, abandoned, some twelve miles from where the murder had occurred. Clear traces of fresh blood were found on the offside running board, and inspection of the car's interior yielded an empty cartridge case under the front passenger seat. A ballistics expert identified the cartridge case as being of a small-arms calibre of a type once used in British service revolvers. However, it was of a rare pattern which would eventually be of help to the prosecuting counsel. The investigation, employing more than a hundred full-time, and many more part-time investigators under the direction of Scotland Yard, dragged on for four months. There were no leads and it was beginning to look as though the case would never be solved.

Sillitoe and his colleagues of the Sheffield police, remote from the area of enquiries, had nevertheless followed reports of the case with interest. But for one of Sillitoe's recently-instituted traffic offence reports, the case of the Gutteridge murder might never have been resolved. By this new system, all motoring offences were reported to him, to ensure uniformity of prosecutions. The report in question concerned a routine traffic offence, involving a speeding motorist who had forced a van off the road, causing superficial damage. The van driver had had words with the other driver but was unable to get his name; however, he took note of the other's licence-plate number. When a check through the records revealed that the vehicle was fitted with false number plates, Sillitoe insisted that the car owner be located. So began a hunt through Sheffield's Attercliffe district, the area in which the violation had occurred. The matter seemed of sufficient importance to Sillitoe for him to assign the investigation to Superintendent Hollis of the Sheffield CID.

From the barest description of a passenger in the car, given by the van driver, a constable on point duty noticed someone he thought fitted the description and got in touch with him. Thus was forged the first link in a bizarre chain of events which led to the arrest of the constable's murderers—for there were two men involved—Browne and Kennedy.

Browne owned a garage in Clapham, London, and made a business of working on stolen cars to disguise them. He had sold such a car, a Vauxhall saloon model, to a Sheffield butcher named Currie, whose premises were located in Attercliffe. Currie was the passenger whose description had been given by the van driver. Currie, a man with a police record, had actually made meat deliveries to the Sheffield police headquarters in the stolen car. Alerted by the beat constable, police mechanics inspected Currie's car and were able to identify it as having been a stolen vehicle. Hollis intensified his enquiries and it was then that the astonishing facts came to light. Currie, put in a panic because of Hollis's persistent enquiries, asked to see the chief constable in private and was duly conducted into Sillitoe's office. As Sillitoe records, the butcher's opening words were:

'I know why you're so hot on these Attercliffe enquiries, sir, but I want you to know that I had nothing to do with the murder.'

To his credit, Sillitoe concealed his surprise, and replied, poker-faced, 'Naturally, with your kind of record, Currie, you don't want to be mixed up with anything you are not responsible for, particularly murder.'

The visitor went on, 'I wasn't in the car—not when Kennedy and Browne shot him. I didn't know about the job until Browne came up here to ask me to take the revolver he used on Gutteridge—he said if the police jumped him for anything he didn't want to have it on him.'

In a short time Sillitoe had an outline of the Gutteridge murder as given to Currie by Browne, and sufficient information to identify both Kennedy and Browne. Immediately Currie left his office, Sillitoe contacted Scotland Yard. A short time later Browne was arrested in his garage by five police officers from the Yard, and Kennedy's arrest followed within a few days in Liverpool where he was on his honeymoon. During the trial Browne made a clumsy attempt to shift the blame on to Kennedy for the actual shooting, but fingerprint evidence on the murder weapon clearly identified Browne as the killer. Both men were found guilty and subsequently hanged. The Sheffield butcher, Currie, as a result of Sillitoe's intervention, received the £2,000 reward offered by the *News of the World* for information leading to the arrest of PC Gutteridge's murderers.

Not all of Sillitoe's life in Sheffield was taken up with combating crime. Devoted as he was to his job, he still found time for social activities; and while he no longer participated in the more strenuous sports of soccer, rugby, tennis and cricket, he did take up golf. He attended public and civic functions, not out of any great liking for socialising but because it was expected of him. The running of their home life and the children's upbringing continued to fall upon Dollie, though these days his salary made it easier to employ and enjoy the luxury of domestic help. He also used some of his men in a servant capacity, and a young constable was often to be seen pushing one of the Sillitoe offspring in a high-sprung perambulator—a uniformed nanny in the best

English tradition. The constable was PC Deacon, who was to join what became the Sillitoe entourage, which followed him to Glasgow and later to the Kent Constabulary. It would be easy to criticise Sillitoe for making use of his policemen to carry out domestic chores, but the practice was a common one, and Sillitoe would almost certainly have looked upon it as his right to make use of his men in this way.

Towards the end of the following year a delegation from the City of Glasgow visited Sheffield to review the city's police organisation, equipment and facilities. Sillitoe's reputation had spread far and wide. Glasgow, racked with crime and lawlessness, was, moreover, in need of a new chief constable; the city fathers had, therefore, an ulterior motive in visiting Sheffield.

Chapter Eleven

The Sillitoe Tartan

The Sillitoe family arrived in Glasgow one late November night in 1931. The only person to meet them was Percy's new second-in-command, Assistant Chief Constable Williamson. The departure from Sheffield that morning could be described as emotion-packed, and it is pretty certain that Sillitoe was feeling at one with the world. The large gathering of well-wishers that crowded on the railway platform to see them off came as a complete surprise. The unsuspecting Sillitoes, shepherding the children, had hurried to the station in ample time to catch the mid-morning northbound express. The children in their Sunday best, Dollie arrayed in a new hat and coat, and Percy outfitted in business suit, light topcoat and bowler hat, were all victims of the deception. The police band, hidden from the view of anyone approaching the platform, struck up 'For he's a jolly good fellow' immediately their departing chief appeared in sight. The well-wishers—men in and out of uniform, a sprinkling of wives, and a number of civic officials—enjoyed the spectacle of Chief Constable Sillitoe for once taken utterly by surprise. One may be sure that the spontaneous gesture, the music and the happy atmosphere brought a lump to Sillitoe's throat, for he was a sentimental man and nothing touched his emotions more than public recognition, which he craved as a flower craves sunlight. It was a rousing send-off, lined with the smiling, grinning, cheerful faces of men who would remember him not as the stern disciplinarian he was, but for the inspiring leadership he had given, and they had deserved. As the train steamed out of the station with the band playing 'Auld Lang Syne', Percy leaned out of the carriage window and waved his hat. He waved it until the platform disappeared from view and nothing was left but a pleasant memory and the musical rattle of wheels on the track joints.

So began what in many ways was the most satisfying and enjoyable period of his life. At the age of forty-three he had command of the second largest police force in the United Kingdom, in the 'Empire's Second City', with a force of almost 2,500 men; an astonishing achievement, considering that he had begun his career in the British police less than nine years before, with a force at Chesterfield barely numbering sixty. Now, with the experience of Sheffield behind him, he had no illusions about the immense task he was about to take on.

Glasgow, with its cobbled back streets, its slums and stately mansions, its bustling industry and thriving commerce, was not only rampant with every type of vice, corruption, graft and the viciousness of gang warfare; it was also a city divided by sectarian rivalry, a division which affected every institution the city hugged to its throbbing bosom. In Glasgow, the mere disclosure of the school one attended was sufficient to bar certain jobs and to guarantee consideration for others; it was a city in which acknowledged support for a soccer team (Rangers or Celtic) was as good as a public confession of faith.

It was clear then that whoever succeeded to the top police post was doomed to labour under the most trying conditions. To maintain strict impartiality, Sillitoe, from the start, had to use all his tact and wit. To add to the difficulties of his task, he had enemies within his own camp: with one exception the Glasgow press, together with a certain faction of the corporation council, was opposed to 'going across the border to find a chief constable'. In the light of subsequent events that opposition is not hard to understand, but this was not so obvious when Sillitoe first arrived.

In late 1931 police forces throughout the country were still in a state of ferment. In mid-1931, a national committee headed by Sir George May had begun a study on government spending, the study to form the basis of an austerity measures programme needed to counteract the weakening of the pound sterling on the world monetary market. One of the May Committee's recommendations was a $12\frac{1}{2}$ per cent cut in the salaries and wages of all public employees. In the September of that year, at Invergordon, a number of naval personnel of the Home Fleet had demonstrated against any pay cuts, and discovered that the intended cuts were already public knowledge. Trenchard, contending with reorganisation of the Metropolitan Police, had deferred announcement of the pay reduction because it was thought that this would be the last straw to break the camel's back and bring about a full-scale strike. Nearer, home the Lord Provost of Glasgow, Sir Thomas Kelly, publicly announced that the new chief constable would be affected by the cut in pay '. . . as would every other member of the Glasgow police force.' Again publicly, Sillitoe accepted this as 'a most necessary measure'.

Having given this demonstration of his leadership, Sillitoe began the task of reorganising the Glasgow force with the same drive and energy with which he had made his mark at Sheffield. Of his whole period as Chief Constable of Glasgow one has an impression of great enthusiasm and vitality. He comes across at times like an avenging angel—the drawn sword in one hand laying low the foe, the scales of justice firmly gripped in the other. Whereas during his years in Sheffield one can admire his administrative and organising skill (and wonder at times if he was not a little haughty), his career in Glasgow, on his own admission, was the happiest, most contented period of his life. No one was neutral or indifferent towards him during those thirteen years. He inspired people to admire or detest him: there was no halfway house. The Communists came to loathe him, the IRA terrorists to fear him; old ladies to adore him; criminals to respect him; the poor and poverty-stricken to thank him; prostitutes to look upon him as their father confessor; and the ordinary man to regard him as a champion without equal. For a man whose primary concern was the maintenance of law and order, Sillitoe's concern for the underprivileged, the unemployed and decent ordinary people, was unusually sensitive. According to the McGlinchey Papers,* 'Sir Percy often attended funerals of poor people found dead who had no known relatives, and gave the few strangers that attended a meal and a drink out of his own pocket.' The chief constable would often say a few words at such funerals and, being known to take his time, there was a story circulated that on one occasion when he was 'saying a few words' a voice was heard to ask why

---

* James McGlinchey, a native of Paisley and occasional journalist, first met Sillitoe during the Glasgow Empire Exhibition of 1939. Following a series of interviews with pensioners, ex-policemen and in old people's homes, he wrote a series of reports detailing Sillitoe's activities, and these are now with the family papers.

it was taking so long, and another voice replied, 'The deceased was so good they're having doubts about burying him.' In co-operation with social workers in the city, Sillitoe started a marriage guidance council and brought dissident couples before the council for help; he had a better record for healing broken marriages than many a clergyman. His achievements on a strictly social level (including marriage guidance councilling, helping rehabilitate prisoners from Barlinnie Prison, organising an annual outing for poor children of the city, and helping the marchers of the Great Hunger March) were equal to those in the police field. All this the citizens of Glasgow took years to appreciate, but among them, even today some forty years later, he is remembered as a remarkable man.

Sillitoe's introduction to the city officials at the swearing-in marked the launching of his Glasgow career. His introduction to his subordinates came a short time later, in a less formal way. The occasion was the annual police concert, attended by the upper echelons and officials of the Police Committee as well as the rank and file members of the force. It was pretty general knowledge that sweeping police reforms were in the offing, and most people who had taken the trouble to acquaint themselves with Sillitoe's achievements in Sheffield knew that he had been brought to Glasgow for this purpose. Sir John Cargill, chairman of the Police Committee, gave the first public intimation of the impending reforms when he alluded to the sweeping measures needed to cleanse the corruption in the police department and other institutions of the city: 'It is an old saying that a new broom sweeps clean, and no doubt Captain Sillitoe has brought the new broom with him in his kitbag from Sheffield. But probably no one knows better than Sillitoe that he has not come here to be the head of the Cleansing Department. . . .'

Sillitoe, outfitted in a new uniform for the occasion and carrying a peaked cap specially ordered from London with the finest display of 'scrambled eggs' on the peak which anyone had seen in a long time, had little to say except to thank the speaker for his kind words. This time he even omitted the piece about 'hoping that when they got to know one another better. . . .' Since he must have known he would soon be using his own make of the 'Geddes' Axe', there was some reason for thinking that the less he said the better. There were those in the audience, mostly senior officers, who knew only too well what Chairman Cargill was spelling out. Sillitoe's first action in Sheffield had been to purge the force's senior officers, and they probably had a fair inkling that the pattern would be repeated. However, for the time being no moves were made on either side to resolve the situation.

In early December the police headquarters were transferred to the new building. Sillitoe's office was a spacious room on the first floor, at the head of a flight of stairs. Visitors who wished to see him first had to check with a sergeant who sat at a desk in the corridor, barring direct approach to the chief constable's office. Sillitoe's office was comfortably furnished, with wood-panelled walls, a carpeted floor, leather armchairs and a glass-topped desk. On the desk and adorning the wall were photographs of Dollie and the children. It had the appearance of a senior executive's office in any wealthy commercial or industrial enterprise. From this room Sillitoe conducted his operations over the next thirteen years.

The first and most massive task before him was, as at Sheffield, the streamlining of the force under his command. But, as expected, the necessary preliminary to that was to ask those officers and men with more than thirty years' service to submit their resignations and accept retirement. They had been prepared for this, as I have noted; indeed, a half-hearted attempt at resistance began as soon as he started to ask for resignations. No one knew better than the senior officers the extent to which the force had become top-heavy. But there is good reason for believing that Sillitoe got the Glasgow appointment above all because he was the only one among the many hundreds of applicants who had demonstrated his ability to carry out a purge of the police force itself, as well as to deal firmly with street gangs.

When one superintendent, who had been with the force since 1908, retaliated by taking his case to a sympathetic press, Sillitoe swiftly launched a counter-attack. He summoned every available man to a meeting at St Andrew's Hall and there laid his cards on the table.

In the interests of efficiency, he told them, reform was inevitable. For anyone reaching retirement age and able to draw the maximum pension, it would be mandatory to leave the force. There was no other way of ensuring promotion from the lower ranks. Furthermore, that promotion would in future be based solely on merit. The reception of this statement—a spontaneous roar of approval from his listeners—left no doubt that he had won the day. Nothing else mattered; the rank and file were with him, and he took this as his mandate to create a new force. From that time on, all resistance to his reforms was effectively negated. The superintendent who had publicly declared himself 'grossly insulted' left quietly and was not heard of again.

Sillitoe thus made it clear from the start what his men must expect of him: he would be a hard taskmaster but not an unfair one. At the same time, as though to sweeten the pill, he offered a reward to any among them who could produce an acceptable plan for reorganisation of the numerous divisions. The five guineas was eventually paid to an ordinary police constable for the plan upon which Sillitoe's 'Reform and Reorganisation' report was based later in the year.

Throughout the spring and summer of 1932 Sillitoe concentrated on this main task of planning his reorganisation scheme, without which it would be impossible to conduct a concerted attack on the gangs.

He despatched two superintendents to Sheffield to study the methods and procedure he had introduced there, and brought to Glasgow a trio of young men who had worked for him in Sheffield. One was Sergeant Hammond, the fingerprint expert, who was given the task of setting up a similar fingerprint record system for Glasgow; the second was Sergeant Robinson who headed the gang-busting flying squad; and the other was Sergeant Bill Deacon, a mechanical transport expert. (The reader will recall that Deacon was not without experience in the care, maintenance and handling of the Sillitoe baby carriage.)

In September 1932 Sillitoe presented his long-awaited report. It was based in part on the submission of the constable who had taken up the chief's invitation to recommend reorganisation of the divisions. 'The large number of divisions is unsatisfactory for many reasons from a practical police point of view,' he wrote, 'and even to the lay mind it must be obvious that much duplication of work is caused.'

In support of his argument for reforms and change he drew a comparison between Glasgow and other large cities. He noted that in the Metropolitan London area there were only twenty-three divisions with an average division strength of 870 officers and men; in Liverpool (whose population was about equal to that of Glasgow) there were seven divisions with an average divisional strength of 321 officers and men; in contrast, Glasgow in 1932 comprised eleven divisions averaging a mere 208 officers and men. Sillitoe therefore proposed to reduce the eleven divisions to seven and to rearrange the divisional areas. Each division would now be responsible for a given stretch of the River Clyde. The reduced divisions would release valuable property for other uses; the total value of the released properties was shown on the corporation books as amounting to £121,804.

Sillitoe had already instituted the police box system in Glasgow, but on a modest scale. The full programme for police boxes would be costly, and he therefore proposed to complete it over a five-year period. The increased divisional areas also created problems; dispensing with so many buildings meant that they would require a large fleet of vehicles to provide increased mobility. He reported:

> In these days of motor banditry and frequent smash and grab raids on business premises, it is really alarming to know that in Glasgow, the second city of the Empire, and with over a million inhabitants and an enormous floating population, the police force is equipped with only five patrol vans and four cars which could be used solely for police purpose. Such a state of affairs is false economy and greatly handicapped the force in its combat with crime generally. It is therefore of paramount and vital importance that a patrol van and a fast touring car should be allocated to each of the divisions.

He also recommended that even before the divisions were altered four patrol vans, two small cars for despatch and six fast motor cars of the touring type be bought at an estimated cost not exceeding £6,000.

The scheme for reorganisation embodied the adoption of a new type of police box. The object would be to provide each beat constable with a miniature police station of a design unlike anything in use elsewhere. There were 323 boxes planned, each to be equipped with a microphone and loudspeaker connected to the appropriate division HQ. Each box would also include a small separate cubicle for use of the constable, affording him some privacy to make out reports and to relax while he ate his lunch. At selected stations there would be detention space for anyone a constable might wish to detain until a police patrol van could be summoned to remove the prisoner to headquarters. The cost of the boxes would amount to £36,000.

The greatest saving to be realised, he argued, would result from the reassignment of officers among the reduced divisions. In support of this he offered the following comparison:

	Authorised	Existing	Reduction
Asst. Ch. Consts.	2	1	—
Superintendents	13	14	4
Chief Inspectors*	50	49	26
Inspectors	109	103	21
Sergeants	200	204	5
Constables	1,915	1,918	25

Although two assistant chief constables were already authorised, only one was on the force. Sillitoe said that with the higher ranks in numbers, two assistant chief constables would be needed: one to take charge of the uniformed branch and the other to oversee the CID. He believed that a reduction in the number of chief inspectors would not mean a falling-off in efficiency, for there was no reason why the 'officer on duty' could not be an inspector. The net saving to the corporation would amount immediately to £32,395 per annum, but to this figure he would add a further saving of £6,863 by dispensing with the services of civilians such as messengers, assessors, clerks and 'casualty surgeons'. A significant portion of the extra saving would come from those additional payments 'made to senior officers for extra services', a practice to be discontinued.

It was perfectly obvious to the Police Committee that Sillitoe's plans would mean a major contribution to the city's strained operating budget, as well as bringing about a vastly improved efficiency. Nevertheless, there was opposition from one quarter: when the Chief Constable's report came up for discussion, Bailie Strain,† one of the people who had opposed his appointment, voiced his objection to the retention of the force's mounted police section which he believed to be an outmoded and useless arm of the force. Strain reminded his colleagues, 'When Sillitoe appeared before the magistrates as an applicant for the post of chief constable, he was closely questioned on this point, and he indicated that he was more interested in mechanical transport,

---

* The original report referred to lieutenants. Here, Chief Inspectors has been substituted as the present-day equivalent.

† 'Bailie' is the Scottish equivalent to the English alderman.

and that the mounted police were only an ornamental body. He also replied that, were the police under his control, he would at the first opportunity disband the mounted section.'

Strain made no attempt to disguise his dislike of the new chief constable. That dislike did not stem purely from a clash of personalities which sometimes occurs between certain men on sight; Sillitoe was a threat to the position which Strain and a small group of his colleagues had fashioned for themselves. Strain was a vociferous and outspoken critic of Sillitoe; he championed the cause of those who were to be 'pensioned off', he criticised the police boxes as an unnecessary expense, he opposed the reforms on the grounds that they were destructive to the morale of the force and would, therefore, do more harm than good. Furthermore, he only rarely put in an appearance at those civic functions attended by the chief constable, thereby lending credence to the view that his opposition was not entirely based on sound economic and political judgement but had a personal flavour. However, for the moment, at least, Bailie Strain and his associates, sniping from entrenched positions, were unassailable.

Despite these tactics, the corporation accepted Sillitoe's recommendations and gave him the authority to put his plans into effect. Choosing his officers for the enlarged divisions with care, personally superintending the changes and working long hours to ensure that everyone knew what was expected of him, he gradually altered the character of the Glasgow force.

Sillitoe had already established himself as a stern disciplinarian, but reports of his early years in Glasgow indicate that he reached a new plateau in this regard. Constables leaving their division headquarters, instead of ambling off to their beat areas as before, now marched in groups of three and four with strict military precision. Sillitoe prowled the streets at night—according to one story, dressed as a workman—to discover for himself if his men were doing their jobs properly. The free and easy days of the pre-Sillitoe era were no more; sergeants and constables who used to slip into the local for a free pint now found it unwise to do so, for they never knew when the captain (as he was still known) would be in the vicinity.

Any officer discovered drinking on the job or otherwise not doing his job properly would find himself brought before Sillitoe the following day. Sergeant Arnot, a police constable at the time, came before Sillitoe this way. He recalls, 'The captain told you the time and the place and it was no use denying it unless you wanted to be thrown out (of the service).' Asked what punishment Sillitoe meted out, Arnot said, 'That depended very much on the charge and circumstances.' I got off with a warning and was told not to be such a bloody fool.' In spite of his experience, Arnot thought highly of Sillitoe and felt him to be a very fair man. 'Sir Percy was interested in his men. When one of the wives was sick he often gave her husband a few days or a week off with pay to get home and look after the family.'

Percy's own family was growing up fast. Audrey was a teenager and the two boys were old enough to move about the city on their own, certainly of an age to be thrilled to visit the police headquarters to see their father. An early recollection of Richard Sillitoe's is vivid enough to provide an insight into his father's personality as seen by a child. Richard, in blue blazer, grey shorts, knee-length socks and peaked cap, with school satchel slung over his shoulder, summons the courage to ask his father for pocket money. His brother, Anthony, is with him; they have talked the matter over and decided which one should do the asking. So, climbing the stairs of police headquarters with some trepidation (they often visited their father in the office), they approach the duty sergeant's desk near his door. At the last moment there is some doubt as to whether they should see him. Is it wise? How can they tell what mood he is in? Experience and the sergeant are their teachers.

'Is our dad in?' they ask.

The sergeant looks at them and rubs his chin. Their decision depends on his reply. If he says, 'Well, he came upstairs whistling today so I suppose he's in a good mood,' they know it will be all right to see him; but if the sergeant says, 'Not a sound all the way up today, kids. You'd better take care,' they have to think again. This day the sergeant winks to let them know he understands, so they open the door and enter. Their father's mood has been correctly divined. He asks them about school and what they are up to. It is a friendly family meeting and Richard feels confident. He asks if his father could let them have money; there is something he wants to buy.

'How many times have I told you that I don't have money! Your mother's the keeper of the family purse, so if you want pocket money you must ask her.' So often over the years did he drill this fact into the children that it became a family law.

Father had no money, mother did; father was a penniless chief constable, mother kept the family. Evidently, Percy had not forgotten his own mother's money problems or the part his father played in them. All this time, incidentally, the Sillitoes continued supporting Percy's mother.

Percy was totally absorbed in his work. He rarely romped or indulged in play with the children, and his only concession to relaxation himself was on Sunday mornings, when he played golf. Malcolm McCulloch, the chief clerk at headquarters during Sillitoe's tenure of office, and who succeeded him as chief constable, had the job of accompanying his chief around the golf course, a task he loathed. One day he remarked to Richard, 'What's wrong with your father? Why can't a man have his Sunday morning in bed? Why does a man have to get up on a Sunday for *his* golf?'

As a public speaker, an enthusiastic Rotarian and an important public servant, Sillitoe was in demand at numerous social meetings, clubs and businessmen's gatherings. The industrialists and business community members were anxious to know what sort of man the new chief constable was. Sillitoe, equally anxious to make himself known, accepted as a necessary duty the dinner meetings he was invited to attend. Typical of this side of his life was his address to the Institute of Engineers and Shipbuilders at 'an informal luncheon' at the Ca'doro Restaurant, Glasgow, in November 1932. The Institute represented an important section of the business community, providing work for many thousands of the city's breadwinners.

Sillitoe used every opportunity to expound new ideas in public; whether his own or borrowed from elsewhere, these were many and varied. To the Institute of Engineers and Shipbuilders on this occasion he put forward what was then a revolutionary idea for the automatic control of traffic.

He may have been thinking of Toll Cross, a particularly intricate city intersection where traffic jams frequently occurred. Toll Cross, which lay on the route from the Sillitoe home to police headquarters, was in the form of a St Andrew's Cross. At these converging thoroughfares, four sets of tram tracks crossed, while yet others ran parallel along the outer lanes. At any time of the day—and especially during rush hours—the constable on point duty, elevated above the traffic on a wooden platform, was the busiest man in Glasgow. It was at Toll Cross that Sillitoe once lost his temper, the shortness of which he frequently betrayed, but rarely to the point of firing on all cylinders.

It was an early spring morning, with torrential rain thrashing down like splintered glass. Richard, then about eight years old, was in the car being driven to school by his father who, in turn, was on his way to headquarters. His father was in uniform, and Richard was huddled in the front passenger seat, conserving heat against the raw morning. At Toll Cross, the milling, noisy traffic was jammed almost to a standstill in a hopeless tangle.

Somehow Richard's father, getting angrier by the minute, managed to manœuvre the car to the constable's point box. Winding down the car window, Percy cocked his head out and, in a cutting tone, shouted, 'What the bloody hell are you waving your hands about like that for? Don't you know how to direct traffic?'

The point man either didn't understand or was past caring. He merely glanced down, formed inaudible words with his lips and hooked a thumb. The 'be-on-your-way' message was unmistakable, and the blaring horns, the headlights of the early morning traffic and the rain somehow made it seem worse. Sillitoe thrust his head out further, the gold braid of his peaked cap clearly visible. 'Do you know who I am?' he rasped with chilling coldness. 'I'm the chief constable of Glasgow.'

The constable calmly leaned over the rail and glowered back. In a broad Glasgow accent he said, 'You can be the monarch himself, mon, for all I care. Now bloody well clear off and let me get on with my job.'

This was too much. In a flaming temper, Sillitoe switched off the engine and got out of the car. Without a raincoat, his black baton tightly gripped in his fist and with the rain piercing the black twill uniform about his broad shoulders, there was no mistaking his identity now. He signalled the constable to get down, eyed the man with a face to match the thunderous clouds overhead and, like a knife cutting into an apple, he said, 'Report to your duty sergeant and tell him to send a replacement—immediately! And report to my office tomorrow morning at ten o'clock sharp.'

The constable saluted stiffly, turned and marched off in high dudgeon. Richard, still huddled in the same position, watched the distorted figure of his father through the windshield as he mounted the dais. The black leather baton began jerking in decisive movements and, miraculously, the traffic began to flow through the congested crossroads.

The next morning on the dot of ten the constable, a man in his mid-thirties, was ushered into the chief constable's office by the sergeant on desk duty. On Sillitoe's otherwise barren glass-topped desk lay the police officer's personal file, unopened, but before the chief could say a word the miscreant spoke.

'I'm very sorry, sir, but it gets a bit hectic out there at times and I was bloody angry. I meant no disrespect, sir. As I said, I'm very sorry.' To the man's utter astonishment, Sillitoe laughed.

As he later told the story to his family at the meal table, the constable showed commendable courage in getting in the first word. Percy owned that he was more in the wrong than the point man, although he made no mention of this during their interview. According to him, all he said was, 'All right, constable; we all lose our tempers at times, don't we, and I suppose a policeman's as human as the next.' Dismissed, the constable turned to leave, but Percy called him back to say, 'By the way, just watch your language in future, will you?' The constable's face relaxed—they both knew what he meant.

Before Sillitoe had been in office a year, he had one more innovation to his credit. This was the chequered black and white headband for the peaked cap to make the wearers easily distinguishable in the dark. This chequered band, known as the 'Sillitoe tartan', first introduced into the Glasgow force then spread to other police forces in Scotland. It spread later to mobile officers and is now in general use throughout the country.

Chapter Twelve

'Just for the Joy-Ride'

Sillitoe's decision to visit the United States of America to study police methods there was a new departure for the chief constables of Great Britain. In the 1930s this was not surprising. The British constabulary system being one of the country's most cherished institutions, it was a popular belief that no one had anything to teach the British policeman—was he not already second to none? Sillitoe did not share this opinion; he believed that there was much to learn from the US police system.

Although there were other outstanding men in the field of US law enforcement, there was no one as innovative and original as August Vollmer. This famous American policeman, a pioneer in the development of modern police methods, was known in the US as the 'Father of the modern cop', and had so much in common with Sillitoe that it was inevitable that they would one day meet.

August Vollmer (1876–1955), former Chief of Police of Berkeley, California, was appointed Professor of Police Administration at the University of Chicago in 1929. He established the first police training school in America, developed the first American '*Modus Operandi*' file through which criminals could be identified by their method of operation; put his officers on bicycles in 1908, on motorcycles as early as 1912, and then in automobiles (the Ford Model T) which he equipped with crystal receiving sets and headphones, the police messages being broadcast by a friend of his who was an amateur radio operator; and opened the first crime detection laboratory. He applied physical and social sciences to crime detection and prevention, and took a practical interest in the social side of police work. In fact, Vollmer was to the US police system pretty well what Sillitoe was to the British constabulary. Like many specialists in other fields, these two men paralleled each other's work with uncanny accuracy, though they were more or less unaware of the other's existence and achievements until they met in late 1932.

In that year, Vollmer made a world tour to study other police systems, and his itinerary included London. While there, he learnt of Sillitoe's work and wrote to ask if he might visit Glasgow. Sillitoe assured him that he would be welcomed. During the ensuing visit, the professor invited Sillitoe to attend the next annual meeting of the International Association of Chiefs of Police, which was to be held in Chicago the following August. Sillitoe made up his mind to attend the convention, but he had first to justify the trip to the Police Committee.

Objections were of course raised to the proposed tour on the grounds that the police budget did not allow for such an expense; also, the police reforms and reorganisation, which were not to be instituted overnight, required Sillitoe's constant attention. It was even suggested that Glasgow's chief constable wanted to visit the United States at the city's expense 'just for the joy-ride'. He was ready for them, however.

Glasgow, he pointed out, had important international responsibilities through its shipbuilding industry and mercantile trade. The city's contacts with other ports and foreign places were equal to, if not greater than, those of the ports of London and Southampton. The growing drug traffic in America, international gold smuggling and other contraband, and related criminal activities, all pointed to a rising internationalism in the world of crime. The obvious answer lay in forging closer ties between the world's law-enforcement agencies; without that co-operation and frequent exchange of ideas, police officers everywhere would find themselves outmanœuvred in their efforts to combat crime.

By the time he had marshalled his arguments there was majority agreement that he should go, on the understanding that he would submit a full report on his return. To this suggestion, which he had made in his original proposal in any case, he readily agreed.

Dollie was to take the children to Elloughton during his absence, a plan which suited him admirably since it meant that he would not have to spend time with his in-laws himself that year. On 23rd July 1933, Dollie and the children watched and waved as the *Tuscania*, with Percy on board, slipped its moorings and steamed down the Clyde, to dock in New York six days later.

The Association of Chiefs of Police had thoughtfully arranged for Sillitoe to be met in New York by an official who was, as it happened, not himself directly connected with the organisation. They could have chosen a more suitable welcoming committee, for this individual, discussing the reason for Sillitoe's visit, told him he could expect to learn nothing from the American police. 'The police are ineffective,' he said in a pessimistic tone. 'There are too many darned politicians in this country.' Sillitoe thrust this information to the back of his mind, but later he had reason to recall what he had been told.

He flew from New York to Chicago in one of the newly commissioned passenger-carrying flying machines. It was his first experience of an aeroplane and though the noise of the engines and vibration made conversation difficult he found it exhilarating. Flying appealed to his spirit of adventure. The fortieth Annual meeting of the International Association of Chiefs of Police also got off to a flying start, at the Sherman Hotel in central Chicago on 31st July. Mayor Kelly was there to make the opening address and to welcome more than a thousand police chiefs to the city.

It is certain that no one—Sillitoe included—missed the point that the gathering was being held among one of the highest concentrations of gangsterism in the American midwest.

The gangsters, about whom Sillitoe soon got to know a great deal, differed only in degree from the razor-flashing hooligans of Sheffield and Glasgow. These were the mobsters, the racketeers and 'syndicate' gangsters whose web of crime was as widespread as the great US railroad system. These were the men who controlled the race tracks, prostitution, drug-trafficking, the extortion racket and 'murder incorporated'. However, in having to deal with their respective gangsters, the British and American police were faced with much the same law-enforcement problems.

In the spacious conference rooms of the Sherman Hotel Sillitoe listened to the technical papers centred on the conference theme 'The modern criminal and the modern policeman', and mingled with his US counterparts from New York, Denver, Los Angeles, Boston, Washington, New Orleans. In the early years of its history the IACP, despite its name, was almost exclusively composed of US and Canadian police officials. In 1933 there were a modest 111 foreign members. Today there are more than 9,500 members in 64 nations.

'JUST FOR THE JOY-RIDE'

J. Edgar Hoover, by then a household name, attended the 1933 conference. Conspicuous by his small stature among big men and surrounded by his devoted lieutenants, the FBI's director commanded attention and respect. His federal officers, commonly known as 'government men', were not yet known as G-Men; that label was not attached until the following month, when government men surrounded and cornered George 'Machine-Gun' Kelly in a house in Memphis, Tennessee, and he implored them, 'Don't shoot, G-Men; don't shoot!'

By 1933 the exploits of the young and brilliant law-enforcement officer, J. Edgar Hoover, Director of the Federal Bureau of Investigation, had spread far beyond the shores of continental America. His reputation, while founded on the substantial ground of a sound administrative ability in organising the fledgling FBI, also stemmed from the successes of his dedicated agents in quelling the unprecedented crime wave which was sweeping America at that time. Sillitoe was among the people Hoover met at the Convention, and they afterwards maintained a correspondence which lasted for the rest of their lives. This meeting was to be mutually beneficial many years later, when Sillitoe was Director-General of MI5, and relations between the two countries, in the intelligence field, reached a low point as a consequence of the activities of Messrs. Burgess, MacLean and Philby.

Sillitoe was not content merely to attend the conference; he had to find out at first hand what went on in the city. As host force to the international convention, the City of Chicago Police were only too willing to open their ranks to their foreign visitor. Also, there is no doubt that Vollmer, now a professor but working closely with the Chicago City Police, had much to do with the Glasgow chief's friendly reception.

The Chicago police headquarters was an almost brand new, thirteen-storey building at the corner of 11th and State Streets. The city fathers had spared no expense in equipping it as the nerve centre of one of the country's largest police organisations, situated as it was in the centre of an ocean of crime. Its spacious floors were outfitted with the most modern equipment that money and technical know-how could provide: a radio communications centre, fingerprint laboratory, ballistics department, science laboratory and a file of criminal records equal to those of the FBI. What he saw was enough to open Sillitoe's eyes in envious wonder. And as though to top off this hive of police industry, the pinnacle of the building carried a single flashing blue light, the city symbol of security.

During one of his frequent visits to the city headquarters Sillitoe had the opportunity to accompany officers on an investigation. A call was received to say that a man had been shot, and investigating officers, with Sillitoe in tow, sped to the scene of the crime. This turned out to be a small Italian restaurant in the central district. The victim, a middle-aged man, had been gunned down while he was eating a meal. He lay conscious but badly injured, surrounded by a knot of curious onlookers. When asked to identify his assailant he proved unco-operative, refusing to give any information because, he said, he would almost certainly be killed by the gunman or his associates if he decided to give evidence. As Sillitoe later reported the incident, the victim said he knew that the courts would deal leniently with the gunmen if caught and certainly let him off with a probationary sentence. The Chicago mobsters, it should be noted, were early pioneers of 'legal aid services', a system of bribery which virtually ensured security in the courts of law to their own kind. In the face of the victim's adamant refusal to help, all the police officers could say was 'OK, we understand'. The man was escorted to the nearest hospital for treatment and the police returned to headquarters.

Percy Sillitoe was saddened by this experience. It brought home to him, as no amount of conventioneering could have done, the sense of frustration under which the US city police laboured in the early thirties. What point was there in being the best equipped police service in the world when they lacked the co-operation of those they sought to protect? A village constable on a bicycle, armed with nothing more than a pencil and notebook, was more effective by far than an entire city police force if he had the confidence of the villagers.

On another occasion, riding as an interested passenger in a patrol car, Sillitoe witnessed the death of a bank robber who, having just emerged from the building when the police arrived in response to a station alarm, was running along the crowded thoroughfare. The patrol car set off in pursuit and an officer, leaning out of the vehicle firing his revolver, brought the bandit down with a chance shot. Yet not all of Sillitoe's time with the Chicago police was spent on patrol. He spent a great deal of time touring headquarters and inspecting the facilities. What he learned of a new invention, the polygraph (the lie detector), wireless transmitters and receivers, US fingerprint practice, and yet another intriguing device which has since become known as the breathalyser, he covered in a report he submitted to the Office of the Secretary of State for Scotland upon his return from America.

It was a measure of his forceful personality that, though a virtual stranger, he made an impact upon the delegates—and this had very little to do with the fact he was from overseas. True, there was a measure of novelty attached to his having journeyed from Scotland, but he was not the only foreign visitor. It is evident from reports of the conference that Sillitoe's exploits with his new-found friends in the Chicago police were bandied about the convention floor and talked about with bemused admiration. When he was not in the conference rooms or in bed he was roaming the streets of the metropolis, at police headquarters, or touring in a patrol car.

When, at the closing banquet, he was quaintly introduced as 'Chief Sillitoe, Constable of Scotland' and called upon to speak, he rose to his feet without hesitation. To his surprise, the entire assembly rose with him and enthusiastically applauded. Sillitoe's eyes could be warm or chillingly cold; the unexpected compliment that his hosts and fellow delegates had paid him was overwhelming and he responded in kind.

'As a mere Briton, may I say this? We have watched the stranglehold of depression that has got your country with the sincerest sympathy, and can only hope that it will soon break into a glorious sunshine of prosperity.' There was another outburst of clapping. Sillitoe went on to tell them what he thought of American hospitality in terms which, even if they do sound patronisingly smooth to the unsentimental ear, were warm and sincere. 'As a mere Briton', 'You wonderful people' —his phrases have the cloying quality of cream dispensed with a ladle, but no one seemed to mind; in fact the enthusiasm of his audience found expression in thumped tables, tinkled glasses, hand claps and shouts of Bravo, all of which pleased him immensely.

It was a long and enjoyable evening. The master of ceremonies, responding to his remarks, assured him that the depression was on the wane. An old-timer, the MC reported, had told him he had been through several periods of depression and none had ever lasted longer than it had taken him to wear out two pairs of pants. 'I'm on my second pair now, and the seat's so thin,' he said, 'when I sit on a dime I can tell whether it's heads or tails.'

During the course of the convention Sillitoe received numerous invitations to visit other US cities, but his time was limited and he was forced to decline most of them. He had, however, mapped out a tour with the help of Vollmer, whose connections were nationwide, to take in Los Angeles, Berkeley, Portland (Oregon) and New York.

His travelling companion for the first leg was to be the Chief of Police of Los Angeles. But it was not to be a happy journey. On the last day of the convention the Los Angeles chief received a telephone call to inform him that he had been replaced during his absence. A new mayor had been elected and, in accordance with the prevailing practice of the day, the mayor had appointed a new chief, a friend according to Sillitoe himself who understood that the appointment was made in consideration of political support received during the election campaign. Sillitoe was disgusted, and publicly said so whenever the opportunity to do so presented itself. Police appointments made on the basis of political patronage were, he thought, a most invidious practice.

As an official guest of the City of Los Angeles, Sillitoe could not of course speak his mind on the matter during his stay there, although he later dwelt on the subject with reporters in Berkeley, Portland and New York. It evidently troubled him greatly that fine and conscientious men should be treated with such cavalier disregard. He expressed surprise on learning that, for one reason or another, the City of Los Angeles had replaced its chiefs of police sixteen times over the past twenty years. (One must note that Sillitoe's first two chief constableships in Great Britain lasted fourteen months each!)

He said goodbye to his unfortunate travelling companion at the airport, where he was met by Assistant Police Chief Finlinson, Harold Lloyd, the film comedian, himself an amateur criminologist and friend of Finlinson, as well as the usual battery of news-hungry reporters. Sillitoe was a find for them, nor did he disappoint those reporters who tagged along on his tour of the Los Angeles police facilities, the Hollywood film studios and other sights.

There were a number of US practices which Sillitoe viewed with concern, believing them to be at the root of the extreme violence and lawlessness in US cities, and he was only too ready to express these views on behalf of the American police officer who, he believed, was unable to speak his own mind, for fear of courting official displeasure and unfavourable public comment.

'Wire-pulling and interference with the police and judiciary,' Sillitoe told Los Angeles reporters, 'are responsible for the rising wave of lawlessness.' Taking murder as an index of crime, he made a comparison. 'In Glasgow last year [1932], there were four murders leading to four arrests and four convictions. Three were domestic-quarrel slayings and the other involved three youths in the hold-up of an inn-keeper.* In Los Angeles during the same period, there were 74 murders, 60 arrests and 40 convictions.'

Asked to explain the obvious disparity in crime rates between the two cities, which were of comparable size, Sillitoe said, 'There are two important factors. I gather that here in America, a police chief is not always free to administer the law, and that this condition is fostered by a privilege-seeking element among the public. In Great Britain, police chiefs, magistrates and judges are appointed by the Crown and can order such meddlers from their offices. And the British public simply won't stand for anything approaching looseness in law enforcement.'

It must be said that the 'Doyen of British Chief Constables' (to quote the Pictorial Weekly of 25th June 1927) sometimes leaned a little too heavily on his own sense of British fair play, and this was one such time. He knew that the facts were simply not as he had made them out to be, playing down the state of lawlessness in Glasgow when he took murder as an index of crime and quoted comparative figures between the two cities. Enough has been said of the shocking state of affairs in Glasgow in the early thirties to establish that it was far from being a law-abiding and peaceful city; on the contrary, it had more than its share of vice, corruption and crime. If differences between US and British crime statistics are to be explained, one must seek for the answer in the more fundamental psychological differences between the two nations. That is, conceived in revolution, nourished on violence, and volatile in its emotions, US society swings between much greater extremes of violence and passivity than that of the British Isles. Sillitoe clearly ignored the broader aspects in considering this question.

Another point: the American system of law-enforcement appointments was not as lax as Sillitoe supposed. Although it is true that, even today, appointments can be terminated with each election and change in the political power-base, the practice is not

* From the Los Angeles *Sunday Morning*, 5th August 1933. Sillitoe probably said 'publican'.

widely used. This is because most appointments are subject to confirmation by the political sub-division's governing body—city council, county council, state general assembly and, in the case of the Federal government, the United States Congress. This process effectively limits the probability of a chief executive replacing his predecessor's appointees with a 'friend of his own'. One must therefore conclude that Sillitoe, in condemning the whole system of law-enforcement appointments, leapt to a hasty conclusion on too superficial an understanding of that system and with the personal acquaintance he made of a single officer who suffered as a result of it.

As Sillitoe must have been aware, the British system can work the other way; the best example of this is perhaps to be found in the case of his predecessor at Sheffield, Hall-Dalwood. Because this chief constable's appointment was for life, we will probably never know what problems that city council had in replacing an executive so patently unable and unsuited to continue his duties. A system in which chief constables, magistrates and judges are appointed for life is not without its pitfalls and disadvantages.

However, his views on the US system are important as an indication of his personality. In some respects he could be as inflexible as reinforced concrete. He was ready to grant that the US police service, with its imaginative and innovative technical advances, was far ahead of the British system, but he tended to make unfair comparisons between the two systems in pointing to differences which didn't exist. For instance, comparing the British policeman with the US patrolman, he was convinced that the patrolman led a boring existence in patrolling his beat. This, he was fond of arguing, was because of the American tendency to specialise, so that whenever a US patrolman came across evidence of a crime he merely reported the fact to his superiors who assigned the investigation to specialists. The British constable on the other hand, he said, became personally involved in the investigation with the help of other police specialists. In fact, in 1933, there was virtually no difference between the American and British beat systems except, perhaps, that US officers were becoming more mobile.

Still in Los Angeles, Sillitoe was questioned, interviewed and his opinion sought on every conceivable subject. Kidnapping, a crime of which he had no experience, was, he had learned, very much in vogue in the US, where the authorities were extremely disturbed. At the Chicago convention a government representative had turned up from Washington to deliver an after-dinner speech in which he had declared that the Administration (Roosevelt's 'New Deal' administration, elected in 1932) were determined to stamp out the evil with the same ruthlessness with which such crimes were perpetrated. The speaker had made an appeal to the local judges that all kidnapping cases be handed over to the federal courts, whose judges were, like their British counterparts, but unlike many of the lower courts judiciaries, free from reproach in the execution of their duty.

Commented Sillitoe to a reporter, 'We haven't any kidnapping law because we never have kidnappings. In Scotland we would have to charge a person with assault or holding a person against his will—if we had any such crime.'

But if Sillitoe deplored the incidence of kidnapping in America and sympathised with law officers on the sheer scale of crime with which they had to contend, he found much to admire in the American way of life. The 'push-button society', with its labour-saving devices, made a lasting impression on him. In Berkeley, California, he stayed with friends who had power-operated hide-away beds and an ironing board which folded into a wall recess; even the simple foot-operated trash receptacles and similar pieces of household gadgetry were completely new to him and, he thought, should be made available to the British housewife.

Travelling from Berkeley to Portland and then to New York, Sillitoe was received with the same courtesy and overwhelming hospitality he had experienced everywhere; given every facility to ask questions, inspect and make notes on how the city police departments operated, he felt that the tour had been worth while.

It was in New York that he acquired one of the main things he was seeking: an example of a small broadcast-receiver set for use in patrol cars. Such a piece of equipment was not available from British manufacturers, a lack that he was determined to rectify as soon as he got home.

Having travelled more than 6,000 miles, mostly by air, on his twenty-two-day-long tour, the sea voyage on the homeward-bound *Tuscania* was a welcome rest. His second-in-command, Assistant Chief Constable Warnock, the police procurator-fiscal, James Langmuir, and a small group of reporters joined the *Tuscania* at the mouth of the Clyde for the remaining part of the journey up-river.

Sillitoe once said, in answer to a reporter's question on the subject of personal publicity, 'I cannot bear to see my name in print.' It was an illuminating comment, considering his consistent behaviour on this score: publicity was the one thing he made no attempt to shun, and, over the years, he developed quite a knack for backing into the limelight. In any case, Sillitoe submitted himself to a barrage of questions and a lengthy interview from the reporters who had joined the ship with Warnock and Langmuir.

Summing up his tour, he said, 'The feeling is strong in America that there is so much political jobbery that a man cannot look for justice today, and public-spirited citizens would fain see British practice followed in the judicature and in such matters as police appointments.'

Despite his honest criticisms of the differences between the British and American systems of police appointments and, to some degree, methods employed, Sillitoe regarded the American policeman as a hero. 'He does his work honestly against great difficulties and in frequent danger,' he said. 'Undoubtedly many people carry firearms and, with the variation in law between the various states in this regard, any partial prohibition or control is hopeless. If (the police) only received the support of the judiciary, the American policeman would be as effective in preventing lawlessness as anywhere in the world.'

We are left with the question as to whether Sillitoe learned anything from his American tour that he could apply to the maintenance of law and order in Glasgow, in his fight against crime in that city, what methods he discovered as peculiar to US law enforcement which would be applicable to his own experience. In other words, was the trip justified? Or had he in fact gone for the joy-ride as had been suggested when he brought the subject to the attention of the police committee? On the positive side, he undoubtedly got an insight into the technical and scientific advances achieved by US police by 1933; he got first-hand information on a number of technical innovations such as the breathalyser, polygraph and Hollerith data retrieval system as testified in his subsequent report to the office of the Secretary of State for Scotland. He met a number of influential people such as J. Edgar Hoover, federal government officials and police chiefs of some of the major cities, and his acquaintance with them would be useful in the years to come. There is, however, no real evidence that he discovered anything of US police methods or applied them, if he did learn anything, to his own situation and work. His biggest gain was in getting a good grounding in wireless equipment and related communication practices, which he certainly applied as soon as he returned to Glasgow.

Home at last, feeling fit—except for a slight touch of rheumatism—and with a tan from the California sun, Glasgow's returned chief constable felt nothing but satisfaction as a result of the tour. It had been a fascinating, informative and enjoyable experience—but Sillitoe, at least, would not call it a joy-ride.

Chapter Thirteen

C Division Specials

Like all modern cities, Glasgow needed room to grow, and during the early thirties its expansion followed the southward curve of the River Clyde in its reach for the sea. Housing developments were a pressing necessity, and the corporation made serious efforts to relieve the congestion of the slums by construction of new housing estates, such as Knightswood, to its west. The slums, however, remained untouched and continued to spawn fresh waves of sons and daughters. These sprawling areas, containing row upon row of tenement dwellings, ill-lit terraces and back alleyways, were breeding grounds of every type of vice and poverty.

Immediately following his return from the United States, Sillitoe set about dealing with the problems of Glasgow with renewed vigour. There was massive unemployment and hunger marches to contend with, gang warfare, corruption in high places, and the usual slop-bucket of crime, the remedying of which could be a soul-destroying task for an ordinary man. But Sillitoe was no ordinary man. His force was reorganised, there were fewer divisions, and there was an emphasis on speedier communications. The division headquarters were now equipped with police vans and fast touring cars, a large number of police boxes had been installed and the response to calls for help now took a matter of minutes. The professional lawbreakers had to think of new ways to offset the advantages Sillitoe had given to the side of law and order. He also began equipping his patrol cars with the radio transmitters he had found in use on the other side of the Atlantic. 'The City of Berkeley,' he reported to the Police Committee, 'has dispensed with foot patrols altogether, and they have been replaced entirely by motor vehicle patrols.'

While he did not envisage going to the same lengths with his own force, he was determined to have the best equipment that the city could provide. He contacted a number of electrical equipment manufacturers and invited them to inspect the sample radio transmitter he had brought back from New York. He then looked around for a supplier capable of equipping the entire fleet with suitable communication equipment. He achieved one of his firsts among British chief constables when the system was installed by Marconi; it eventually covered Argyllshire, Lanarkshire and Dumfries. By the outbreak of the Second World War he had a VHF station in operation. The Home Office said it wouldn't work; it did, of course, and when Sillitoe formed his 'Clyde Patrol' (a fleet of motorboats manned by civilians to patrol the Clyde during the war) each craft was similarly outfitted and included in the communication network.

Command of the fleet of fast patrol cars satisfied one of Sillitoe's few passions. In most things he was a man of moderation: he smoked little, enjoyed good food and an occasional drink, but nothing to excess, and as to his relationships with women (a necessary question to be asked in biographies), Dollie was his good companion, and he neither needed nor sought any female companionship. If he had a weakness, it was for fast, sporty cars, and of these the Alvis held pride of place. The machines he chose for the Glasgow fleet were Alvis Speed Twenties: high-performance models, low-slung, with spoked wheels, soft tops and large chrome headlights mounted on a crossbar skirting the radiator. Sillitoe's enthusiasm for fast cars and, perhaps, the fact that his drivers took time to get used to them led to initial difficulties.

In March 1932 the Sillitoes had rented Tapston House in the village of Kilmalcolm. Kilmalcolm lies a few miles to the southwest of the city and for a period a driver was required to call at Tapston House in the morning to drive Sillitoe to the office. For some reason, carefully trained though they were, the drivers seemed to lose their heads whenever they had the chief constable as a passenger. According to Sillitoe himself they became reckless, lost their sense of reason and were a menace to life and limb. They raced other vehicles on the road and overtook with dangerous abandon; in the city limits, they bypassed trams which had stopped to take on or discharge passengers and were known on occasions to mount the pavement in their anxiety to deliver their chief to the office in record time. Sillitoe cautioned and upbraided them to no avail. One driver after another abandoned all caution the moment the chief constable stepped into the car. He finally summoned Sergeant Deacon, who, it will be recalled, was in charge of transport.

'Deacon,' he said, 'why the hell can't you get me a decent driver? They're all stark raving mad.'

'I don't know, sir,' Deacon replied. 'You seem to have an odd effect on them. They just seem to lose control of themselves when you're with them.'

'Well, do something,' Sillitoe demanded. 'I'm sick of risking my bloody neck every time I get into a police car.'

Deacon said he would see what he could do. He found a man renowned for his imperturbability and put him through his paces. Only when he was quite satisfied did he tell Sillitoe that he thought there would be no cause for complaint with the new driver. The driver was therefore instructed to be at Tapston House at the appointed hour the following morning. He was a punctual and conscientious constable. As he was about to set off for Kilmalcolm the following morning, however, he came across a stray dog. There was ample time before he had to be at his destination, so he put the sorry-looking creature into the back of the car and took it to the local dog pound before continuing on his way.

Sillitoe, impeccable in his uniform as usual, eyed Deacon's latest choice with a critical eye as he climbed into the back of the car and gruffly bade him good morning. To his vast relief he had a sedate ride into the city. It seemed that a safe and reliable driver had been found at last; but there was still something wrong. For a time Sillitoe had no idea what was bothering him. He certainly felt uncomfortable. He was unaccountably itchy and scratched himself a few times in an exploratory way; there was an unusual smell, too. As they were approaching the city centre, his curiosity got the better of him and he tapped the driver on the shoulder.

'There's a strange smell back here. Any idea what it might be?'

The driver barely moved his head. 'Oh that, sir,' he replied matter-of-factly; they might have been discussing the weather. 'I picked up a stray dog on the way over and dropped it at the pound.'

Sillitoe exploded. 'Stop this bloody car,' he barked. 'Stop it right away.' He scrambled out on the pavement. Shaking his baton at the driver, he said, 'Clear off. Get this bloody car fumigated, get it fumigated immediately. What do you think it is, the corporation muck cart? Jesus Christ in creation!' And with that he slammed the door and strode off to the office in a fuming temper. That morning, he was not whistling happily to himself as he mounted the stairs. Nevertheless, despite the unhappy beginning with Deacon's latest choice, Sillitoe found him to be a first-rate chauffeur and kept him on

The emphasis on motor transport had little if any effect on the foot patrols, and those policemen pounding the beat continued to have the daily contact with the public that they had always had. The Depression was a way of life for thousands of families in Glasgow—the common experience of all European cities during these years—but, unlike most, Glasgow had early fostered a vocal and well-organised Communist Party in its midst. Prominent amongst the Scottish CP leaders was William (Willie) Gallacher, who was to be the first Communist Member of Parliament, representing the mining district of East Fife for many years. When Lenin visited Scotland as a political refugee it was the Gallachers who took him into their home in Paisley. Gallacher was the 'prominent member of the Communist Party' referred to in Sillitoe's autobiography who, delivering an inflammatory anti-government speech on Glasgow Green, incited his audience to attack three plainclothes policemen, resulting in serious injury to all three.

At one time public meetings were held daily on Glasgow Green, one of the city's main public parks and Scotland's equivalent of 'Speaker's Corner' in London's Hyde Park. Partly as a consequence of the roughing-up of the three plainclothes men, but more as part of an overall campaign to hold the Communists in check, Sillitoe used his influence to have a by-law passed prohibiting such meetings. The ordinance, carefully worded to permit religious meetings, gave rise to the creation of what became known as 'tramp preachers', a phrase first introduced by Gallacher. Whenever tramp preachers—who were, of course, the regular Communist speakers—espied a constable approaching their meetings they immediately started offering up a prayer. Supporters who were parties to the deception then asked the constable to remove his helmet in the hope that he would be embarrassed enough to leave them alone. The ruse frequently worked.

Persistent among the Communist agitators working to stir up the city's battalions of unemployed was Guy Aldred, one of the more colourful characters whom Sillitoe was fond of recalling in later life. Aldred, a Londoner, moved to Glasgow in the mid-twenties and soon established a name for himself as a pamphleteer and broadsheet writer, selling copies for a penny an issue. Aldred attacked anything and everything with a savage streak of humour. As chief constable, and therefore a prominent representative of the establishment, Sillitoe came in for some of Aldred's most bitter attacks. He was never more vitriolic than when Sillitoe joined the Highland Institute, an organisation catering to the more affluent residents of Glasgow.

The Institute's annual Highland ball was a grand affair, to which everyone of importance flocked in the full regalia of his respective clan. Up to the time of Sillitoe's appointment the chief constables had been Scottish, so in Sillitoe's case there was some difficulty as to what he should wear. To quote from the McGlinchey papers:

> You could hire for the evening a full dress down to the fearsome dagger 'dirk' stuck down your hose. A local Jew, also a member of the Institute, would supply you for a fee a suitable tartan outfit if you had no tartan of your own—and he had a selection of vivid and chequered tartans to chose from. Sillitoe chose one that would've stopped the traffic on sight.

On the night of the ball it was noted that for a man of his height and build, Sillitoe had very spidery legs. Aldred, in his next broadsheet, quoting a well-known phrase from a Scottish vagrancy charge, said that the chief constable, with those legs, should be charged 'for having no visible means of support'. Aldred was also pleased to point out that as the chief constable was so fond of charging local gangsters with 'carrying a lethal weapon likely to cause bodily harm', he should himself be charged for 'carrying an offensive weapon—namely, the dirk'. These poisonous darts aimed from afar did Sillitoe little damage, even though they continued to issue from his pen until the outbreak of the war. It is interesting to note that Aldred ceased his propaganda efforts soon after the war began—following the party line no doubt—and took up other activities (he founded a marriage bureau, and by all accounts it prospered).

The Communists used every trick they could devise to stir

up the unemployed and, of these, that of infiltrating meetings and attempting to heckle into submission those speakers who did not satisfy their tastes was the most common. Here again Sillitoe came in for his share of harassment. We have already noted that he participated in many activities outside his normal police work —marriage guidance counselling, youth programmes and prisoner rehabilitation work (of which more will be learned in due course), and he was also known to be a willing public speaker.

When church ministers in one district organised a series of public lectures to help occupy the unemployed, Sillitoe was asked to participate and agreed to deliver an address on his favourite topic—'Big Game Hunting in Africa'. Considering the circumstances, the subject could not have been more ill-chosen or out of place. Nevertheless, he was assured of a packed audience when listeners filled the New Patrick Picture House to hear him speak—and the Communists turned up in force with some of their most experienced hecklers to take him on. There was a band in attendance and after a few suitable numbers the chairman, the Rev. Hugh MacDonald, stood up to introduce the chief constable.

'He came here very early this morning . . .' he began, only to be immediately interrupted by a shrill female voice shouting, 'He should have stayed in bed!' This was a signal for supporters to offer a stirring rendition of 'The Internationale' and, in a display of Christian good manners, the chairman was good enough to wait until they had made their offering complete before finishing his introduction (not without further difficulty). He then beckoned Sillitoe to take over.

Percy began his address, bearing with initial goodwill the gibes of the hecklers, then broke off to ask for the footlights to be turned off, wishing, he said, to see the people he was addressing. He had used the same device when he first spoke to the police assembled in St Andrew's Hall, but this time there was a different response.

'Use your baton,' a heckler shouted. 'Awa' back to England', 'Awa' back to Sheffield' were shouts heard above the booing and catcalls. Sillitoe smiled.

'I am perfectly willing to listen to you,' he said, 'but if you won't listen to me I'll sit down.'

Those wanting to hear what he had to say were in the majority and called out for him to carry on, but the interruptions continued with remorseless and perverse intent. Sillitoe did his best to make himself heard above the noise of the hecklers on the one hand and the shouts of encouragement of those who would have order on the other. When he then told them he would tell of the time he shot a bull elephant, another strident female voice screamed, 'Tell us the one about the three bears!'

'I frankly admit that I am not a professional speaker,' Sillitoe continued, 'I only came here this morning . . .'

'You're a professional bobby,' someone shouted.

'. . . but if you arrange for another meeting and have a better lighted hall, I will willingly come down and address you again.'

Shrugging slightly, Sillitoe then turned to leave the stage, and only now realised how few were those who had effected the disruption—his supporters gave him tremendous applause. But he should have realised before he started that he was not there to address Rotarians or members of the United Empire League. There is no record of his returning to address the unemployed again; besides, there were other things, for which his efforts were better appreciated, to keep him occupied.

The hunger marches which took place almost daily at this period, and mass meetings in George Square were accompanied by outbreaks of violence reminiscent of the General Strike of 1926. As much as he sympathised with the protesters, Sillitoe nevertheless insisted that the marches and meetings be orderly.

His own explanation of how he eventually succeeded in controlling the demonstrations and achieved some measure of orderliness is fairly straightforward. This, briefly, was that he instructed the division superintendents to be responsible for those contingents of marchers which formed in their division areas, placing police at the head and tail end of the columns, and maintaining this formation when it reached the central assembly point with contingents from other districts. This achieved the effect of boxing in the entire demonstration. Troublemakers, he recorded, were then more easily dealt with by putting them into conveniently-located police vans. He omitted, however, to mention the important contribution to his police system of an extra division which came to be known as 'Sillitoe's C Division Specials'.

The C Division Specials had nothing to do with the uniformed 'special constable', that well-known feature of the British constabulary system whereby civic-minded citizens, acting part-time and unpaid, assist the regulars. The C Division Specials constituted Sillitoe's intelligence-gathering service and, as such, were a race apart from the ordinary specials, not to mention the regular PCs on the beat.

Every police force depends to some extent on information provided by law-abiding and conscientious citizens who are doing their duty to the community when they report an occurrence. Indeed, it is confirmation of public confidence in a police department when the citizenry offer information without fear. In the mildest sense, anyone who offers information to the police, and therefore informs, is an informer. However, what the police call 'informants' are, quite specifically, suppliers of inside information about crimes performed or planned. They are clearly distinct from the general public who may casually report some suspicious sight, or who give information in response to investigations in the form of eye-witness reports. Informants—narks, snouts, grasses—are usually underworld characters or persons in frequent contact with the police who report what they know, not what they happen to have seen, and are usually paid for their reports or receive some consideration in return.

The origins of Sillitoe's C Division Specials are obscure, but it is thought that they began to be recruited during the early days in Glasgow when Sillitoe first came up against extreme left-wing agitators. McGlinchey, who seems to be more than usually well-informed on the subject—journalists frequently use the same sources as the police and are themselves a rich source of information—maintains that the ranks of C Division included barmen, ex-cons whom Sillitoe helped over the years, prostitutes, a number of ex-boxers, and an ill assortment of gangsters through whom Sillitoe established a wide information network to keep him abreast of what was going on in the city. The name, C Division Specials, applied as well to the special irregulars who, supplementing the regulars, he used to beat the battling street gangs at their own game. One ex-boxer, noted for his cauliflower ears, and who went under the name of Deaf Burke, was certainly of this number. Burke was recruited and sent out with the police contingents in furniture vans to fight the gangs, a subject more fully discussed in the next chapter. Of Sillitoe's C Division intelligence network, McGlinchey says:

> 'Reformed ex-cons, the professionals'—prostitutes—'barmen, barmaids and publicans were recruited. They were never seen

talking to a policeman, nor did they ever set foot inside a police station. They all used the phone; nothing was ever written down on paper. (Sillitoe) got most of it himself direct, at the office, and that information covered everything from titbits to large jobs in the making. For instance, coin meters for gas and electricity were frequently robbed so anyone who offered too many shillings (or pennies) for his drinks at a public house, especially if he was not a regular, was not there long before he had a hand on his shoulder wanting to know how he had come into so much small change.'

Sillitoe was to use his C Division with increasing effectiveness throughout his career in Glasgow, especially in combating IRA terrorists in the late thirties. At the outset, however, the Division's special talents were well occupied by the fight against the disruptive influence exerted by Communist agitators. One of the earliest examples of usefulness of the network concerned the case of an agitator, Peter McIntyre who, aided and abetted by his friend Aldred, was one of the main organisers of the hunger marches. Following Sillitoe's return from his American tour, McIntyre planned a march during which there was to be deliberate provocation to generate a riot. Information coming to Sillitoe from a number of C Division sources confirmed that there was mischief in the making. One of these sources was a former Communist sympathiser, a woman acquaintance of McIntyre, with whom the chief constable came in contact after the New Patrick Picture House incident.

Now Sillitoe could identify with the poor and unemployed to the extent that he could understand their expressing dissatisfaction with 'the system', but he had no scruples about dealing with those of McIntyre's stamp, who deliberately conspired to cause trouble. In his view, McIntyre was a dangerous agitator from whose machinations the man in the street ought to be protected. Wondering how to nip McIntyre's scheme in the bud, and learning from his source that he was in arrears with his rent, Sillitoe invited McIntyre's landlord to pay a visit to his office. He without difficulty persuaded the property owner to seek an eviction order. When McIntyre was served the order he determined to put up a fight, and had his supporters ram a sizeable tree—with considerable foliage attached—through a rear window of the house, and through the hall and out through the front door, to prevent the bailiffs from entering the premises to enforce the eviction order. It was a useless gesture, however, and served only to delay the eviction.

For Sillitoe the step was a drastic one to take, yet, so far as one can gather, the planned riot did not take place, and from then on the marches, though they continued at regular intervals, became more orderly affairs. Of McIntyre no more was heard, but it is thought that he left Glasgow for other parts. If so, he was the first of a long line of people who did so after crossing swords with the city's chief constable.

One further example of C Division at work concerned a police operation mounted following receipt of information concerning a burglary. This time, Sillitoe was contacted by a prostitute for whom he had once done a good turn. At one of the public houses she frequented in connection with her work, she overheard the conversation of three strangers who were planning a large burglary, and who intended leaving the country on the overnight ferry to Belfast. She was unable to give the location of the intended break-in, but she provided an accurate description of the three conspirators. Officers were despatched to the ferry to await the arrival of the burglars. For three nights the police waited in vain. Sillitoe contacted his informant, but she insisted that her information was accurate. Sillitoe told the CID plainclothes officers to wait, even though no reports of large break-ins had been received from the time he received the initial information. The three men were picked up when attempting to board the ferry four days later, and an inspection of their baggage revealed a large jewellery haul from a country residence in Renfrewshire.

It will be recalled that Bailie James Strain was one of the councillors who had opposed Sillitoe's appointment, and later objected to his visiting the United States of America on the grounds that he had nothing to learn from such a visit and was only going for the joy-ride. Early in 1933 Strain was caught red-handed taking a bribe. Sillitoe rarely concerned himself with the detailed investigation of crimes, but this particular case was distinguished by, first, the obvious animosity of Strain towards himself, and, second, corruption in the corporation—something which he had long wanted to expose. That graft and corruption existed, that it was widespread, that a number of officials was involved there was no doubt in Sillitoe's mind. For a long time the newspapers had speculated about it, rumours of graft were persistent in the ranks of the police, and there was much talk that it existed in the city, but no concrete evidence came to light to justify the claims that were frequently made. However, it is well known that if anyone wanted council consideration for anything, then Bailie Strain was the man to approach.

As a member of the licensing committee for street vendors and market stallholders, Strain was able to offer licence applicants better positions in return for a fee which he shared with two of his colleagues. It was a petty sort of graft, but the income was regular and the practice well organised, though this was never brought to light in the subsequent court proceedings. However, one stallholder who had been offered a better position for her stall for a fee to Strain of £25, reported the offer to the police. When the matter came to Sillitoe's attention he took charge himself.

The stallholder was instructed to proceed with the deal. She was supplied with marked banknotes, to be handed over during a meeting in a restaurant as specified by the committee members. The trap was laid with two police officers in attendance and sprung according to plan. Two Bailies, Strain and Ritchie, were taken into custody and charged. The third member of the trio escaped arrest by a hair's breadth because, being detained elsewhere on other business, he telephoned to apologise for being late and was given warning of the police trap. Strain received a prison sentence; Ritchie got off by the skin of his teeth, for no sound reason that one is able to discover other than the fact that he had a fine war record.

The conviction of Strain exposed a hairline crack in the veneer of respectability disguising the corruption on the corporation, but Sillitoe had to wait another eight years before he was finally able to prise the crack wide open.

One of the subjects with which Sillitoe chose to concern himself about this period was the lax licensing laws governing the operation of licensed premises in the city—hotels, public houses, clubs—and the incidence of drunkenness.

There were 1,524 licensed premises in Glasgow in 1933: 1,180 public houses, 261 grocers, 70 clubs and 13 hotels. The opening and closing hours varied to such an extent that it was possible for some citizens who were club members to have virtually unlimited time for drinking. It is quite evident from Sillitoe's annual report for 1933 that he objected to the operation of private clubs with different opening hours from those of the public houses, because this gave these privileged members an undue advantage over the ordinary citizen in the matter of drinking. In cases where there were infringements of the licensing laws or brawling, he had the premises raided, employing a strategy that may seem familiar to those who have seen films dealing with America during Prohibition.

He had his police concealed in furniture vans, which were then backed up to the door of the premises to be raided. Then the doors were opened. Everyone in the premises, without exception, would be taken into custody and the place closed for the night. McGlinchey says:

'He used more than furniture vans, some times an ambulance or ordinary commercial vehicle was put into service. With the vehicle backed up to the doorway of the pub, his "specials" rounded up all the customers and returned with them to the central police station. As the Glasgow drinker was not going to lose any drinking time they soon told who caused the disturbance, and, after obtaining witnesses, Sillitoe had the innocent boozers driven back, not to their "local" which remained closed for the night, but very near their own area where there were plenty more pubs still open.'

Again, he was using an unconventional but highly successful method to deal with a vexing problem. He also brought about by this means a considerable reduction in the incidence of drunkenness. His raiding parties on establishments which contravened the licensing laws were so successful that he was able at the end of 1933 to report to the corporation:

Prosecutions for drunkenness during 1933 were 5,674, which was a decrease of 401 over the previous year.

I am still of the same opinion that I expressed at the annual licensing court in April 1933, that there should be the same hours of opening on Saturday as on other weekdays.

To my mind and from practical experience I am satisfied that the more equal the two periods of permitted hours the better, and to have in Glasgow on the one weekday (Saturday) when people are more free than on any other, six continuous permitted hours for drinking cannot be considered under any circumstances to assist restraint. I venture to suggest also that the interest of the general public in this matter must be considered, and that it is unreasonable that a person who requires alcoholic refreshment with his Saturday lunch cannot obtain it.

He went on to say that his programme of vigilance with respect to the licensing laws over the past year had been very effective: 'It will be seen that drunkenness has now ceased to be a problem to the police, for, when compared with 18,709 proceedings for drunkenness in 1920, the figure for 1933 becomes almost negligible.'

Of all the aspects of the city's licensing laws and drinking habits, he was most unswerving in his condemnation of the drunken driver. 'It is the duty of the police to enforce the law and protect the public against the offending motorist.' Of 78 motorists charged in 1933, only one had received a prison sentence (60 days) while the remaining 68 actually convicted were let off with paltry fines, the great majority not exceeding £10, which he thought was ridiculous. In discussing the treatment of offending motorists in his 1933 annual report, Sillitoe directed his opinion at the city's magistrates who evidently took due note: the following year, fines were increased and many more offenders went to prison.

In a remarkably short time Sillitoe had succeeded in curbing Communist activities in the city, reducing drunkenness to manageable proportions, and affecting sweeping police reforms with the accent on scientific modernisation. Superficially—and in the main, it must be owned—these achievements stemmed from the force of his personality and the use of the legal processes at his disposal, but his formation and use of that intelligence network referred to as the C Division Specials, should not be underestimated. It was a 'force' which he continued to use over the years, and it is a testimony to his stature as a brilliant and dedicated public servant that he never misused it. The tact and delicacy with which his network was used to serve the public good deserves both praise and approbation. In unscrupulous hands such 'instruments' lead to the police state; for evidence one need only look to the rise of Hitler's Third Reich.

Chapter Fourteen

Gangsters and Barking Dogs

Sillitoe, the most prosaic of men, revealed his personality in many ways. Despite the dearth of private papers, his character shines forth like the edge of a finely-cut diamond in his numerous official reports. In one of his early Glasgow annual reports he raised an issue which many discussed in private but did not have the courage to bring into the open, until Sillitoe showed the way: this concerned the relationship between the level of crime and unemployment. One commentator, reviewing his report, made the following observation:

> No city can afford to be indifferent to the picture of the community presented each year in the police returns. For the modern chief constable in any considerable city works on a large canvas in publishing his record. His duties take him far beyond the mere recital of the figures of crime, delinquency and accident. He has not only to describe his organisation and justify his arrangements, but it is possible for him to place a finger here and there on the assembled tables and charts and thus to draw attention to social trends and to indicate possible reforms. The annual report for the City of Glasgow . . . is distinguished by this vitality. Sillitoe's conclusions bear striking witness to the administrative ability and understanding of the city's problems which have already marked his work in Glasgow.

The commentator was referring to the statistics of crime which Sillitoe had presented. These were in two categories: first, an analysis of the number and types of crimes against persons and, secondly, a similar analysis of those against property. He showed that while there was a marked decrease in the former, there was an alarming increase in the latter. In 1931, there were 7,626 property crimes; in 1932, 13,559. An equally impressive leap occurred in 1933. Discussing the significance of this disturbing trend, Sillitoe reported:

> Many of the younger generation have drifted into crime owing to present-day conditions. Their parents may be able to provide them with a home and clothing, but are unable to supply them with the pocket money they require for amusements. As they have never known the discipline of work they fall into criminal habits as the opportunity offers.
>
> There can be little doubt that the increase of crime in the city is due in some measure to the difficult times through which we are passing, and that unemployment is the main factor, especially in the case of crimes involving the dishonest appropriation of property.

It was Sillitoe's firm conviction that reduced unemployment and regular wages would automatically result in a decreased number of arrests and convictions. He believed that a living wage was the best incentive to good conduct—a view widely held today, but not so popular in the thirties. Crimes associated with the affluent society had yet to be experienced. The pressing demands of industrialists and mine owners in the twenties and early thirties for lower wages led, in the long run, to increased expenditure by the community for the prevention and detection of crime which would probably not have arisen if normal economic conditions existed.

This was the situation as Sillitoe saw it. He felt that his duty was to translate his words and opinions into action, even if no one else agreed with him. In this regard he was confronted, first, with the problem of ending the reign of terror imposed by the street gangs, and then of demonstrating by his own good example that to catch and convict lawbreakers was not enough. Something had to be done to dissuade them from breaking the law in future. Many police officers of the day shared Sillitoe's views on this subject, but none practised what they preached to the same degree as Sillitoe, and, in America, August Vollmer.

Sillitoe's own account of how he throttled the gangs is exciting, but he did not record how he organised the police machinery to deal with them, and pursued a systematic plan to put the gangs out of business with the long-range objective of winning public co-operation. First, he studied the composition and organisation of the gangs to understand the problem with which he had to deal, and then made his plan. The police files were full of reports of gang incidents and gang warfare; they were a rich source of information to put the subject in historical perspective, and the experiences of long-serving officers who had had to deal with them over the years helped to provide him with a comprehensive picture.

The gangs had their beginnings in recognisable form in the 1880s with numerous references in newspapers of the day to a gang known as the Penny Mob. The name derived from the fact that a levy of a penny a week was imposed on members, who were numbered in the hundreds, to pay the fines of those hauled before the magistrates. At the turn of the century new gangs came into being and were identified with particular sections of the city as well as by name. In the east end there was the Ping Pong gang; in the north end, the Hi Hi; in the southern districts, there were the South Side Stickers, the San Toy, the Village Boys and the Tim Malloy gang. During the 1920s, new gangs appeared in place of the older gangs which passed into oblivion through loss of leadership or simply disintegrated with the passage of time. Gangs holding sway in the 1920s included the Redskins, the Black Hand, the Parlour Boys and the Beehive gang. By the time Sillitoe arrived in the city, two very large gangs, the Norman Conks and the Billy Boys, were operating. They were each able to muster between three and four hundred members. As with their predecessors, the new gangs were partly motivated by religious prejudice. The Norman Conks (derived from the Norman Street district where they were concentrated and, allusively, from William the Conqueror), loosely followed the Roman Catholic persuasion, and were in continual conflict with the Protestant Billy Boys. Both gangs operated in the east end of the city. The Norman Conks were led by Bull Bowman and the Billy Boys by William (Bill) Fullerton.

Originally known as 'Keelies' but, by about the turn of the century, called 'Neds' by the police, the public and themselves, the Glasgow gangsters have been credited with using the cut-throat razor as their principal offensive weapon. This is in fact a a popular misconception, generated by such fictional works as *No Mean City*.* Some, it is true, did carry razors; Aggie Reid, for

---
* Longmans, London 1936.

a time one of the leading lights of the Redskins, was known to use the cut-throat razor, but it was not the most popular weapon. As a general rule the gangsters preferred beer bottles, primarily because there was no law against carrying them. More important, they served the dual purpose of being used as clubs and, when the need arose, could be broken off at the neck, producing jagged edges which could be employed with devastating and disfiguring effect. The favourite weapon of the Norman Conks was a forty-two inch long pickshaft, while Neds from the Knightswood Estate, however, preferred a sharpened bicycle chain, which could be wrapped around the gangster's neck and concealed under the coat lapels, to be brought into action with a swift movement of the hand and delivered on a backhand swing.

In each gang there was a hard core without the existence of which rank and file gang members would have drifted to other gangs. The core contained a number of more conventional criminals including housebreakers, pickpockets, smash and grab robbers who carried out their operations under the protective panoply of gang *esprit de corps* and so had a shield of silence against police investigators. Around this core the main body provided a formidable force that could put to the field to fight other gangs. Skirmishes occurred often, pitched battles less frequently, but throughout the early thirties brawling and senseless attacks between rival gangsters, frequently involving innocent citizens, were endemic to city life. The same sordid state of affairs existed in, for example, Sheffield, but the Glasgow Neds outstripped their Sheffield brethren so far as frequency and level of their internecine warfare was concerned. Perhaps the sectarian character of the Glasgow conflict lies at the root of its degree of intensity and, though it may be unpalatable to some, the fact remains that what took place in Glasgow in the thirties was very similar to the present unhappy situation in Northern Ireland.

Whereas the Penny Mob imposed a levy of a penny a week on gang members to pay fines, the gangs of the twenties and thirties demanded tribute from local shopkeepers for this purpose. Any shopkeeper who resisted had his premises ransacked, his stock piled in the centre of the store floor and his windows smashed, as well as getting a beating himself.

To deal with the city's gangsterism, Sillitoe first had to demonstrate the effectiveness of his police administration by delivering a series of knock-out blows and, secondly, to win public support to keep them from forming new gangs. Neither of these long-term objectives could be achieved overnight. His short-term plan involved punitive measures to put the police in a dominant position. In an interview with a reporter of the Glasgow *Sunday Mail* in early 1934, he said:

> 'We are determined to fight the city gangsters with the utmost ferocity. These hooligans are most unemployable louts from the slum districts whose education and environment have given them a complete contempt for the law. They are craven-hearted rats when alone. They find their courage in numbers, and they fight with iron bars and knives and with their boots. We are out to teach them that they must take heed of the law.'

The new police boxes and radio-controlled patrol cars help speed up communications and the ability of the police to respond to calls for help. Sillitoe's intelligence network was another source of information in the campaign so that, the *Sunday Mail* reported, 'he is informed long before the event of any political, religious or gang disturbance is likely to take place'. Sillitoe even managed to recruit Aggie Reid of the Redskins (by that time dispersed) into the ranks of the C Division Specials.

A large map of the city was mounted on the wall of the operations room at police headquarters, and a similar map of each divisional district, manufactured on a scale of twenty-two inches to the mile, was provided for each division HQ. The maps, each ten feet high, showed every building and dwelling, and pin-mounted flags were used to designate occurrences. For example, a red flag was used to show a burglary, and stuck in the map at the building location which had been burgled. If the break-in was done at night time a black tip was put on the pin head; for a day time burglary a green tip was used. The date and a code letter was written on the flag to indicate how the job was done according to the *modus operandi* classification. For smash and grab raids, motor thefts and gang incidents different coloured flags were used. The maps showed the pattern of crime and incidents in each district, and the city as a whole on the headquarter's operations map, which helped the administration in the matter of disposition of its forces.

The fingerprint department under Hammond's direction was located above the operations room at central headquarters. By 1934, the department was thriving with many successes to its credit. One of their best coups was in connection with a smash and grab raid on a jeweller's shop in the city in late December of 1932. The raider had thrown a brick through the jeweller's window and made off with a haul from the window display. Fingerprint experts were despatched to the scene, but failed to find a single print on the broken glass which might give a clue to the raider's identity. They sifted the debris with care and discovered spots of blood, indicating that the robber had apparently cut himself. A constable found a small sliver of skin lying on a polished shelf. In the headquarters laboratory the skin was photographed and enlarged and sent to the fingerprint files section where assistants spent the next few days comparing the blown-up photograph with their records. Finally, by narrowing down the field of search by means of the *modus operandi* file, one was discovered that tallied. The owner of the fingerprints was arrested, charged and convicted.

Over a period of several weeks a clearly discernible pattern of incidents showed up on the operations map. There were clusters of flags in the Norman Street district (home area of the Norman Conks) and Abercrombie Street district (home ground of the Billy Boys). The leaders of these two gangs rarely overlooked an opportunity to do battle, to ambush and inflict injury on the enemy. There was a long and sordid history over the years of battles lost and won by both sides. In January 1932, for instance, the National Unemployed Workers' Movement (a Communist-inspired organisation) prepared a march that was to lead the procession through the Abercrombie Street district. Learning of this, Bull Bowman of the Norman Conks mustered three hundred of his armed followers and tacked themselves on to the tail end of the march. Fullerton, however, leader of the Billy Boys, managed to gather two hundred of his followers together and waited for the main body of the procession to pass. Just as the antagonists let fly with their pickshafts, a police sergeant and five constables detached themselves from the main parade and rushed into the open space separating the two sides. The police officers received flying missiles from both sides. Sergeant Daniel McKay got a pickshaft in the face, Constable Hughes had fingers on both hands broken in the first volley, and half a dozen plate glass windows behind them disintegrated. The two gangs then moved in for close quarter fighting with their beer bottles, spare pickshafts and other assorted weaponry, while the small group of police officers in the centre defended themselves as best they could and eventually managed to fight their way out of the mêlée. Outnumbered and outfought, the Billy Boys who had gone into combat with shouts of 'God Save the King' were left to lick their wounds after half an hour or more fighting, which only ended with the arrival of a large body of police reinforcements. The Norman Conks returned to their home territory flushed with victory.

Fullerton's Billy Boys might have had their revenge but for Sillitoe's improving the efficiency of the force. Over a period of many months in 1934, the police moved quickly enough and in sufficient force to prevent minor outbursts developing into large battles, though they could always be sure of trouble every Sunday when the Billy Boys had their church parade. Fullerton had organised a drum and fife band, and the route chosen for the parade took the Billy Boys into the heart of enemy territory through which of course the band played such noble marches as 'The Battle of the Boyne'. Such provocation brought its weekly shower of bricks and glass and buckets of piss from the upper windows of houses in the enemy camp.

The time came towards the end of 1934 when Sillitoe decided to put an end to the Sunday church parades; even they were getting out of hand, and there was no telling when the pitched battle of Abercrombie Street would be repeated. Together with Inspector James White who commanded the division in which both gangs operated, Sillitoe decided to lay a police ambush. Two furniture vans loaded with police officers and a number of picked C Division Specials were driven to the vicinity of Celtic Park and there parked in strategic positions. A large contingent of mounted police were moved into position up a side street and out of sight of the procession route, while two officers were posted in a conspicuous position to intercept the approaching column.

The Billy Boys, two hundred and fifty strong, accompanied by their followers and led by Fullerton's 'spit and dribble' fife band playing a stirring rendition of 'The Sash My Father Wore', bore down on the waiting officers. The tight formation, flanked by guards armed with their pickshafts to ward off enemy attacks, marched with cocky abandon, and the officers had no time to deliver their 'break-up' order before they were pushed aside as bothersome but harmless interferers. This was the signal for the concerted police attack. 'Sillitoe's Cossacks' (as the mounted police by this incident became known) swept out of the side street at a canter, the horses' hooves clattering over the Glasgow cobblestones, and cut the column in half. With riot batons drawn, the concealed police charged through the van doors and surged into the Billy Boys without waiting to form a fighting formation. With the mounted police fanning out and among the gangsters from the centre, the first contingent of foot police struck the head of the parade; the second waded into the severed tail half. The Billy Boys had been taken by complete surprise and had no time to recover from the initial shock. The clash of batons and pick-shafts, the shouts and curses and cracking of skulls added to the confusion. The only gang member to escape injury was the bass drummer who squeezed into his drum and there remained until the fighting was all over; that was ten minutes after the first charge. The police did not come out of the fracas unscathed; there were many injured among them, for the Billy Boys had put up a strong resistance. The entire gang was rounded up and bundled off to division headquarters where charges of disturbing the peace and 'assaulting police officers' were laid.

From this time on the police gained the upper hand. With Sillitoe's backing they clamped down on any breach of the peace with force, and offenders received the stiffer sentences for which Sillitoe had asked of the magistrates. A few weeks after the police ambush, Fullerton was charged with assaulting a police officer and given a one year prison sentence. Leaderless (for no one arose to take Fullerton's place) the Billy Boys fell apart as a gang organisation and, without them, the Norman Conks lost the *raison d'être* for their existence and they, too, disintegrated.

Nevertheless, throughout the balance of 1934 and the early part of 1935, the police had to deal with sporadic outbursts of gang violence in other parts of the city. There were, at the same time, attempts by smaller gangs to fill the void created by the break-up of the Conks and Billy Boys, two of the most vicious and mercurial gangs ever to flow through the streets of Glasgow. But it was the killing of a good Samaritan working man, Charles Smith, by three hooligans which rang the death knell of the gangs for the remaining years of Sillitoe's chief constableship.

Two brothers, John and Andrew McNamee, and a man named Kennedy attacked a rival gangster with knives and an iron bar. A passer-by intervened to help the victim and was struck down by Andrew McNamee wielding the iron bar. It was at this point that Charles Smith, returning home from his day's work, stopped to help the passer-by. The attack had taken place outside Smith's house. He stooped down to comfort the injured man and a moment later John McNamee turned and plunged his knife into Smith's back. Smith died instantly; the knife pierced his heart. Smith's fifteen-year-old daughter, Mary, witnessed the slaying and identified the killer at the trial, held on 3rd April 1935 at the Glasgow High Court before Judge Lord Aitcheson. For his crime McNamee was sentenced to fifteen years in prison, the harshest sentence dealt out to any gangster up to that date.

Sillitoe had worked hard to gain public co-operation in dealing with hooliganism. By the end of the McNamee trial, the general public was only too willing to come forward with information to help keep the gangsters subdued, so that Sillitoe had every reason to believe that his long-term objective of winning active support from the public had been achieved.

Many of the gangsters, law-breakers and criminals of the city served their sentences in Barlinnie Prison, near Glasgow. The governors of Barlinnie had previously had very little to do with the chief constables, but Sillitoe set out to change the then prevailing relationship in a serious effort to rehabilitate the prison inmates. He began by taking his lantern slide projector to the prison assembly hall, and the police male voice choir, to entertain the prisoners. He started and encouraged sports events between the various prisons in Scotland, arranging both home and away soccer matches. Because a certain number of spectator prisoners were permitted to accompany their teams, the privilege of doing so became an incentive for good behaviour. Also, through his contacts with the city's social workers, he helped a number of prisoners' families, providing them with food and clothing and sound advice. In what he did for the prisoners, he showed his interest for the rehabilitation in a practical way. Yet there were some for whom no amount of help would cause a change in their intractable attitude towards society. The really difficult offenders, the ones who returned to prison again and again, the ones who would not respond to any gesture of kindness, these were they with whom he tried another ruse.

Sillitoe was known to have had some gangsters committed for observation to a mental institution where they were confined for a period beyond their sentence. They were then released on the threat of being permanently certified should they for any reason be returned to jail. This was undoubtedly highly illegal, paralleling present day Soviet practice for dealing with dissident intellectuals, though there is no evidence that Sillitoe employed this tactic with any intent of permanency. It did, however, cause some gangsters to leave Glasgow permanently.

Sillitoe's threat to have habitual offenders certified was not confined to the hooligan element. One person who underwent this treatment was a retired barber named Petre, nicknamed 'The Clincher'. Petre was a Communist agitator and an associate of McIntyre. His speciality was a rather wicked and malicious contempt for the city council, delivered almost daily to his Glasgow Green 'congregation' from his tramp preacher's pulpit. He was obviously a powerful and convincing speaker, for he had a large following, and was frequently charged with attempting to incite a riot. Charging the city council with corruption (and subsequent events proved him right in this charge), incompetence, lack of concern for the thousands of unemployed, and with serving the industrialists at everyone else's expense, Petre managed to stir up a wave of council antagonism. In a country renowned for free speech, he nevertheless succeeded in making such a nuisance of himself that Sillitoe caused him to be confined in Forest Hall, a local mental institution, for a period. His confinement did little to curb his tongue or his activities, however, for he continued to harangue the crowds on the Green for many years. Even afterwards, the Clincher, tub-thumping on the Green, claimed that he was the only man among them who was sane and had a certificate to prove it, which, he would say, was more than any of his listeners had.

One of the more colourful prisoners in both Barlinnie and Peterhead jails at various times was the safe-cracker Johnny Ramensky. He served the usual 'lag' apprenticeship of reformatory school, Borstal and prison, and for a short time, following a spell in a Borstal institution, he worked in the coal mines of Lanarkshire where he learned to handle explosives, a skill which was to lead to his serving more than forty of his sixty years behind bars. He was exceedingly fit and kept up his exercises with a religious devotion: he spent part of his yard exercise each day walking on his hands for fifteen minutes at a stretch, including a climb up the thirty or more steps to his cell. There was a purpose behind this, of course, which was to keep himself fit for his cat-burgling activities. He was the only prisoner to escape twice from Peterhead Prison in Aberdeen, and still holds that dubious record so far as is known (though it does not appear in the Guinness Book of Records). He did this by swinging hand over hand along the bottom girders of the steel bridge connecting Peterhead Prison to the mainland. During the Second World War, he made a number of parachute drops into occupied France on secret service missions. According to McGlinchey, it was Sillitoe who recommended Ramensky for this work. Ramensky was fond of telling the story of how he was taken to Berlin to blow open Hitler's safe in the Reichstag.* There is no real evidence for the truth of the story, but it should not be considered entirely apocryphal, because Richard Sillitoe recalls his father mentioning Ramensky's war work long after the family left Glasgow and there was no reason why Percy Sillitoe should have known anything about the safe-cracker's war activities unless he himself had been involved in some way. Apparently, the Allies searched in vain for a means of opening the safe without damaging the contents and finally called upon Ramensky to do the job. He agreed to do it on condition that he should perform the task alone, and, having been supplied with all the equipment for which he asked, the door was blown open and the contents removed intact. Ramensky died in 1972, shortly after being released from prison for the last time. Perhaps the truth about his activities will never be wholly known.

Sillitoe's unrelenting efforts to rid the streets of the gangs and to make them safe from gang terror brought him repeatedly into the national spotlight. The mere mention of his name in the national press was sufficient to prompt readers to nod their heads in recognition and perhaps comment, 'What's the captain up to this time?' It came as little surprise when, in 1934, the national press began speculating that Sillitoe would succeed Trenchard as Commissioner of the Metropolitan Police, the country's highest police post. Society magazines began printing Dollie's photograph in their 'portrait galleries' and the columnists assiduously searched their newspapers' files of back numbers for that material without which the columnist is unable to effect his nodding acquaintance with the famous and obscure alike. But speculation came to nothing; Trenchard remained chief of the

---

* In *Mostly Murder*, published by George G. Harrap & Co. Ltd, London 1959, Sir Sydney Smith places the scene of this exploit in Rome.

Yard and Sillitoe soldiered on in Glasgow for many more years.

One of Sillitoe's more curious foibles was an obsession with his height. Although, as has already been observed, he was himself unusually tall, he disliked being overlooked by anyone, and even wore boots with extra high heels to add to his stature. At the rehearsal for the 1934 inspection by the Scottish Inspector General of Constabulary, Brigadier-General Dudgeon, he came face to chin with a 6' 8" constable from Aberdeen. The following day the PC found himself transferred to a desk job at headquarters, and from then on he was excused all parades. Percy's phobia about his height extended to his own family. He often boasted that his sons would never be as tall as himself—Richard did reach the same height as his father, but the latter always contended that he won by an eighth of an inch.

His concern for his height was nothing but vanity, an aspect of his personality which had a lot to do with his competitive spirit. He was keen on sport of every description, and in this connection McGlinchey recorded the following reminiscence:

> I heard an old man in a pub saying that Sillitoe fancied himself as a chess player. The pensioner's brother was an amateur champion in the thirties and belonged to a working man's club. The chief constable often went into the club and had a game. The man said Sir Percy was no mug at the game but was ... too quick a mover. He said that Sir Percy never studied a minute and in his opinion would have been a good chess player if only he had taken more time over his moves. But he was the worst loser. When Sillitoe was hopelessly beat he would say, without turning a hair, 'What about making it a draw?'

Sillitoe was never a worse loser than in the celebrated 'Case of the Barking Dog', a court action in which he himself was the plaintiff. Kilmalcolm, where the incident occurred, is a beautiful Scottish village on the River Gryfe, a tributary of the Clyde and a well-known salmon stream. In this village stood Tapston House, the residence rented by the Sillitoe family shortly after they had moved to Glasgow. There is no doubt that the villagers of Kilmalcolm, accustomed to poaching the salmon to their heart's content, resented the presence of this high-powered officer of the law in their midst—though that was not the only reason. The growing number of wealthy tradesmen from the city, industrialists and other outsiders who settled in the village during that period disturbed its placid tranquility, so far as the old residents of the village were concerned. One cannot doubt the possibility that there was considerable animosity towards the newcomers, and one must be suspicious of collusion to provoke legal action.

Tapston House stood opposite Dinnistoun Farm, the property of a small cattle farmer, Angus James Miller, who kept a number of collies for working around the farm. Miller had a licence to maintain a kennel and, in the autumn of 1933, bought a couple of collie pups because, he said, the regular work dogs were getting old. There was no other house between Tapston House and the farm, which were separated only by a road and an open field. The prevailing wind blew from the farm to the house and the pups barked during the night hours, disturbing Sillitoe enough to telephone Miller to complain.

Miller, who appears to have been a reasonable fellow, at first expressed his regret and offered to have the dogs destroyed, though this may have been a piece of heavy-handed Scots sarcasm which flew over Sillitoe's head. He said he did not want them destroyed; he only wanted them kept under control. There were more telephone calls. Finally Sillitoe said he was sick of continually ringing up to complain of the dogs and asking that they be kept under control. Miller, in turn, said he was sick of being rung up in the middle of the night and that he was going to do nothing further in the matter. In short, the relationship between farmer and chief constable became a belligerent one as their conversations became more acrimonious.

Following Sillitoe's decision to take legal action, the dogs no longer barked, thereby indicating that they could be kept under control. The action, heard at the Greenock Sheriff Court, was for an interdict (an injunction in English law) against Miller because of alleged annoyance caused by the barking of the dogs belonging to the farmer. The complaint was for 'material discomfort, annoyance, disturbance and inconvenience as to constitute a nuisance for those residing in the vicinity'.

Giving evidence, Sillitoe said that the maids and the children had complained about the barking of the dogs and the annoyance this caused. He agreed that there must be a certain amount of legitimate barking on a farm, but this was not what he was complaining about. The annoyance occurred during the night between 11 p.m. and 2 a.m., when no cattle were being taken into or out of the farmyard. Asked if he was aware that following his complaint one of the dogs had been shot and the other removed, Sillitoe said he was not.

'Why did you not close your windows to reduce the noise of the barking?' Miller's counsel asked.

'Why should I?' Sillitoe replied.

'You would rather suffer the nuisance than reduce the ventilation?'

To this question Sillitoe gave no answer; this was hardly surprising because there was too much laughter for him to be heard. Even greater amusement was caused when a police sergeant from the Kilmalcolm Police Station testified to the number of complaints made by Sillitoe, and quoted a sample entry from the station record, 'Captain Sillitoe off at the deep end again.'

In defence, Miller said that he used a collie sheep dog for rounding up the cattle; this was a highly-trained and prize-winning dog, Laddie by name. He said he was quite willing to give the court a demonstration any day to show that it did not bark when controlling either cattle or sheep. He agreed that he did own a couple of collie pups at the time of Sillitoe's complaint, and still did own one—but it could hardly be called a pup now, some months later. He thought it might have barked at night, but not, in his opinion, excessively.

The outcome of the court action was that Sillitoe lost the case, much to his chagrin. He hated being a loser, but there was much more to it than losing the case. When it became known that the chief constable was residing outside the city limits, in direct contravention of an ordinance which specifically stated that corporation employees must live in the city, a hue and cry went up. 'Why should Sillitoe be exempt from the laws he is supposed to uphold?' the detractors asked. So, in addition to the loss of face attached to losing the court action, the Sillitoes were forced to move. Percy had originally turned down the city's official residence for its chief constable in favour of Tapston House. The police committee now agreed that the official residence should be renovated, and in the interval, a period of about eight months, the Sillitoes moved into the Buchanan Arms Hotel, Drymen.

The hotel was owned and operated by a friend of the family, John Grant, who was also the owner of the famous Grant Whisky Distilleries. The Buchanan Arms at Drymen was located a little more than a mile from another salmon stream, which suited Sillitoe, who was exceedingly partial to fish and had salmon placed before him almost every day. Like everyone else, he thought that something ought to be done about the blatant poaching, to which the local stream was particularly subject. What he didn't realise was that the hotel staff were the main culprits, poaching the fish so that the important guest might have fresh salmon as often as he desired.

Despite these personal difficulties, Sillitoe continued without interruption to wage his war against rowdyism and lawlessness. It was during this period that he was threatened with personal violence—the only time during his entire career when this occurred.

As I have mentioned, rivalry between supporters of the Rangers and Celtic football clubs was energetic and incessant, and fighting between supporters of these two famous Scottish teams got out of hand time and time again. The warring factions resorted to bottles, clubs, chains and all the instruments of gang warfare; the brawling became so dangerous that Sillitoe determined to put an end to matches between the two teams. He called in the club managers and warned them of his intentions. They were furious, and the press reacted with shock to the chief constable's intractable stand in the matter. Following its public disclosure, Sillitoe received an anonymous threat, warning him that if he stopped a Rangers–Celtic match he would be killed.

Percy was unconcerned for himself, but he feared for the safety of his family; from then on and until the storm died down, all mail arriving at the house was inspected for parcel bombs and the children warned not to open anything themselves. Richard remembers the arrival of one parcel which had no positive identification as to its sender. The house was then vacated and the parcel removed by the police arson squad. However, Sillitoe refused to be intimidated by the threat, and developed tactics for controlling the spectators at Ibrox Stadium, which proved in the end to be effective. Uniformed men mingled with spectators in the stands, and the ring of constables on the outer perimeter of the field moved constantly around on the lookout for disturbances. Large contingents of reserves were held out of sight of the spectators so that, in the event of the slightest hint that a pitched battle might develop, the reserves appeared to materialise out of thin air, swarming on to the field to deal with the troublemakers.

It became standard practice to compel anyone making a nuisance of themselves to report to police headquarters each Saturday afternoon for the next four weeks and to remain until the match was over. The opinion of one pensioner who remembers those days was, 'Those who had to report to headquarters never returned a second time.' Sillitoe preferred meting out this kind of treatment to hauling offenders before the magistrates.

When soccer matches were in progress at Ibrox Stadium, Sillitoe would arrive at the grounds in his chauffeur-driven Alvis, always in uniform himself, and wander about talking to policemen on duty, like a conscientious engineer checking on the pressure of the boiler. Said ex-Sergeant Arnot of Sillitoe and the football crowd, 'He was a stickler for people behaving themselves, but never really malicious with the football fans. He never was a vindictive man and liked sport himself too much to deny others the pleasure.'

A few months after the dust had settled on the football fracas, Richard contracted scarlet fever, a frequently fatal illness in the days before the discovery of antibiotics. This, however, turned out to be one of the rare occasions—in Richard's view—when his father showed any real concern for him as a child. When Sillitoe learned that his son was so desperately ill that he was not expected to survive the night, he went immediately to the Glasgow Royal Infirmary where the boy was confined and spent the night at his bedside. There, he held his hand and talked and talked to him through the long hours, willing him to pull through. Years later, discussing the illness with his son, Sillitoe said he was convinced it was his being there, willing Richard his own strength, that gave him what he needed to survive the crisis. After that single all-night vigil, it seems, their remote and somewhat detached relationship was resumed, not to alter again until after Sillitoe retired from MI5.

Chapter Fifteen

The Common Touch

Compared with the early days of his reign as Glasgow's chief constable, the period from 1935 to 1938 was, for Sillitoe, a relatively peaceful one. By 1935, his police machine was running with a quiet and smooth efficiency, much of which was due to his skill of defining responsibility and delegating authority to his subordinates. He was never idle himself, yet he found time to travel about Scotland and England to meet with his fellow chief constables of neighbouring constabularies. In this, he worked hard to develop co-operation between the various police authorities, and he was only too ready to offer the assistance of the specialist departments of the Glasgow police when called upon for assistance. Discovery of the Ruxton murders (among the most gruesome of British murder cases) on 29th September 1935 was a good test of this co-operation, for the investigation involved a number of police authorities (those of Dumfriesshire, Glasgow and Lancaster), Scotland Yard, and the famous pathologists, Sir Sydney Smith and Professor John Glaister of Edinburgh University.

On that day, a Sunday, a woman strolling with her dog across a bridge over Gardenholme Linn, a small stream in Dumfriesshire near the village of Moffat, looked over the parapet into the gully below and saw a human arm protruding from the bank. Summoned to the scene, the police discovered the dismembered remains of two bodies, strewn along the stream bed in seventy separate packages. This human debris included two heads and one trunk, but everything had been so expertly mutilated it was difficult to tell even the sex of the victims. In fact, it was at first thought that one was male and the other female. Every possible means of identification had been severed from the bodies—eyes, ears, noses, scalps, muscles, sexual organs and large areas of skin and flesh. However, the murderer had made the error of parcelling the dismembered remains in identifiable wrappings; these included newspaper, straw, articles of clothing, and bedsheets. One of the newspapers was a 'slip' edition of the *Sunday Graphic* dated 15th September 1935. (A slip edition of a newspaper is one prepared for limited circulation in a particular locale—in this case for Morecambe and district near Lancaster, and only 3,700 copies had been printed.) From this fact, and a recent report in a Glasgow newspaper, it was discovered that two females had been reported missing from Lancaster. One was Isabella Ruxton, the commonlaw wife of Dr Buck Ruxton, and the other, a maid of the Ruxton household, Mary Rogerson. Within two weeks of the discovery the doctor was arrested, but it still remained to positively identify that the dismembered remains were those of Isabella Ruxton and her maid. While the Dumfriesshire police pursued other lines of enquiry, fingerprint experts from the Glasgow police were called in.

With the arrest of Ruxton, Hammond, in charge of the fingerprint section it will be recalled, had free access to the Ruxton house where he spent eleven days gathering finger, thumb and palm prints from household utensils, fixtures and woodwork about the house. With these he was able to make a positive identification of the body of Mary Rogerson. He also found what appeared to be a number of thumbprints from the victim's right hand. The badly decomposed right hand was not found until 4th November, but Hammond and his assistants, with considerable skill, managed to get a dermal print of the thumb which matched with two thumb impressions found in the house. The Ruxton murders trial was the first occasion on which dermal prints were offered as evidence of identity in a British court of law. Other means used to identify the murder victims included superimposing a photographic negative of one skull on a photograph of Isabella Ruxton taken shortly before her death. Ruxton was found guilty of the murders and hung.

Sillitoe was only indirectly connected with the Ruxton enquiries, though he followed the investigation with interest. That he was no great detective himself is certain, for he never actually demonstrated any marvellous gift of deductive logic in solving any crimes. The reputation he left behind rests entirely on his administrative record, and as an administrator and organiser he was superb. Outside his police work, he was an unpretentious person with simple, ordinary tastes and, furthermore, while he had few friends they came from all walks of life. Deacon, discussing his former chief, summed up Sillitoe's friendships when he said, 'Distinct from those of equal rank, he did not look for friendship in the upper crust; he set out to make friends for their own sake.'

One acquaintance he did not set out to develop into a friendship was Himmler, whom he met in 1937. Audrey Sillitoe, then sixteen years of age, was studying at Freiburg University at the time, and her parents decided to pay her a visit. When Dr Gregor, then the German Consul in Glasgow, heard of the impending trip he suggested that the Sillitoes should journey to Berlin as guests of the German government and meet with Himmler. Even at that early date—the Nazi Party had only been in full power some four years—Hitler's war machine was being revved up for the coming conflict. Fully aware of the situation building up in Germany, Sillitoe accepted the invitation that he might, as reported in the Glasgow press, take the opportunity 'to study methods of the German police' under Himmler. Audrey met her parents in Cologne and the three of them travelled to Berlin where the arranged meeting with Himmler took place. What benefit Sillitoe derived from the meeting is not known, and if he submitted a report to the Home Office the details were never made public, but knowing of his propensity for gathering information it is certain that he did not return empty-handed.

The Empire Exhibition, which opened in Glasgow in the spring of 1938, was the gleaming jewel in Sillitoe's police crown. He established a special unit for policing the Exhibition, with its headquarters in the grounds. In spite of aches and pains, which he put down to rheumatism, though he went so far as to seek the help of masseurs, he appeared at the Exhibition daily, and spent long hours wandering among the exhibits and attending official functions. He was always on hand to escort members of royalty and important dignitaries who frequently visited Glasgow during the six months the Exhibition was open. He loved spending his time in the African pavilion where he was able to practise his linguistic abilities with the attendants, performers and entertainers, much to their delight.

During the next two years, there were sporadic outbursts of IRA activity which kept Glasgow police occupied, and Sillitoe's intelligence network was given its acid test. He wrote, 'The

Glasgow police began to suspect that their city was being used as a supply HQ by the IRA,' and there is every reason to believe that that suspicion was based on information received from his intelligence network. The most dramatic arrest concerned a gathering of Irish dissidents in an assembly hall in the city, which the police raided just as the meeting was getting underway. This led to a series of searches in the homes of those caught in the net and further arrests followed. Explosives, detonators and fuses were found, and these helped convict such terrorists as Gill, Carson and O'Hara, who each received lengthy prison terms. What is not so well known is how Sillitoe got on to the terrorists in the first place.

His network of C Division Specials was widespread. From among the thousands of Scots-Irish living in the city, he was able to gather intelligence from as far afield as the Irish ports of Belfast and Dublin. One evening in the spring of 1939, shortly before the assembly hall raid earlier mentioned, a coffin was shipped aboard the overnight ferry in Dublin, bound for Glasgow. The coffin, bearing the name of a woman, was accompanied by two young nuns. One of Sillitoe's observant 'specials' noted that the coffin was not accompanied by any male mourners which, for some reason, struck the special as rather odd. Because of the large passenger list and the fact that it was an all-night sailing, the nuns were put in a four-berth cabin with two female passengers—one of whom was Sillitoe's intrepid special. During the night one of the nuns was seen with her wimple off and 'she' was shaving.

The following morning, after the ferry docked, the 'nuns' were quietly arrested and the coffin opened. Neatly packed inside it was a cache of small arms, ammunition, grenades and explosives. Strange to say, the two IRA men were never sent to trial, but a short time later the much-publicised raid on the assembly hall took place, and the IRA movement in Glasgow was nipped in the bud. One may reasonably conclude that the 'nuns' had turned King's evidence.

In the interests of giving some form to Sillitoe's Glasgow activities, numerous items have only been given passing mention: such things as his concern for the welfare of the police themselves, important though they were in the Sillitoe scheme of things, may be taken for granted as occupying much of his time. He encouraged sports, recreational and educational activities, and brought in experts to teach his men to defend themselves, to improve their skills and to make them better policemen all round.

He had a knack for summing up a subordinate's personality, of recognising strengths and weaknesses and leadership qualities. Bill Deacon said, 'Sillitoe sorted out the right person for the job. If he did well he would leave him alone, but if he didn't he would throw him out.' The fact that Sillitoe would unhesitatingly 'throw him out', as Deacon explained what happened to those who didn't come up to expectations, indicates that Sillitoe was not infallible in selecting men for promotion.

One of Sillitoe's most impressive achievements was on behalf of women police. No one worked more assiduously than he to gain public recognition of their value to the constabulary system. Those few who were brave enough to take their place alongside the men in the early thirties were intrepid pioneers of the women's liberation movement. When they first joined, according to McGlinchey, 'They were a strange sight. They took to the beat with their long skirts sweeping the streets and wearing long, wide tunics; they were a formidable sight, but when they were put on plain-clothes duty they were hard to spot.' Just as Sillitoe had got the plain-clothes officers to wear less noticeable clothes than the belted trenchcoat and felt hat, he had the plain-clothes women officers dress in ordinary clothes, which made them difficult to recognise for what they were. 'At one time,' McGlinchey reports, 'there were numerous complaints from women of being accosted in Glasgow's central railway station. Shortly after Sillitoe put his plain-clothes policewomen on the job, resulting in a large number of arrests, the trouble ended.'

With the war creeping closer during the closing years of the decade, Sillitoe was far-sighted enough to realise what would happen to the efficient police force he had so carefully built up: it would disintegrate. He knew that he would not be able to prevent the younger and more valuable members from joining the armed forces—and it would not have been in his nature to try. On the contrary, he helped them prepare for the inevitable day when they would be gone by, encouraging them to join reserve training units and to start a rifle club. Many became territorials or joined the auxiliary reserve forces, such as the famous 602 Squadron Air Reserve, which shot down the first enemy bomber over Edinburgh. For those who joined the reserves, Sillitoe instructed superintendents to change their duty schedules to allow them to attend training camps or weekly drills. At the same time he began a campaign to encourage more civilians to join the regular specials under Commandant Colonel James F. Daly. Civilian car owners were formed into a mobile branch and, as I have already mentioned, a number of motor launch owners were formed into a special section for patrolling the busy shipping lanes of the Clyde; this section became known as the 'Clyde Patrol'. When war was declared, the younger regular police officers joined the armed forces and their places were taken by the specials without any disruption to the services provided to the city, thanks to Sillitoe's planning.

In 1939 he extended his specials' recruiting campaign to women, with the creation of a Women's Auxiliary Police Corps under Bailie Violet Roberton, a popular woman councillor who became the WAPC's Commandant. Wearing the, by then familiar, Sillitoe tartan on the hats, WAPC volunteers became a regular sight about the sandbagged offices of police headquarters. Both Dollie and Audrey joined the auxiliary force, Dollie as assistant commandant (a flagrant example of nepotism of which Sillitoe was guilty on more than one occasion) and Audrey as a driver. From a small group of twenty, the WAPC soon grew into an indispensable force numbered in the hundreds, and took over many police duties.

The day war was declared was one of the rare occasions on which Sillitoe was late for an appointment; demanding punctuality in others, he was punctilious about this himself. Ex-Inspector Douglas Grant* was on duty at headquarters that fateful Sunday, 3rd September 1939. Commenting on this occasion, he said, 'The Prime Minister was due to broadcast to the nation at 11 a.m. For several days before then we had been fitting black-out curtain to the windows while workmen were engaged in protecting the building with sandbags. The Air Raid Precautions organisation (ARP) had been set up for some time and Sillitoe had told two constables to be at headquarters at 10 a.m. that morning, when they would be promoted to sergeants in the ARP department. The officers arrived as instructed and waited for the chief constable. We were listening to the broadcast and I have no doubt that the chief constable was also listening, but where I have no

* Author of *The Thin Blue Line* (a history of the Glasgow police). John Long Ltd, London 1973.

idea. In any event, he evidently forgot about the appointment. Shortly after the broadcast the two men became fed up and decided to leave. They were halfway down the stairs when the front door burst open and in came Sillitoe. Suddenly realising he had overlooked his appointment with them, he said, "I'm so sorry, gentlemen, that I have kept you waiting, but as from now you are both promoted to the rank of sergeant. Good morning." '

His longing for public recognition met crowning success when a knighthood for his services was conferred on him in the 1942 New Year's Honours List. He was the first Scottish chief constable to be honoured in this way. Upon his return from the investiture at Buckingham Palace, he was the guest of his senior officers who presented him with a canteen of cutlery. In paying tribute to his chief, Assistant Chief Constable Warnock said, 'Greater progress has been made in the past ten years than in the previous thirty. He has been responsible for bringing the police services of the whole of Scotland up to date with what he has achieved in Glasgow. I make no bones about saying that, and for this reason I think he is a worthy recipient of the honour conferred upon him by the King.'

Warnock's speech in praise of his chief might make a fitting conclusion to Sillitoe's career in Glasgow. However, in addition to the day-to-day experiences of his remaining period in Glasgow he had two important experiences; one illustrates his tenacity, the other an intractable and less pleasant side of his nature.

He had suspected for years that corruption lurked beneath the surface of city life and plagued the corporation. Rumours of petty bribery, hints of influence-peddling and stories of a larger corruption, connected with securing municipal contracts for the supply of materials and services, seemed to wax and wane over the years with persistent regularity. Where these stories and rumours came from and who started them was something no one knew; yet they circulated among the ranks of the police and were alluded to in the columns of the press without anyone offering real proof that they had any foundation in fact. Nevertheless, the rumours were strong enough to justify a suspicion in the minds of the police hierarchy sufficient enough that they should not be ignored nor entirely dismissed as malicious talk. Since that initial surfacing in 1933, when Sillitoe had caused Bailie Strain to be convicted and jailed for extortion of the market stallholder, no further developments occurred to prove one way or another that the wrong-doing was more widespread than was brought out at Strain's trial. Indeed, following this city bailie's conviction, the Scottish Secretary of State, Sir Godfrey Collins, had ordered a public enquiry into civic graft, but it had fizzled out for lack of evidence and willingness on the part of would-be accusers to testify. This had scotched the rumours for a while, but within a couple of years they were making the rounds afresh.

Then, in 1941, Sillitoe objected before the licensing committee to the renewal of a licence for the Beresford Hotel on the grounds of an infraction of the licensing laws having to do with serving liquor out of licensed hours. The managing director of the Beresford Hotel was a city councillor, Hugh Fraser, and, unknown to Sillitoe, one of Fraser's fellow councillors on the licensing committee, named Hugh Campbell, offered to ensure that the hotel received its liquor licence in consideration of £120. Fraser, an honest man, promptly reported the offer to Sillitoe, who thanked his golf-course God for answering his prayers to expose the suspected corruption and prepared a trap.

He arranged for two of his police officers to install listening equipment in the hotel room where a meeting had been arranged to effect the transaction. (This must be one of the earliest instances of the practice now known as 'bugging'.) In spite of the ample warning they had and careful preparation, the police plans went awry. To begin with, the bugging equipment with its concealed microphone in the meeting room developed a fault. The fault was traced to the microphone and there was a last minute scramble to make use of the telephone receiver, but this meant leaving the receiver conspicuously off its hook. Then, as a consequence of an error on the part of one of the hotel staff, Campbell blundered into the very room where the bugging equipment had been set up. Explanations of the officers seated by the monitoring equipment failed to allay Campbell's suspicions of a laid trap. He fled in haste, but on his way out of the hotel he chanced to meet Fraser, who now offered the agreed payment. Avarice getting the better of him even in such risky circumstances, Campbell pocketed the money—which was in the form of banknotes that had been marked by the police. The following morning, armed with a search warrant, police officers visited Campbell at his home and discovered the marked notes stuffed up a chimney. For this piece of folly, Campbell was brought to trial, convicted and given a six-month jail sentence—but there was more to come.

While biding his time in Barlinnie Prison, Campbell exposed three other councillors. The first of these was a brittle and fire-eating champion of the people, Thomas Wilson, who had been appointed to the magistrate's bench the previous year; the second was one Bailie Taylor; and the third was Bailie Ritchie who, it will be recalled, had been implicated with Strain in the 1933 scandal but who had managed to squirm his way off the hook. These three were charged with soliciting and receiving bribes totalling £225 from the chairman of the Gas Chambers & Coke Ovens Company Limited, a London firm which had submitted a tender to the city corporation for the supply of fuel to fire the city gasworks. Campbell was brought from Barlinnie to give evidence, and for their efforts Wilson, Taylor and Ritchie were rewarded with jail terms ranging from fifteen to eighteen months.

Public exposure of city councillors involved in bribery and corruption charges led to other, unconnected, charges when victims of those officials who were corrupt felt safe in taking their complaints to the police. As a result, another magistrate, Neil Shaw, was charged with accepting a bribe to influence the licensing court and sentenced to six months in prison. Yet another councillor, Bailie Gemmell, who was in fact no less than chairman of the Police Committee, was indicted by a public baths attendant. Besides being chairman of the Police Committee, Gemmell headed the Public Baths and Fire Department Committees. However, unlike the Police Committee over which he exercised no influence in the matter of promotion, he had power to confirm or deny promotion in these other two departments. In consideration of arranging such a promotion for one George Macguire, a baths attendant, Gemmell demanded payment of £30. In view of what was happening to other bailies, magistrates and council members, Macguire, who was in any case due for promotion, had little compunction about reporting the demand. Gemmell was charged, convicted and sentenced. All this only goes to prove that the US system of government, about which Sillitoe had been so critical, is not alone in harbouring civic corruption. In any case, the persistent rumours and tales of corruption which had circulated over the years proved in the end to be true. The scale and range of that corruption, from small sums to assure promotion to corporation employees to those larger sums for influence-peddling in the matter of supply contracts, was all that had been rumoured.

On the domestic front—that is, in the Sillitoe household—great changes had occurred during the ten years since they had moved to Glasgow. All three children were grown up and in the armed services: Audrey had joined the WRNS, Richard the RNVR and Anthony had become a gunner in the RAF. Both Richard and Audrey managed to get home fairly often and, no longer subject to the strictures of a disciplined home life, felt free to take their friends along. It wasn't long before Audrey began bringing home with fair regularity a young naval lieutenant-surgeon. From the moment the young officer was introduced to the family, Percy took a dislike to him. The root of that antipathy was Sillitoe's assertion that Audrey's friend was indecisive. Percy accused him, for instance, of conducting a two-hour discussion on the paltry matter of buying a suit. Knowing how quickly Sillitoe came to a decision about most things, one can understand how irritated he might become. Given his pride in his ability to sum a man up in a few minutes, it is equally unsurprising that nothing would alter the unfavourable opinion Percy formed, and this uncharitable attitude coloured his behaviour to the young man.

He denied him accommodation in the house, so that Audrey's suitor was compelled to put up in a hotel whenever he visited the city with her. When the visitor did arrive at the Sillitoe home, his host lost no time in leaving the premises to play golf or to return to the office. But Percy reckoned without the tenacity of Audrey's character. It was too much like his own for him to have his own way entirely. When she announced her intention of marrying her suitor, her father became so angry that he lost his temper.

'If you marry this man,' he said, 'you walk out of this house and never come back again.' Audrey retorted that she loved him and that was all there was to it. If her father would not give his blessing to the marriage she would simply get married without it. The more her father opposed her the more solidly she stood her ground. The quarrel became more and more heated until Dollie intervened, a course she took only in cases of dire emergency.

'Tod,' she said, 'if you oppose Audrey, if you dare stop this marriage, I will divorce you. There! I will see a lawyer and I'll divorce you, that I promise.' She had never been so certain of herself since she had returned with Tod from East Africa in 1922 and he had wanted to return there.

Percy softened immediately. 'Come on,' he said, 'this is only a family squabble. Let the matter rest.'

A family squabble it might have been, but Percy realised just how close he had come to breaking things up himself. He gave his blessing to the match, although ungraciously, and the couple became engaged, but the matter was far from ended. Percy yielded no more than he had to and remained obdurate as ever. He swore that he would not sleep under the same roof as his prospective son-in-law and, even after they were married and were living in Coventry, Sillitoe refused to change his attitude. Audrey invited him to stay with them, but he would only go on condition that Audrey's husband was not present. 'I couldn't stand that,' he said. The trouble was that he did not know when or how to bury the hatchet; he could not bear to admit that he was in the wrong, either in his behaviour or in matters of fact. His accusations of indecisiveness were shown to be unfounded in time, for Audrey's husband turned out to be a successful surgeon, well accepted in his profession and required to make decisions quite equal in seriousness to those of his father-in-law.

For a long time now Percy had been making increasingly frequent visits to his own doctor. He became short of breath easily and had aches and pains which he described as rheumatism, but most of all his left knee was bothering him—this was the knee which had swollen to the size of a football soon after he had been cursed by the witch doctor during his service in Africa—and causing him considerable discomfort. Indeed, it had always been a source of trouble, and was the reason he was not as active on the sports field as he might have been. He was repeatedly advised to move to a healthier climate than that of Glasgow. With its damp, cold atmosphere and its foul industrial smog, one cannot wonder at the advice.

Some time towards the end of 1942, Sillitoe was attending an ARP course at Cobham, Kent, where he met a Home Office official, Colonel Vance. They were discussing plans for the amalgamation of various borough police forces into larger units. A pilot project for this was being prepared in Kent. The special reason for choosing the Kent constabularies for the experiment was the long-range plan for the invasion of Europe, at which time large concentrations of men and equipment would require a unified command to facilitate the movement of war convoys. During the course of a conversation they were having over a drink one evening, Sillitoe remarked, 'At long last you people down here have had the courage to get on with this question of amalgamation; of course, it's the only thing to do in the interest of economy and efficiency.' Vance nodded agreement and said he was interested in hearing Sillitoe's views.

'In my opinion,' Sillitoe obliged, 'this should be going on all over the country. For the present, our own Secretary of State—he was referring to the Scottish Secretary of State—'won't face up to it. I don't know whether I'm stepping on anyone's toes, but I imagine the Kent people will have to find a first-class man for this job because of the difficulties with these local boroughs.'

In saying this he had pretty well talked himself into a job. Vance, who seems to have been closely connected with the amalgamation programme, was left in no doubt as to Sillitoe's interest in the job. He had the qualifications to head such an undertaking, added to which the move was a necessity in view of his increasing medical problems, though it is not known if Vance was told or got to know of those problems. It was not long before the offer was made, and readily accepted. The salary was actually lower than that he commanded as chief constable of Glasgow, but there was a challenge once again, a change of scenery and a pleasanter climate.

Sir Percy's farewell party for his departure from Glasgow in February 1943 was held in St Andrew's Hall, where more than a thousand policemen and their families gathered for the occasion. By a stroke of good fortune, the whole of the Sillitoe family was present to listen to Percy's farewell speech. He was sorry to leave, for his time in Glasgow was his happiest and most successful period as a professional policeman.

He would be able to look back on those thirteen years with the sure knowledge that he had subdued the rapacious temper of the city and bequeathed it the legacy of a gentler, more generous character which, in comparison with the heyday of the Norman Conks and Billy Boys, it yet enjoys. There will always be street gangs, but none as violent and bloodthirsty as those quelled during Sillitoe's era. Like Marcus Polinius, the Sabine whom the ancient Romans invited to bring them order out of chaos in the city of Rome, Sillitoe was an outsider; and for this reason he will be remembered as long as the city has a police force.

Chapter Sixteen

Man of Kent

Just one month after the Sillitoes moved to Maidstone, the Secretary of State issued an order for the amalgamation of the nine police boroughs of Kent with the Kent County Police (Sir Alexander Maxwell, the Permanent Under-Secretary of State, was actually responsible for planning the new force). It was an important move. Sillitoe, who had a hand in the planning while still nominally running the Glasgow force, knew before he arrived to take up his new duties exactly what had to be done. Allied plans for the invasion of Europe involved a massive movement of military equipment through Kent, which called for the precise scheduling of those convoys. The amalgamation of the nine boroughs was in fact planned to assist the opening of the invasion operations.

To help him with this side of the operations, Sillitoe brought Deacon from Glasgow and promoted him to Superintendent in charge of traffic. Deacon later said that during the first month at this job his hair turned white. There were daily conferences with the military planners for the movement of traffic: precise timetables had to be drawn up, bridge loadings and specifications obtained and alternative routes to be decided on in the event of disruption of the network by aerial bombardment.

Even while these plans were under way there were other important details to be attended to. One of these was arranging for a tight band of security around the secret preparations being conducted by the RAF for the bombing of the Moehne Dam, scheduled to take place about 16th May 1943. An area of land one mile square was cordoned off to the east of Reculver Towers, Herne Bay, where two poles were erected on the sea wall, the distance between the poles being equal to the length of the Moehne Dam.

Sillitoe was present to see for himself what it was all about. Dummy runs were made whenever the weather allowed, and there was invariably a large contingent of onlookers, consisting mostly of senior RAF officers together with a number of government officials. The Lancaster bombers used in the trials were first seen as specks in the distance as they approached from across the Thames Estuary, a mere sixty feet above the water. The ball bomb was then dropped and would skip like a pebble over the water, hitting the beach to bounce into the air and finish two hundred yards to the south of the marshes. On one occasion the bomb struck a breakwater and was deflected towards the spectators two or three hundred yards away. Almost to a man they threw themselves flat on their faces as the five-ton ball whistled over their heads to land in the Roman ruins opposite the coastguard station. Sillitoe was the exception, for he remained on his feet to watch the lethal missile make its dangerous curve. (The reason for recording this particular incident, when he undoubtedly was in danger and displayed great courage, is that it may be compared with his strange and erratic behaviour some time later when, as a consequence of the 'Doodlebug' onslaught, he began to lose his nerve.)

Sillitoe was fortunate with his new command: the previous chief constable, Major Chapman, had had the foresight to plan a new headquarters building at Maidstone, capable of accommodating the entire headquarters staff required for the enlarged force. The organisation Sillitoe decided upon is not of special interest except to note that he was now an old hand at reorganising and reforming police forces. Although it was essentially a rural constabulary (his previous reforms, of course, having been with urban forces), he knew exactly what had to be achieved to effect unification in record time, and did not have to experiment and change his orders because this or that or the other could not be done. Essentially, he settled on a three-tier system of command, with districts reporting to divisions and divisions reporting to headquarters. The former chief constables of the borough police became assistant chief constables under the new organisation, so that Sillitoe's reforms were carried out with experienced smoothness. At least two of those former chief constables took early retirement, however, and a number of senior officers with them, for despite the pressure of a war Sillitoe insisted on his usual 'purge'. A number of these officers not unnaturally complained that they were still young and active and quite capable of attending to their duties efficiently, but such was Sillitoe's reputation and self-confidence by now that he was unmoved by their protests and they had to leave without redress. (It will be interesting to note how Sillitoe accepted his retirement when he reached his sixty-fifth year.) On the other side of the coin, he showed his consistency by giving a great deal of attention to police welfare and 'conditions of service' reforms, and by encouraging sporting activities and devising training programmes.

Obtaining additional property to that already owned by the Maidstone police, he laid plans for a model 'police village' with accommodation for officers and their families; the field behind his house, on which sheep grazed when he arrived, was turfed and put to recreational use; and to supplement wartime rationing, he encouraged the headquarters staff to keep poultry and livestock of their own. Nor did he confine his efforts to benefit only the Maidstone staff and police school: he spent much of his time in the rural districts, serving the interests of the country policeman. One report, recalling Sillitoe's command, speaks of his indefatigable efforts to improve the ordinary policeman's lot, mentioning that he began a countywide golf tournament so that officers at all levels could get to know one another better; yet, golf being a recreation limited to a relatively-high income group, one tends to think this is stretching Sillitoe's 'goodness' to the elastic limit.

But he was indeed a faithful commander and defender of his men, brooking no criticism of their performance in the line of duty, loyalty or otherwise. His experience with a visiting army colonel was typical of his uncompromising attitude. There were, of course, numerous visitors to the Sillitoe home when they lived at Maidstone, which is hardly surprising in view of the many people with whom Sillitoe had to deal in connection with the planned invasion. By this time, at the age of fifty-five, he had grown more testy than he had been in the old days, and therefore less inclined to forgive shortcomings.

One evening, after dinner, a colonel began boasting of the army's superiority over the police on the sports field. Sillitoe, listening to his guest in silence, became more and more irritated as he reclined in his leather armchair, pinching and rolling one cheek between a thumb and forefinger—a sure sign that he was getting riled. Dollie tried to steer the conversation to another subject, but either the colonel purposely ignored the hint or knew he had touched a sore spot in his host and wanted to explore the possibilities with more needling. In any event, with whitening knuckles and the blood drained from his face, Percy could stand it no longer and lunged into a lightning attack.

'You don't know what you're talking about!' he cried, rising to his feet. 'The army is in full training all the time. A policeman trains in his spare time—and that's on a bloody Sunday afternoon.' He waggled his finger in admonishment. 'And just you remember, the police have turned out some first-class athletes. Don't make statements on matters that you don't understand.'

The colonel, knocked off balance by the suddenness of the attack, looked to Dollie for support, but there was none to be had from that quarter.

'Such bloody nonsense,' said Sillitoe, flopping back into his chair and further silence.

The visitor beat a hasty retreat, quickly excusing himself to attend to other business, and Dollie was left to accompany him to the door. He was never invited again.

The Sillitoe home, provided by the County Police, was near an aerodrome of Bomber Command. During the period of the great daylight bomber raids on enemy territory, regular sorties took off from the Maidstone aerodrome and passed over the house. For weeks at a stretch, Sillitoe made a practice of walking into the centre of the field behind the house during the noon hour, and there he would take a white handkerchief from his pocket and wave it to the departing bombers. Until she found out what he was doing—and that was not for a couple of weeks after Tod began the habit—Dollie was quite mystified. She would stand at the kitchen window and watch him with the utmost curiosity. He never discussed what he was up to, but the next day would quietly leave the house to repeat the performance. Dollie stood it until she could contain herself no longer. Then, on an impulse, she slipped into her coat and followed him some distance behind. The bombers, perilously close to the ground it seemed, with engines roaring as they clawed for height, rose above their heads.

'Why are you waving your handkerchief like that?' she asked when she got close enough to make herself heard.

Tod looked at his wife unsmiling. 'Because a lot of these boys won't ever come back,' he answered. 'They know it, too, and

I'm quite sure they would like to remember that there was someone here to wave them off, wishing them well. It's probably the last thing some of them will remember. Have you got a handkerchief on you?' Yes, she said she had. 'Then wave it, for God's sake.' Dollie took a small handkerchief from her coat pocket and waved it too.

Sillitoe's unstinting if rather sentimental admiration for 'the boys of the RAF', as he referred to them, was not entirely to do with the fact that his son Anthony was a gunner in the air force. He was almost as fierce in his praise and admiration of the RAF boys as he was of his own policemen. When the V1 attacks were under way, he spent many an hour standing on the white cliffs of Dover, watching the infernal machines droning their way across the channel. To combat the 'doodlebugs', every available anti-aircraft and bofors gun in the country was moved to the south-east area where they stood, gun carriage to gun carriage, so to speak, a bristling array of defence against the menace, almost a thousand guns in all. The women ack-ack gunners stationed on the cliff top, pounding away at the incoming low-flying machines, had a critical observer in Sillitoe, who would view the proceedings like a visitor at the battle of Waterloo. Sometimes he would take sandwiches along and a thermos flask of tea. When the gunners were off target, as they frequently were, he heaped scorn on their heads; when they were on target and knocked a V1 out of the sky, he grudgingly acknowledged the fact with a handclap.

'Why the hell can't these women learn to fire a gun?' he asked Richard, who occasionally accompanied him when on leave as he made the rounds of the districts.

Flying bombs were not the only scourge sent to plague the south-east reaches of England. The enemy dropped 'booby-trap' bombs with time-delayed detonators and anti-personnel devices to inflict damage on the innocent and the curious. With the help of his Whitehall and War Office friends, Sillitoe arranged for a reinforcement party of sixty officers, bomb reconnaissance and bomb disposal experts recruited from Durham, Northumberland and Newcastle City, to bolster the Kent force. They remained in the county until the worst of the bombardment was over.

Richard, as already related, joined the Merchant Navy. Once he was home on leave during the height of the doodlebug barrage. He noticed that his father had changed considerably since they had last met, some months earlier; he was edgy and inclined to be nervous. The V1s had begun to affect him. Despite the fact Richard had been through the kind of hell only Merchant Navy men on wartime convoys could experience, his father felt compelled to warn him about the flying terrors. 'Before you go to bed,' he said, the first night Richard was home, 'if you hear doodlebugs for Christ's sake get out of the house and get down flat on your face.'

The next night, as they were getting ready to retire, they heard the familiar sound of a doodlebug approaching; its ramjet engine emitted a staccato 'phut-phut' noise and stopped only when the machine ran out of fuel. Suddenly the noise ceased. Percy was in the bathroom in his underwear, brushing his teeth. He immediately ran out and flew down the stairs, shouting for everyone to make for the shelter. With his toothbrush clutched in one hand and a tube of toothpaste in the other, he opened the front door and leapt into the darkness to land in a heap in the lavender bed. Meanwhile, Richard had sauntered downstairs with his mother hurrying after him, and stood on the front step laughing. Swearing and groaning and dusting himself down, Percy turned on his son in fury.

'Don't stand there grinning like a silly oaf,' he fumed. 'When I tell you to get out, get out!'

In the confusion and uproar of the moment, everyone had forgotten about the bomb, which suddenly detonated with a furious roar half a mile away, sending them all scrambling for cover. Percy was shaken and took a long time to regain his composure. Later, when Richard was alone with his mother and they discussed the incident, she said, 'My God, I never realised how terrified your father is of these doodlebugs.'

Long before D-Day, the military planners and Sillitoe's police staff tested their plans for movement of supplies and routing of traffic by conducting an exercise code-named 'Harlequin'. Basically, this involved the mass movement of men, convoys and heavy equipment such as tank transporters and guns from inland depots to the coastal marshalling areas. All bridge dimensions and loadings were checked, road widths measured and convoy routes worked out. Alternative routes were devised for the heavy transporters in case accidents or aerial bombardment blocked the preferred routes and, throughout the exercise, such occurrences were simulated to test the ability of route officers, military police and drivers to adjust to unforeseen circumstances. All crossroads, converging and diverging points were manned by either control officers or military police, while Sillitoe's civil police manned important thoroughfares and crossroads in the towns and villages. The Harlequin exercise turned out to be a jolly scramble of grand confusion, despite the claim Sillitoe liked to make that it went smoothly. Heavy equipment, re-routed when part way along a chosen route, got stuck making turns on the smaller roads, hump-backed bridges were a problem and long hold-ups were endured by the rear-most drivers. Yet, for all the confusion, Harlequin served the purpose it was intended to serve; many valuable lessons were learned which were put to good use by the planners and control officers during the build-up for D-Day. The exercise exposed the weaknesses of the plan and strengthened the co-operation between the police and the military forces. Afterwards, Sillitoe toured the divisions to speak to the police and to urge upon them the necessity of running a smooth operation. The police, he said to the officers of one division, were not on point duty to argue the toss with the military police as to whether civilian or military traffic had right of way, and there were a number of instances of such arguments. Still, in the main, he was well satisfied with police contribution to the exercise.

With the coming of the V2s (the high altitude rocket bombs, forerunners of the modern space rocket), that same south-east corner of the country which had withstood the V1s became an even more dangerous place to live in. The doodlebugs could at least be heard approaching; with the rockets there was no warning; it was a case of instantaneous devastation. Sillitoe had the basement of the headquarters building at Maidstone converted to an air-raid shelter. It was large enough to accommodate a number of police families, and there they were safe from anything but a direct hit, so while their husbands and fathers were on their tour of duty the families enjoyed the protection of a ready-made shelter.

One evening a report came from the headquarters of Southern Command to say there had been a report of German paratroops dropping into Kent. Would Chief Constable Sillitoe investigate and confirm or deny the information immediately? Sillitoe, in turn, called his headquarters. As a precautionary measure, he ordered a cache of small arms (supplied for such an emergency) to be distributed, but warned the officers on duty that on no account were the families sleeping below to be alarmed. Everyone was on edge, naturally, and those on the roof lookout saw in the moonlit sky a broken cloud formation which did indeed take on the appearance of parachutes. By the time Sillitoe arrived the headquarters was in an uproar because one officer, more edgy than the rest, had panicked and gone to the basement to spread the alarm, terrifying everyone needlessly. When Sillitoe learned what happened, he reached boiling point and gave the culprit a public tongue-lashing.

The point has already been made that Sillitoe did little writing that was not in the official line of duty. The one correspondence he did maintain with some regularity was with August Vollmer at California State University. At one point, the professor wrote offering to send the Sillitoes food parcels, shortly before they left Glasgow for Kent. Sillitoe tactfully wrote back:

My Dear Vollmer,
It was most terribly kind of you to offer to send me something from your Great country that we are unable to obtain over here but as we are definitely getting sufficient to eat, which is the main thing, I feel it would be an abuse of privilege to avail myself of your very kind offer.

Dollie was, and remained, the giver of family news to friends and relations. She maintained a regular correspondence with the children and kept in touch with one of the nannies, a Miss Powrie, who had been with them at Chesterfield, Sheffield and Glasgow, but who had left to get married and return to her native Yorkshire. In one of her letters to the former Miss Powrie, she gave the family news (and a great deal of classified information about military dispositions which was contrary to wartime regulations) when she wrote:

Anthony is a Sergt. Air gunner in the RAF and is due to go out to the Far East any time—an awful thought. Richard is a senior cadet officer in the MN—Merchant Navy—and I enclose a snap of him—the baby you looked after so well. Richard's photo was taken in July in Naples—he is now waiting to go off somewhere again. Audrey's husband is at sea with the Home Fleet and she is now living in Glasgow. It is too risky to bring little Susan—Audrey's daughter—down here; we get plenty of 'alerts' and bangs in this district. I hope you and your family are well.

Sillitoe's service with the Kent County Constabulary brought him into contact frequently with those at the centre of control, both the political leaders and senior members of the armed services. In particular, his frequent contact with members of the wartime coalition government—such people as Churchill, Attlee and Morrison, for example—gave him access to those at the core of national power. His organisational abilities had smoothed the operations connected with the movement of troops and supplies through the county, movement of the D-Day traffic was effected without a hitch, and for this alone Sillitoe merited official thanks and recognition. Similarly, with the constant concern about enemy infiltration of agents along the stretch of coast nearest to Europe, he was often consulted by those officials of the Home Office (and particularly MI5) concerned with national security.

Throughout 1945 he was to be found in London dealing with questions not strictly connected with his duties as chief constable of a county police force. This fact is supported by two reliable reports which indicate the kind of work with which Sillitoe became increasingly occupied. The first, already discussed, concerns the Glasgow safe-cracker, Johnny Ramensky, whose special talents were employed to open the Reichstag safe. Another incident occurred in the summer of 1945 which is singularly odd because of the fact that Sillitoe had no 'official' connection with MI5 until 1st May the following year. That the incident concerns a Canadian who spied in Germany during the war (and he would have been 'controlled' by the SIS or a similar organisation) is even more mystifying, until one relates it to the brief which Sillitoe wrote on Communist organisation and activities in Great Britain for Home Office consumption, a subject we will come to in a moment.

The Canadian operator, identified as Jacques DeRocher, of Bavarian descent, worked in a German labour battalion in France, the Netherlands and along the East German border defences from late 1942 on. In the summer of 1945, DeRocher was flown from Germany to London, where he was personally interviewed by none other than Sillitoe. The former Canadian intelligence officer who provided this information, and had dealings with DeRocher when he returned to Canada, maintains that Sillitoe conducted this interview in his police uniform.

Official confirmation or denial of Sillitoe's involvement in matters of national security prior to his appointment as Director

General of the British Security Services, MI5, is not forthcoming. Nevertheless, one must assume that some special qualities, experience and ability must have led to his being considered for this highest security appointment in the country. There is strong reason to believe that his MI5 appointment stemmed directly from the brief or report Sillitoe submitted to the Home Office, dealing with the potential threat of a subversive Communist organisation in Great Britain. It is quite possible, though one must admit there is no concrete evidence, that the DeRocher interview was a source of information for Sillitoe's 'Communist Organisation' report. Indeed, this is the only rational explanation for that interview. It must be remembered that Sillitoe had considerable experience with Communist agitators and organisers during his Glasgow days, probably more than any other British chief constable. During the closing days of the war there was increasing concern in official circles about Communist activities in post-war Great Britain. At a time when so little was known in the western world of Communist cell organisation—and this before the Gouzenko disclosures in Ottawa in September 1945— Sillitoe was an acknowledged authority.

In a confidential letter from the Home Office, dated 3rd January 1946, the chairman of the Kent Standing Joint Committee was informed that Sillitoe would resign in about three month's time to take up an appointment as a Director on the staff of the Chief of the Imperial General Staff. Whilst the letter did not state the specific nature of his duties, his appointment in fact was as the Director General of British Security Service, MI5. He had been selected by the Prime Minister, with the concurrence of Chuter Ede, the Home Secretary. Sillitoe would take up his new duties the following 30th April. He had yet to perform one more important service as chief constable—a 'Give-Me-Your-Guns campaign', conceived by Sillitoe himself and carried out with characteristic efficiency. In January 1946 he decided it was high time someone took the lead in gathering in the hundreds of firearms, assorted weapons and ammunition which returning servicemen had brought home as trophies of war. There were difficulties to contend with. People appealed against the chief constable's refusal to grant firearm permits; demobilised servicemen protested that they were law-abiding citizens and only wanted to keep their battle trophies as innocent souvenirs; others thought they ought to have protection against burglars; one old man, a veteran of the Boer War, appearing at the Quarter Sessions, said he would be lost without his pistol. Sillitoe was unrelenting. He would have no dangerous weapons in civilian hands. The police intensified the campaign, persuading the public at large that a revolver was not the best defence against criminals. The results were staggering: four hundred rifles, over one thousand revolvers, automatic pistols, anti-tank weapons, sten-guns and ten thousand assorted rounds of ammunition were collected. Commenting on the results of the campaign to the press, Percy said, 'If this is what we have found in Kent, this peaceful corner of Britain, what must the rest of the country be like?'

There was no great fanfare when Percy left Maidstone to take up his new appointment. He submitted his final report to the police committee, expressing his gratitude and thanks for the support, kindness and patience they had shown to him during his term of office. To accommodate the incoming chief constable, the Sillitoes left Maidstone and moved to Eastbourne, which was within easy reach of London.

Never again did Percy Sillitoe wear a uniform.

Chapter Seventeen

The Muttonhead Institute

When he retired from his post as Director General of the Directorate of Security Services (referred to from now on by the British counter-espionage service's popular designation, MI5) in 1953, Sillitoe wrote his memoirs. He was obliged to submit the manuscript to the Home Office for approval, and almost everything of interest about his MI5 intelligence work was rejected. Later, discussing the censorship with a former colleague, he remarked with some bitterness, 'The government tore out the guts of the book and completely emasculated it.' To his family he was equally blunt: 'They've torn the bloody guts out of it, torn it to shreds.' A blander, more acceptable version of the book was produced and this, with official blessing, was finally considered suitable for public consumption.

A comparison between Sillitoe's *Cloak Without Dagger* and Philby's *My Silent War** is well worth making. Philby's work, even to the most casual reader, betrays a serious effort on the part of Philby and his Russian intelligence colleagues to undermine the intelligence efforts of his former British secret service colleagues; in short, *My Silent War* comes across as a woeful psychological exercise, being designed and written for its potentially demoralising value. In the case of Sillitoe's memoirs, it is equally obvious that the British intelligence service (taken as a whole) either missed or ignored a perfect opportunity to inflict psychological injury on the Soviet intelligence system. One imagines that with the subtle use of information available to them, this would have been a relatively easy task.

* Grove Press, Inc., New York, 1968. Philby, a Russian agent, became head of the Soviet Section of SIS (the British 'offensive' espionage service, MI6), and defected to the Soviet Union in 1963.

THE MUTTONHEAD INSTITUTE

But to begin at the beginning with respect to Sillitoe's service with MI5, there were two other contenders for the top post, both long-standing employees of MI5. One was Guy Liddell, who had joined the Service in 1919 and was, by 1945, head of MI5's 'B' Division, the information gathering and assessment unit; the other was one of Liddell's senior officers, Richard (Dick) Goldsmith White (later knighted), a former schoolteacher who had joined MI5 between the wars. Liddell was close to retirement, so was weak in the running. So far as can be determined, the reason why Sillitoe was chosen over his nearest rival, White, was because of his evident knowledge of Communist organisation in the United Kingdom, experience with combating Communist activities, and all round administrative talents. Furthermore, the new government (the Labour Party under Clement Attlee had gained power in the first post-war election) needed a man who could deal with the Americans, who had a broad background and, above all, one with superior organisational abilities. Sillitoe fitted the bill nicely.

The next seven years were to be the most difficult and trying period of Sillitoe's whole career. This was not so much due to any lack of counter-intelligence experience or lack of willingness to grasp a fistful of nettles, as to the totally different type of person with whom he had to deal. Some of those who have commented on the activities and performance of the Secret Service during the first seven years of the cold war have made him out to be little more than a figurehead. Nevertheless, on the word of a number of people who worked with him during this period, his achievements as head of MI5 were no less brilliant than those which characterised his performances in Sheffield, Glasgow and Kent.

There is a difficulty here for the biographer which is best explained by referring to another writer. In his *History of the British Secret Service**, Richard Deacon touches on the subject of 'literary espionage', defined as the gathering of intelligence information from published works. This is an important development for the intelligence expert, he says, in the political, scientific and economic fields. The implication of the statement must be obvious when applied to this part of Sillitoe's life. The point must be made that, although no dark and revealing secrets are likely to be found in this narrative, none of the former employees

* Frederick Muller Ltd, London, 1969.

of various espionage and counter-espionage agencies (not just the British Secret Service) who were willing to comment or express opinion on Sillitoe's work, were prepared to be named or to have statements directly attributed to them. What new information, then, that is revealed must necessarily be taken at face value.

MI5 came into being in 1909, and was headed by Major General Vernon Kell until 1940 when the National Security Executive, under the chairmanship of Lord Swinton, established to review all security organisations in the country, dismissed Kell as no longer being a suitable chief, despite his previous fine record. A caretaker director was appointed and, a short time later, was replaced by Sir David Petrie, who held the office until 1945. The counter-espionage service was created to combat any and all subversive elements which sought, for one reason or another, to destroy the established institutions of the country. Unlike its aggressive sister service, SIS (formerly MI6), MI5 was essentially a policing operation. Under Petrie's leadership, a group of bright young men and women was recruited to rejuvenate the Service, and they did a commendable job. MI5 is reputed to have caught some fifteen spies during the Second World War—an achievement which might be rated good, mediocre or bad, depending on the number of agents who penetrated the nation's security screen, which there is no way of measuring—or if the number is known, it is still under lock and key. Naturally enough, MI5's whole effort during the war was directed against the Axis powers. As the war drew to a close in Europe, a new enemy appeared in the shape of international Communism. The Western Powers must share equal blame with the Soviet Union for the ensuing state of affairs. The SIS created its Soviet Section IX early in 1945 with Philby as Section Head. MI5 had done practically nothing in this direction although an MI5 officer, Roger Hollis, had written a paper prior to Sillitoe's arrival in which he gave a detailed description of the state of the Communist Party in the United Kingdom, but this offered little subversive intelligence. The only other person in MI5, other than Liddell, who could boast a knowledge of Communist subversion was a woman Philby identifies as Jane Archer, but she was transferred to the SIS to bolster the newly-formed Soviet Section.

At the opening phase of the cold war, the intelligence agencies of the Western Powers knew remarkably little of Soviet operaions in the western hemisphere, and any attempt to infiltrate their world was largely negated by Philby's activities. About the only organisation which successfully penetrated the 'enemy' camp was the Royal Canadian Mounted Police.

The first real break, for western counter-intelligence agencies in general and MI5 in particular, came with the Gouzenko disclosures in Ottawa in 1945, a short time before Sillitoe took over command of MI5. On 5th September, Igor Gouzenko, a civilian employee cypher clerk working for the Military Attaché in the Russian Embassy, defected to the west. His disclosures exposed an international spy ring. Among those working on behalf of the USSR, as revealed in the Gouzenko disclosures, was Dr Allan Nunn May who, at that time, was working in England. Formerly, May had spent some time in Canada with the nuclear energy authority. The day Sillitoe officially took up his new duties, 1st May 1946, May was charged and brought to trial at the Old Bailey. It was an auspicious start for the new chief.

At the time of his take-over, the offices of MI5 were located at 11 Curzon Street, off Park Lane. The first time Richard Sillitoe visited his father, he must have been the only person in London who did not know the address: its location had been written out for him on a slip of paper which he promptly lost. Getting into a taxi at Victoria Station, he told the driver his problem and got the answer, 'That's all right, gov, we all know MI5. That'll be 11 Curzon Street you want.'

The main hall of Britain's counter-espionage headquarters was a large, gloomy area, about thirty feet square, with a marble floor. Little light penetrated into it, and the eye had to adjust to the crepuscule before it could discern the peeling white walls and cracked plaster ceiling. In all, it was entirely in keeping with the dingy atmosphere with which such places are endowed by popular fiction.

At the far end of the left-hand wall was a flight of stairs leading to the upper floors, and a semi-circular reception desk, normally manned by a commissionaire. Along the same wall, about halfway from the entrance to the reception desk, there was an enclosed telephone box. Along the right-hand wall, a couple of doors led to offices and at the far end, opposite the reception desk and stair-well, were two lifts—decrepit pieces of equipment and ponderously slow.

Ascending to the first floor via the brass hand-railed stairs or the lifts, one found oneself in a spacious room, bisected by a counter. On the stairwell side of the counter stood two desks, widely separated and set at right angles to it. Here the chief's two women secretaries sat with their backs to Curzon Street, so that whoever entered the main area would be seen by them. To their front were the double glass-panelled doors which gave access to a portion of the main offices housing junior personnel of the Service, secretaries, files and records. At the opposite end of the main room, above the building's entrance, was Sillitoe's blue-carpeted and wood-panelled office. His desk, set at an angle, gave him a view of a large map of the world studded with coloured pins on the far wall (the Park Lane side) and of the window overlooking Curzon Street on his left. Next to the lifts, there was a small reception room for visitors and, next to this, but also abutting the chief's office, was the sanctuary of Sillitoe's executive assistant. There were doors connecting the reception room, executive assistant's office and Sillitoe's as well as a connecting door to each from the main first-floor hall or outer office.

For some reason, Sillitoe's relations with the MI5 personnel were at first dogged by difficulties. A minor but perhaps symptomatic series of incidents concerned the commissionaires.

One day, when he was not yet well known, Sillitoe was leaving the office when he decided to make a local telephone call from the telephone box in the hall. He closed the door but no light came on. The bulb had burned out. He called the commissionaire to know why it had not been replaced.

'Don't ask me,' said the commissionaire. 'That's someone else's job, not mine.' Sillitoe had very little patience with people having that sort of mentality.

'Where the hell do you keep the spares?' he asked.

'There's usually a couple on top of the booth.'

Sillitoe groped about the top of the kiosk, located a replacement and fitted it into the socket himself, made his call and stamped out of the building to his waiting Rolls-Royce.

He was not one to hold a grudge, however, and later got to know the commissionaire, exchanging friendly greetings as he went in and out of the building. A few months later he was surprised to find a new face behind the reception desk.

'Hello,' he said, 'what's happened to Charlie?'

'He was taken into custody last night, sir,' said the new man, grinning. 'Bin running a brothel for months, sir. Couple of streets over the way.'

Sillitoe shook his head and went up to his office, making a mental note to ask a few questions about internal security.

The new commissionaire was as obstreperous as his predecessor. A visitor to Curzon Street presented his credentials to the commissionaire and asked to see the Director, who was expecting him.

'Sir Percy Sillitoe?' questioned the man behind the desk. 'Never heard of him.' (Perhaps security was now *too* tight.) The new man telephoned Sillitoe's office and was heard to remark, 'Then he will have to come down himself,' meaning the Director General. He listened again, eyeing the visitor up and down. Then: 'No,' he said, 'he has no pass so he can't come in without an escort.' Sillitoe's secretary offered to come down, but the commissionaire was adamant that Sir Percy should present himself at the desk to receive the visitor in person. This commissionaire was replaced without further ado by another who showed more tact.

Resistance to the new chief's leadership was evident from the start. It has already been noted that White had high hopes of winning the post, and friction developed between him and Sillitoe.

Without exception, writers (including Philby) commenting on this period of MI5's activities have dismissed Sillitoe's contribution to the Service's successes as insignificant. The general opinion is that Sillitoe, a former policeman, had no idea how to run a counter-espionage organisation. He was, the consensus would have it, a mere figurehead appointed by a Labour government, itself unfamiliar with the delicate business of espionage or counter-espionage. The real work was necessarily left to Sillitoe's 'brilliant' subordinates, Liddell, White, Hollis, Skardon, Collard and the rest. This sort of friction is all too easy to perpetuate, yet the facts speak otherwise. Clearly, Sillitoe was not a man to take a back seat. To have done so would have been completely out of keeping with his character and previous activities, and those who miss this point are guilty of self-deception.

There was, however, some animosity between Sillitoe and the colleagues over whom he was set. A number of them were 'bright young men' recruited during the war from the universities, and they resented the imposition upon them of a Director General who had been a policeman—an archetypally uncerebral profession—as much as he scorned what he called 'Oxbridge types' and 'long-haired intellectuals'. This conflict manifested itself during the early days of Sillitoe's appointment.

One of the first major affairs in which Sillitoe was involved was the investigation, code-named 'Homer', into a leak to the USSR of information about supplies of pitchblende (from which uranium is extracted) from the Belgian Congo to Canada for the Manhattan Project.* (It was as a result of this investigation that Donald MacLean eventually defected.)

In the summer of 1946 Sillitoe, who as head of the Service was directly responsible to the Prime Minister, was summoned to 10 Downing Street to brief Mr Attlee on the latest developments. Asking for the Homer file to be brought to him, Sillitoe hurriedly thrust the papers into his briefcase and went on his way. When he arrived at the Prime Minister's official residence and drew out the file, he was horrified to discover that he had been handed the wrong papers. He apologised profusely and was assured by the Prime Minister, with whom he got on extremely well, that he should forget the error and come back later.

Understandably, Sillitoe was furious with the junior officer who had caused him to waste the Prime Minister's time, to say nothing of making him look a fool. For the culprit upon his return to Curzon Street, there was a public tongue-lashing. Sillitoe did not believe that the wrong file was handed to him with malicious intent, but that the mistake was merely the action of a bumbling incompetent. But from this time on he began to make his presence felt—and there was need of it.

Of the two secretaries in his outer office, the senior handled his correspondence, and was helpful to him in other ways. She proved to be Sillitoe's main support before the arrival of Michael Surpell, his personal assistant, of whom more later, and kept him informed of what was going on as regards 'office politics'.

A few weeks after the incident of the file, and following a particularly gruelling session with Home Secretary Herbert Morrison, Sillitoe returned to the office to be greeted by his faithful secretary with a choice bit of inside information. One of the junior intelligence officers, it seemed, catering perhaps to the derision which had been building up and had apparently infected the greater number of Sillitoe's staff, publicly accused him of spending most of his time on the golf course. According to the secretary, the accusation was something to the effect that, 'Sir

* Code name for US programme for manufacture of the first atomic bomb.

Percy will never show his head around here, chaps. He's too busy on the golf course.'

Sillitoe was already in an irritable mood, and on hearing this story he immediately stormed out of his office, across the main hall and burst through the doors of the general office. He thundered towards the culprit's desk and all but yanked the loudmouth to his feet. Then, before the whole office staff, the typists, secretaries, filing clerks and intelligence officers, who had rarely witnessed such an explosion, Sillitoe vented his fury.

'So it's golf every afternoon, is it? For your snivelling remarks I'd fire you on the spot if I had my way. I can't. You evidently have something in that skull of yours or you wouldn't be in the organisation. Your are bright, I'm told, and intelligent. We need men like you . . .'—Sillitoe pointed his finger menacingly and his steel-blue eyes pierced the young man's skull—'but let me tell you this. Your are a marked man. Don't you ever let me see your face again or by God I'll have your hide.' It was a dire warning which Sillitoe intended for general consumption and, so far as one can tell, it marked a turning point for his 'get tough' measures.

When he got home that evening he was still fuming. 'I sometimes think I'm working in a madhouse,' he told Dollie. 'They're either idiots or muttonheads. I'm not sure which, but now I know what MI stands for; it's the Muttonhead Institute.'

Sillitoe once remarked privately that counter-espionage was the most dreary, uninspiring and over-rated occupation imaginable; even a plumber's career was exciting by comparison. The mystery and excitement of cloak and dagger operations, he said, was more in the public's imagination than to be found in fact, and stemmed from a natural awe of the unknown. While this private view conflicts with his public statement when, of the Service, he wrote, '. . . I felt its popular reputation for excessive secrecy was in no way exaggerated', it must be noted that his written comment referred to secrecy within the Service, and to his difficulty in finding out himself what was going on immediately following his appointment.

From what is known and told of his time with MI5, Sillitoe was responsible for instituting organisational reforms and was among the first of the many government department heads to 'clean house' at the onset of the cold war. The fact is, practically the entire effort of the Service from 1946 on, and until long after Sillitoe's retirement, was directed at identifying and weeding out

Communists from positions in which they posed a threat to national security. One of his first actions after getting settled into the job was to carry out a purge (hardly surprising in view of his record), though not for the same reason which dictated his police purges, namely, to rid the force of senior officers due for retirement. In the case of MI5, he was primarily interested in the political reliability of his staff, and a number of employees were forced to leave for one reason or another. His MI5 purge probably contributed to his unpopularity as much as for the fact he was not 'one of them'. Beginning with those whose credentials were 'impeccable', he carried out a systematic security check of the entire establishment. This was a programme in which the internal security officers combed through each personnel file as though the person concerned was a newcomer; the individual's history was checked and rechecked, membership in clubs, societies and social organisations was investigated anew to ensure that the Service itself was 'clean'. Without this purge Sillitoe could not be sure of his department's ability to provide an effective counter-espionage service. He was strongly supported in this by Mr Attlee, who, in retrospect, probably acted with wisdom in choosing a total outsider to head MI5 at that time.

Having satisfied himself and the Prime Minister that he had a reliable Service, Sillitoe proceeded with the next stage of his elaborate security screening programme, which was nothing less than a total survey of the civil service. For this larger programme, Sillitoe devised the ground plan, interpreted government policy, and gave it impetus. As a result, in the United Kingdom, numerous civil servants were compelled to leave their employment with the government. There were court cases, appeals and minor demonstrations—especially when *The Daily Worker* took up the cudgel on behalf of those severed, but, once alarmed, the government acted with firmness. Considering the many thousands of civil servants who were positively vetted during the period from 1946 to 1950 (and some eight thousand Foreign Office employees in connection with the Manhattan Project leak which reduced the suspects to two, of whom MacLean was one), Sillitoe's programme never reached the dizzy height attained by the McCarthy witch-hunt in the US during the late forties and early fifties. With a less scrupulous man in the driving seat of MI5, the 'programme' in the UK might have taken a similar turn. It is a testimony to Sillitoe's sense of values that he himself said he would rather see one or two spies slip through the net than be a party to the creation of a police state.

That enemy agents did slip through the counter-espionage net is now a matter of known fact; Burgess, MacLean, Philby and Pontecorvo were among the more well known of those who did, but this was not for want of effort on Sillitoe's part or neglect to inform the security sections of other services such as the Foreign Office and SIS. That MI5 provided ample evidence pointing to guilt in the cases of MacLean and Philby is also well known; the problem was compounded by the solid support these 'trusted' employees received from their colleagues in the two services concerned.

Questions naturally arise as to how the detailed business of counter-espionage is carried out. From where is information obtained in the first place? How is it sifted and analysed? What specific contribution did Sillitoe make during his stewardship of the Service? And what organisational reforms did he institute? These are difficult questions to answer because, as with any bureaucracy, the structure and work of MI5 during Sillitoe's era was sufficiently complex as to defy reduction of its inner workings for simple explanation. Nevertheless, on the information of one informant, a reasonable picture may be drawn. Of one thing we may be certain; Sillitoe was never personally involved in an investigation. This work was left to such specialists as William Skardon, who conducted the Klaus Fuchs investigation. Sillitoe was naturally familiar with the progress of particular cases; his role was that of a high-level advocate and advisor to heads of other departments as well as to his own chief, the Prime Minister.

MI5 was responsible for counter-espionage intelligence in the United Kingdom, its possessions and colonial territories, and acted as a central co-ordinating and clearing house for the security services of member countries of the Commonwealth. In those territories for which the Service had direct responsibility, a regional office was established under a Director of Intelligence. Each regional office acted as the eyes and ears of the Service and were to be found in such centres as Nairobi, Singapore, Jamaica, Lusaka and Kuala Lumpa. It was the responsibility of the Director of Intelligence and his staff to maintain a close liaison with military intelligence in his area, with the police and other security services as they were variously constituted. The chain of command which connected a particular regional office with other government departments was an intricate one which varied from region to region depending on the peculiar political-economic-military circumstances of that region. In the case of Commonwealth countries (and with the US for that matter), a liaison officer was located in capitals such as Ottawa, Washington and Melbourne, and dealt with their opposite numbers very much as resident representatives of the Service.

It was the growing body of information, showing the extent of Soviet intelligence operations in the West, which brought about the need for closer co-operation between the various international counter-espionage agencies. This meant even more travelling for Percy Sillitoe, accompanied by his assistant, Michael Surpell, whom he jocularly referred to as 'Sir Pell'. One of Sillitoe's former associates, speaking of his chief's life as head of the Service, said, '... intelligence operations, as seen from Sir Percy's viewpoint, would have little, if any, appeal.' However, his shrewd administration and organising work, while making for dull reading, is something for which he should be remembered, and a good example of that work outside the UK is to be found in the case of the Federation of Malaya, a region for which MI5 exercised security intelligence control.

Field-Marshal Sir Gerald Templer, during the 1946–53 period, was the High Commissioner and Director of Operations. In 1948 the Malayan Communist Party was banned and a state of emergency declared, but the Malayan Security Service was functioning quite separately from the police. Because of this lack of co-ordination, the MSS was proving a totally ineffective instrument against the violent tactics of the Communist Party's tightly-knit organisation. To remedy this deficiency, Sillitoe persuaded the Malayan government authorities to disband the MSS (not to be confused with MI5's organisation in the region) and to bring its staff into the Special Branch (intelligence) as an integral part of the police. Sillitoe appointed a new Director of Intelligence, a former Intelligence Bureau official of the Indian government whom Sillitoe incorrectly identifies as MacDonald in his memoirs. Sillitoe's advice was accepted, and this had the desired effect of achieving a much closer link and a far more healthy co-operation between the Special Branch on the one hand and the uniformed branch, the CID and the army on the other.

Much the same thing occurred in 1952 in Kenya, when that country was struggling with the Mau Mau terrorists under the leadership of Jomo Kenyatta. Sir Evelyn Baring, Governor of the colony at the time of the Mau Mau uprising, asked the British government for Sillitoe's assistance. What Sillitoe found was a complete lack of co-ordination between the security forces, the police and the army. He corrected the deficiency by working out a plan for the integration of all services, similar to the organisation designed for combating the Malayan Communists. Sillitoe's ability to expose organisational weaknesses and to offer remedies was his great strength, and herein lay his undoubted contribution to the forces of law and order.

Popular fiction perpetuates the myth that secret service forces are constantly on the prowl for subversive elements but, as one former intelligence operator pointed out, there have to be reasonable grounds for suspicion in the first place, which brings us to the question of where and when and from what point an investigation begins. Original reports of suspicion and intelligence are brought to the notice of the Service from multitudinous sources, ranging from a concerned citizen to the qualified intelligence of a liaison officer working closely with the security forces of a foreign but friendly power such as the US. When the Service has something to go on it may act, but not until then may the vast resources of the organisation be brought into play. During Sillitoe's period of office, the main concern being centred about Communist activities, there was a constant flow of suspicious reports directed through military intelligence, Scotland Yard, county police headquarters and security sections of other governments departments. MI5 makes use of all these sources, assigning seconded police officers, full-time field operators and senior investigators as the particular case demands. Reports are routed to the various internal sections of MI5 which file, analyse and inform others of their findings. There are routine assignments such as that of watching the employees of unfriendly embassies. Periodically, we learn of wholesale withdrawals of foreign embassy staffs or certain individuals. These are the end results of months of patient watching and reporting by field operators, which go to make up a composite picture of subversive activities.

Typical of the cases dealt with during Sillitoe's era is that of William Marshall, a member of the Diplomatic Wireless Service, who was employed as a radio operator and Foreign Office employee in the British Embassy in Moscow. Upon his return to

England in 1950, following two years' foreign service, he was discovered in the company of a Second Secretary of the Soviet Embassy who was himself being routinely followed by MI5 scrutineers. With this knowledge it was a simple matter for the investigators to identify Marshall and check his history. He was arrested and charged, tried at the Old Bailey and sentenced to five years' imprisonment.

In another case a young soldier, Trooper Dewick of the Royal Armoured Corps, a former member of the Communist Youth League, was reported to the authorities by a suspicious adjutant, Captain W. F. Cornish. Dewick's piece of treachery involved stealing technical reports on the performance of armoured fighting vehicles being used in the Korean conflict. His intent was to hand these reports over to his Communist friends. His case was investigated by Skardon and this led to Dewick's arrest. His activities were nipped in the bud; nevertheless, he was tried and sentenced to twelve months' imprisonment.

In the case of Klaus Fuchs, the scientist involved in the Manhattan Project and betrayed atomic secrets to the Russians, there is contrast with the cases of Marshall and Dewick. Information concerning Fuchs's complicity first came to light through the FBI. The Americans suspected a leak of atomic secrets and informed the British. As happened in the case of the Homer file (resulting in MacLean's defection), the final suspicion coming to rest on Fuchs was a time-consuming job on the part of MI5 investigators. The narrowing down and elimination of suspects employed the energies of numerous agents: a detailed file on every person connected with the case, the 'tailing' of those under suspicion, cross-checking and analysis of reports all constituted a major investigation. Naturally, all these cases came to Sillitoe's attention although he was not personally involved in any of them.

The third Director of MI5 was, it is safe to claim, the least pretentious of the three. Although he did not go out of his way to advertise himself, neither did he cling to the notion that he must disguise his position with elaborate denials or by travelling incognito. There was little purpose to be served by denying what the press already knew. Furthermore, whether he was liaising with the Americans or intelligence services of member countries of the Commonwealth, he was as outspoken in his opinions as he had always been. For a period after the McCarthy hearings had abated, the US Congress did much soul-searching as to what should be done about Communism in their country and, early in 1950, brought in anti-Communist legislation which outlawed the Party. During his visit to the US in October 1950 to attend the 57th Convention of the International Association of Chiefs of Police (he was still a member), Sillitoe warned his listeners that the new legislation would drive the Communist Party of America underground, thereby making it doubly difficult for US law-enforcement agencies; and that, of course, is what happened.

If he was able to exert enormous influence on the government security authorities of so many Commonwealth countries and colonial administrations, his influence on his immediate family was still almost nil. Audrey had, against her father's wishes, married the man she loved; the boys went their own way; and Percy showed little interest in how Dollie managed their home life. He lived for his work and little else. Even on his brother, Hubert, the church minister, Percy was unable to exercise his otherwise iron will. Hubert frequently visited his brother at Curzon Street, turning up in a shabby coat and battered moth-eaten old hat. Percy would rave at him loud enough for everyone to hear. 'The least you can do is get rid of that flaming rotten old hat.' But it had no effect. Percy always dressed himself with impeccable taste.

Sillitoe spent almost eight years as the head of MI5 and when he finally retired, at the age of sixty-five, he did so without any of the banqueting and public speeches which accompanied his leaving other appointments; however, he was far from ready for retirement, as subsequent events were to prove.

Chapter Eighteen

The Diamond Syndicate

'Things are getting too hot. At the mines. I don't like it at all. There's been a big intelligence man down from London. You've read about him. This man Sillitoe. They say he's been hired by the Diamond Corporation. There've been a lot of new regulations and all the punishments have been doubled . . .'

'So?' said the pilot. He paused. 'Do you want me to pass this threat back to ABC?'

'I'm not threatening anyone,' said the other man hastily. 'I just want them to know that it's getting tough. They must know it themselves. They must know about this man Sillitoe. And look what the Chairman said in our annual report. He said that our mines were losing two million pounds a year through smuggling and IDB and that it was up to the government to stop it. And what does that mean? It means "stop me"!'

Thus Sillitoe is introduced in the first chapter of Ian Fleming's novel *Diamonds Are For Ever*.* Fleming's fascination with diamonds spanned a period of many years. When he began working on his latest novel Fleming managed to get an introduction to Sillitoe, who had been engaged by De Beers Consolidated Mines the previous January to head up the famous diamond-smuggling investigation. The two met in July 1954. Sillitoe was able to give Fleming considerable background material which helped lend the novel an air of authenticity. In fact, Sillitoe turned out to be one of the few real-life characters mentioned in Fleming's Bond novels.

Diamonds Are For Ever was first published in 1956. Just a year

* Jonathan Cape Ltd, London 1956.

later, Fleming embarked on a series of articles for the *Sunday Times* dealing with the actual diamond case in which Sillitoe had been involved. The articles, based on the supposedly factual account of the investigation, were later published as *The Diamond Smugglers*.* Material for the articles was supplied by a deputy director of the organisation set up to make the investigation, identified under the pseudonym John Blaize. In real life, this was John Collard, a solicitor and former employee of MI5, reputed to have worked with Skardon on the Fuchs case in 1951.

The job of setting up the diamond-smuggling investigation organisation was originally offered to Sir William Stephenson at a fee of a million dollars plus unlimited operating funds. The former chief of British Security Co-ordination (the British counter-espionage organisation based in New York during the war) turned down the offer. De Beers then advertised in *The Times*, but disclosed no hint as to the organisation's identity nor the nature of the assignment.

In August 1953, Sillitoe reached the retirement age of sixty-five, quietly left MI5 and opened a sweet shop in Eastbourne. To open a sweet shop was the oddest, most irrational act in Sillitoe's whole life. It is the kind of thing one would expect of a sergeant-major or chief petty officer, but in Sillitoe's case it was so out of context with his character, the only explanation must be that he was totally unprepared for his retirement. And whatever the reason for it, the venture was so far from his liking that it folded within two days of being opened.

For the next few weeks, he worked on his memoirs, becoming more and more depressed and obsessed with the idea that he had gone to seed. The period from August to December 1953 was one of great bitterness for him. This once famous policeman loathed the idea of sinking into obscurity, of feeling that he was no longer needed. His former police colleagues ignored him, no one sought his advice; he railed against the press for ignoring him, too. He spent idle days doing the *Daily Telegraph* crossword puzzle or mooching around the house; he moaned about 'the public's lack of gratitude.' He became as 'blue' as he had been in those far-off days when he returned from East Africa to seek his first appointment as a chief constable. His favourite expression at this time was 'The King is dead, long live the king', and almost as frequently was heard to say, 'No one wants me, I might as well be

* Jonathan Cape Ltd, London, 1957.

dead.' Privately, he took his retirement as badly as any of the police officers he had forced to leave the service during his 'purges'. Not only was he miserable himself, he made everyone else's life miserable, too, and Dollie's most of all.

'My mother,' says Richard, 'was at desperation point herself, with father moping about the house all the time and, on seeing the advertisement, urged my father to answer it, especially with his experience in Rhodesia.'

Dollie read the advertisement out aloud: a position was vacant for a high-level civil servant who had a top security experience, was able to negotiate with senior executives and senior government officials, and who had a working knowledge of Rhodesia. Percy said he would not lower himself to submit a resumé, but agreed to write a brief note in which he would express his interest in discussing the position. As to his credentials, he referred the would-be employers to *Who's Who*. Back came a speedy reply from Sir Reginald Leeper, Chairman of the London Committee of De Beers, inviting him to visit the offices of the Diamond Trading Company in London.

Sillitoe was certainly the ideal candidate for the job and De Beers lost no time in making arrangements for him to fly to South Africa. His first journey was made to Johannesburg in mid-January, and he met Sir Ernest Oppenheimer, the Chairman of De Beers, in Cape Town.

Oppenheimer was more than Chairman of De Beers; he was the acknowledged ruler of a vast empire of mining companies, trading concerns and associated marketing organisations which, over the years, had acquired a virtual monopoly of the free world's diamond production and, thus, could dictate the price. Bound together by common interests, agreements and interconnecting equity share holdings, this empire has long been known simply as the Diamond Syndicate. Only once during its long history have the closely-guarded inner workings of the Syndicate been subjected to public scrutiny; this was in 1929 when Otto Oppenheimer, the brother of Sir Ernest Oppenheimer, was charged at the Old Bailey with conspiring with others to defraud The United Diamond Fields of British Guiana Limited, as a result of which the company went bankrupt.

No sooner had Sillitoe arrived in the Union than an enterprising reporter from South Africa's *Die Transvaaler*, smelling a story, picked up the former counter-espionage chief's trail. The following day, the newspaper ran a speculative front-page story to the effect that Sillitoe was in the country to organise an espionage ring.

Sillitoe had called on the Union's Commissioner of Police, Major-General J. A. Brink, at his Pretoria office to tell him in confidence of the purpose of the visit. Questioned by *Die Transvaaler's* reporter in Cape Town, Brink said he was aware of the Britisher's presence in the Union, but that he had come on a short holiday. The reporter was not satisfied, and followed the mysterious visitor back to Pretoria and then to Johannesburg, where he finally ran his quarry to ground in Oppenheimer's luxurious residence at Inanda at the north end of the city. Here, in the early evening, the reporter entered the house via the kitchen entrance and sent one of the servants into the drawing room to announce his presence. With some difficulty, he obtained an interview and was able to elicit an admission from Sillitoe himself that his visit was in connection with diamond smuggling. This explanation was no more acceptable than that given by the Commissioner of Police and was dismissed in a second newspaper report the following day as a smoke-screen for other activities.

> No country has more experience of combating diamond smuggling than the Union, argued *Die Transvaaler*, and it would be easy for the Oppenheimer organisation to find retired police officials in the country who had more experience of diamond smuggling than Sir Percy.

The reporter was both right and wrong: right on the point of experience and wrong about the smoke-screen. There *was* a smoke-screen all right, but what it concealed neither *Die Transvaaler* nor Sillitoe himself could have known at the time, and indeed there has been no satisfactory explanation until now for the massive diamond-smuggling investigation.

During his meeting with Oppenheimer at Inanda, Sillitoe was told that a Communist-directed diamond-smuggling ring was working in the west on an international scale; its agents, operating from a number of European capitals, were directing the flow of illicit diamonds from the Syndicate's numerous diamond mines in various African countries to Communist bloc industrial centres where they were desperately needed. Sillitoe's job was to set up an organisation to counteract the ring's operations. All necessary resources would be at his disposal: money, equipment and, of course, all the powerful political influence the Syndicate could bring to bear. From this time on, all of Sillitoe's old enthusiasm returned. Filled with zeal, and a firm conviction that he was once more fighting the continuing battle against Communist intrigue in the western hemisphere, he returned to London to discuss the subject with his friends in Whitehall, and to formulate a plan for attacking the problem.

Die Transvaaler's lead in questioning Sillitoe's activities in the Union was quickly followed by the national and international dailies in Africa, Europe and the US. The *Rand Daily Mail* vied with other African newspapers in demanding a satisfactory explanation of Sillitoe's comings and goings over the next several weeks, their guesses ranging from 'spy rings' to 'an investigation of race relations in the Union'. The following month, in February 1954, the London *Daily Mail*, under the banner headline 'DIAMOND CHIEFS CALL SILLITOE', disclosed that it all began with a 'conspiracy' reported to Scotland Yard by a city company claiming an annual loss of £750,000. The newspaper further reported that a senior police officer was to fly to Accra on the Gold Coast to investigate, while another was to visit Ottawa and New York, where the illicit diamonds were being sold. Although this latter information was not in accord with the Communist intrigue information given to Sillitoe, it is typical of the speculative information offered to satisfy a voracious public appetite.

It is interesting to note that in the many news stories which quickly followed on the heels of the first newsbreak, estimates from 'reliable sources' of losses attributable to smuggling activities rose astronomically. Experts were soon available to substantiate the sudden deplorable state into which the diamond industry had fallen. All of these experts, with the sole exception of an American economist, Professor Frank Pick, were connected in one way or another with the Syndicate. Chester A. Beatty, Chairman of Consolidated African Selection Trust (a Syndicate member), said that production in Sierra Leone was down some £430,000 as a result of the smuggling; David Marais, President of the World Federation of Master Diamond Cutters, put the figure at more than a million pounds sterling annually; The *Sunday Times* upped the estimate to £2 million; Pick revised this to £5 to £11 million; and by July 1954, the London *Daily Herald* raised the value of smuggled gems to a whopping £30 to £50 million.

In 1953, the diamond sales of the Union of South Africa amounted to £62·2 million, of which some £17·8 million were industrial diamonds. The American economist Pick put legal imports into the US from the sterling area at £22·8 million.

By the time Sillitoe made his second visit to Johannesburg in connection with the case, he had a clear idea of how he intended to set about his task. First of all he proposed to establish in Johannesburg a headquarters for the African operations with regional offices in London, Antwerp, Beirut and Zürich. Overall operational headquarters were to be located in Eastbourne, where the former MI5 chief had already installed Bob Buchanan (Dollie's old flame) and a secretary to collate the reports he expected to receive. Buchanan, it seems, had fallen on hard times, and Percy was able to extend a helping hand by offering him a job. Like a firefly on a summer's night, Buchanan casts a brief light at this time, but is not heard of again. As a result of his efforts in London, a number of MI5 operators were released from duty to join Sillitoe's new organisation, the International Diamond Security Organisation (IDSO), at attractive salaries. His basic organisation plan having met with Oppenheimer's approval, Sillitoe installed his deputy director with an assistant in Johannesburg to run the African headquarters, and staffed the regional offices with regional directors, each of whom were to have autonomous responsibility for recruiting local operators and conducting local investigations under Sillitoe's overall direction. In addition to senior people (regional directors and their assistants), a large number of policemen were recruited, and at the height of its operations the IDSO was employing hundreds of full-time and part-time operators—at enormous direct cost to the Syndicate.

Besides those directly employed by the IDSO, the police forces of France, Germany, Belgium, Holland, the United Kingdom, the Union of South Africa, the BSAP (Rhodesia) and other African countries were involved in varying degrees. With Interpol making its services available to IDSO and the police forces of member countries, the whole diamond-smuggling investigation was to be a massive operation, serving national as well as commercial interest.

At the regional level, ample funds were made available to recruit local help and to pay informers in a bid to gather diamond-intelligence information. One of the field operators recruited in South Africa, J. H. du Plessis, formerly with the South Africa diamond police, records in his sensational and racy account of the affair, *Diamonds Are Dangerous*,* that safe havens (houses and apartments) were established to provide operators with a meeting place where they could discuss business with informers and make transactions with which they became involved.

Through the organisation Sillitoe conducted his investigation on three levels. The first was on the existing security arrangements at the mines; the second, among the IDB (Illicit diamond buying) operators; and thirdly, along any international routes by which the supposed diamond-smuggling ring disposed of the gems they gathered. Until he knew the extent and range of the smuggling operation, he would not be able to deal with it to put it out of business.

Apart from setting up the organisation, his first move was to make an extended tour of the major diamond-mining centres to meet with mine managers and their security staffs. Even before the tour began, the new organisation ran into trouble. Brink's assistant commissioner, Brigadier C. I. Rudemeyer, who was in charge of South Africa's diamond police, took umbrage with Sillitoe for not calling on him. In fact, Sillitoe had tried to contact the Brigadier, but without success. Secondly, because creation of the IDSO implied a criticism of Rudemeyer's diamond police, the assistant commissioner was most disgruntled. 'There is no organised smuggling of uncut diamonds out of the country,' he told reporters. Further, he was surprised that Sillitoe had not called on him, because no activity in connection with IDB could take place without his knowledge. This misunderstanding was later cleared up and the diamond police of the Union eventually proved most co-operative. The security organisations of the various mines were less willing to accommodate the new organisations, resenting as they did this outside intrusion into their exclusive sphere of operations.

By the time Sillitoe returned to England some seven weeks later, he had travelled more than thirty thousand miles, having visited Dar-es-Salaam, Pretoria, Johannesburg, Lusaka, Accra, Leopoldville, Yengema, Freetown, and a host of smaller diamond-mining centres. Considering the fact that he was in his sixty-sixth year, and his health was failing, he weathered the gruelling

* Cassell & Co., London, 1959.

journey well. He was having respiratory problems; in Johannesburg, which is some six thousand feet above sea level, he had difficulty breathing, and then there was an increasing worry about his right knee (the same one which had given him so much trouble in Tanganyika almost fifty years before); it swelled again occasionally, making even a gentle walk painful.

The newspapers were still interested in diamond-smuggling copy, and almost weekly there were press reports of dramatic arrests, of secret gangs being hauled before the courts, and of imminent large-scale police raids. In fact, during three full years of intense activity, investigation and co-operative effort between police departments and the IDSO, not more than half a dozen people were charged with smuggling diamonds. It is at this point that one must question the *raison d'être* for the creation of the IDSO. Measure of the success or failure of the privately-financed investigation can only be decided on the basis of the primary objective, if one knows or can determine what this was, and whether or not this objective was achieved. According to Sillitoe's terms of reference, he was dealing with Communist intrigue and this is clearly confirmed by the only two published accounts of the investigation. First, in his account, du Plessis says:

'. . . certain of my superiors made it clear to me that without the incredibly huge flow of illicit industrial diamonds from Central Africa to behind the Iron Curtain, the development of the Russian H-bomb would have been delayed by many years. Diamonds, thousands upon thousands of industrial diamonds, helped to make the precision tools and instruments which made the Russian H-bomb, helped make the precision tools and instruments which made the Russian armaments the formidable giants they are now. Diamonds, tiny industrials and huge and exquisite gem-stones, have helped (and still are helping) finance anti-west uprisings in Greece, in the Lebanon in Syria, in Algeria, in the Far East—in a dozen other places which are hotspots of trouble today.'

Similarly, the significant passage in Fleming's report of the investigation, *The Diamond Smugglers*—which is liberally sprinkled throughout with references to Communist intrigue—is:

The black market in diamonds grew with the white, and De Beers simply had to try to cut it down, both as a service to various countries and companies involved in the Diamond Corporation, as a natural commercial operation against a competitor and—and this is not quite so incidental as you might imagine—as a patriotic duty; to stop this huge gun-running operation through the Iron Curtain, because industrial diamonds are one of the sinews of armaments.

Fleming went so far as to publish a map showing 'trade routes' of smuggled diamonds from the various centres, graded in three levels to show the relative volume of traffic. The heaviest, boldest flow converged on Moscow from the European centres of Antwerp, Zürich and Berlin, with a direct connection from Monrovia in Liberia. As with the other material on which Fleming based his account, the map was supplied by the ex-MI5 operator Collard.

Was the Communist element, then, the real purpose behind the diamond-smuggling investigation? No, it was not. The charge of Communist involvement was undoubtedly the greatest hoax of the mid-fifties. Discovering this during the course of his investigation gave Sillitoe a twinge of conscience which had some bearing on the ultimate outcome of the affair.

Contrary to the impression created by Fleming and du Plessis —albeit unwittingly in both cases, because neither writer had a technical background—and generally accepted at the time, diamonds are not essential to the armament industry. Indeed, diamonds for general industrial use are very much over-rated, as even the most junior engineer must know. They may be used to a limited extent for grinding wheels, drill bits and for optical instrument applications, but as for manufacturing an H-bomb, 'to make the precision tools and instruments which made the Russian armaments the formidable giants they are', this is utter nonsense. The hardest materials encountered in nuclear energy applications would be uranium oxide (the common uranium fuel), uranium carbide, plutonium, and deuterium, none of which require a diamond cutter to be worked. Plutonium, the heart of the atomic bomb, or deuterium, for the H-bomb, could be cut with carbon-tipped tools, which have been in use for the past thirty years.

Besides, the Russians had an adequate supply of diamonds from their own fields. The Soviets announced the discovery of diamonds in Siberia as early as 1953, although the discovery and development of the Russian diamond deposits occurred some few years earlier, probably in 1950. Needless to say, no one in the West took the announcement seriously. In all probability, the Siberian discovery was only made known in 1953-4 to scotch rumours of Soviet involvement in the alleged smuggling activities from the Syndicate's mines. The USSR diamond mining centre is at Mirny, Siberia (present population 25,000) and whilst 100-carat stones are not everyday discoveries, large finds are frequently made. It needs no mastermind to calculate what the Mirny diamond output would be. Experts agree that Siberian diamonds are every bit as good as the best stones found in South Africa. Clearly, the Soviets had sufficient supplies of diamonds to satisfy their industrial needs in 1953-4.

What of their alleged political interest in diamonds from the West? Again, this hypothesis will not hold up. They were not likely to exchange their 'foreign currency' holdings for diamonds to 'finance anti-west uprisings in Greece, in the Lebanon, in Syria, in Algeria, in the Far East', as du Plessis states because, as must be patently obvious, it would be more expedient, cheaper and safer for the Russians to use diamonds from their own sources —if indeed they were so naïve as to use diamonds for such purposes.

In the end, not one shred of evidence was discovered during the investigation to implicate the Soviets or to support in any way the theory of Communist intrigue. The undue emphasis placed on Communist interest in Western diamonds makes the Fleming and du Plessis accounts suspect and points to an ulterior motive on someone's part. The map so thoughtfully produced for Fleming by Collard was a red herring. The ex-MI5 operator may have made the map in good faith; if so it was the faith of blind conviction—blind, that is, to the facts. In any case, the Collard map helped to effectively hide the real motive behind the creation of IDSO and its activities.

On the evidence of a former director of IDSO (who declines to be identified), on the evidence of subsequent events and acceptable corroborative information to be found in *The Diamond Smugglers*, the primary objective earlier mentioned can be defined. This objective, which we can now pursue, was a bid on the part of the Syndicate to wipe out a collective and independent diamond-mining operation being conducted in Sierra Leone.

The situation in Sierra Leone (formerly a British colony) was rather special, indeed it appears to have been the nub of the whole operation, the chief reason for setting up the IDSO in the first place. Sierra Leone Selection Trust had two large concessions in the territory: one centred about Yengema and taking in the upper reaches of the Sewa River, the other in the areas of Banguma, which lies somewhat to the south of Yengema. However, large tracts of diamond-bearing soil existed—mostly along the river beds—and these were being mined by local villagers, who were channelling the fruits of their labours across the Liberian border to be marketed through Monrovia on the coast. Liberia had no diamond mines of its own; what it was able to offer was a legitimate outlet for Sierra Leone diamonds on the world market.

Another important factor was that the Syndicate's diamond clearing house in London was a huge 'dollar earner' for the sterling bloc. Those stones filtering through Monrovia not only meant there was no dollar-earning contribution to the sterling bloc, but that the trickle, if allowed to go unchecked, could grow; given the help of more sophisticated equipment, local diggers could increase their output and threaten the Syndicate's monopoly position.

Sir Ernest Oppenheimer, perhaps remembering his brother's earlier bungling in connection with the British Guiana diamond fields, was determined to tackle this new assault on the Syndicate's seemingly impregnable position with a shrewder game play. By employing the former chief of MI5, and so getting the active co-operation of the British government, Oppenheimer achieved an advantageous position without recourse to price-fixing, as had been done almost thirty years before.

Thus, what Sillitoe was duped into doing, under the blanket coverage of an international smuggling operation investigation, was to expose and define the specific dealers and dealings in Liberia. Then, when the British government was heavily committed to the operation through the loan of MI5 staff, it was persuaded to participate in the next phase of Oppenheimer's plan: literally to corner the IDB market with funds supplied by the British government; in other words, the British taxpayer's money, amounting to a million pounds. Syndicate funds for this purpose had been provided to Sillitoe's field operators on a more modest scale and they, through contacts made in various African centres, vied with the regular illicit diamond buyers on behalf of the Syndicate, to beat them at their own game. In the case of the funds supplied by the British government, the entire sum was handed over to a co-operative diamond dealer in Liberia, who cornered the Sierra Leone export market and so funnelled that territory's diamonds into the Syndicate's hands. Of this part of IDSO's operations, the Director earlier mentioned says:

> 'Its primary task was not to produce evidence on which to prosecute smugglers but to detect the source of the vast leakage into the illicit market which was at that stage threatening the world price of diamonds. That task we achieved—the leakage being through the illicit diggings in Sierra Leone into Liberia.'

Having successfully re-routed the 'illicit' diamonds, the Syndicate persuaded the government of Sierra Leone and the Sierra Leone Selection Trust (under the chairmanship of Phillip Oppenheimer) to licence, and therefore 'legalise', the local diggers, and to funnel the entire production through the Syndicate's 'official' clearing house in London. Says the former IDSO director: 'In this way, to the best of my recollection and belief, diamonds valued between ten and twelve million pounds were channelled back into London during the following twelve months. This measure sealed the main source of leakage, thus completing the main task for which IDSO was formed.'

For the duration of IDSO's three-year existence, Sillitoe put his heart and soul into his work. He carried out a systematic and detailed investigation, co-ordinating the work of his regional offices and collating the information gathered by the field operators. He consulted with Oppenheimer frequently and was invariably received with the utmost kindness and hospitality at Inanda. Nevertheless, two matters which troubled him gradually assumed increasing importance. First, it became increasingly clear to him that there was no evidence of an 'international diamond-smuggling ring'—unless one considers those people in Sierra Leone and Liberia exercising their free-enterprise rights. The fact that so few people were charged—and only then for diamond packages of relatively small value—bears this out. He knew that Interpol, the national police forces, and the well-organised diamond police of the Union were quite capable of dealing with large outbreaks of diamond smuggling. Knowing that there was no Communist intrigue, he *must* have reached the conclusion that the organisation he set up was an instrument to serve strictly commercial ends. Secondly, there was growing opposition to the IDSO from within the Syndicate itself.

Strangely enough this opposition came primarily from Oppenheimer's son, Harry, who is the present chairman of De Beers and its associated companies. While Sir Ernest was intent on preserving the Syndicate's monopoly position, Harry took the view that there were more than enough diamonds for everyone, and the measures taken by his father to protect the industry were unnecessary. Such diametrically-opposed views affected Sillitoe's relationship with those who supported the current chairman, including Harry himself. On this subject, the IDSO director earlier quoted says:

'The fact that we worked directly to Sir Ernest created, not unnaturally, jealousy and antagonism on the part of the consulting engineers and general managers of the various mines who regarded any criticism or recommendations on our part as a reflection on their own efficiency. Harry Oppenheimer was conscious of these likely repercussions (from the beginning). These led to the inevitable unpleasantness and would have continued to do so if IDSO were to do its job properly.'

All this led in the end to the disbanding of IDSO. An official spokesman of De Beers to whom these conclusions were put replied, '. . . it is close enough to the truth to be credible', which was as far as one could get to positive confirmation of the facts from the De Beers organisation.

Sillitoe returned to his retirement distinctly unhappy with the closing down of the IDSO's operations, despite the fact that his task, clearly successful and complete, was made increasingly difficult and frustrating because of Harry Oppenheimer's uncompromising attitude. A number of the London directors of the Syndicate were opposed to the break-up of IDSO on the grounds that there was a continuing need for an international security organisation. Who could tell where fresh diamond deposits were going to be discovered, to pose a fresh threat to the industry? But Oppenheimer was too strong a chairman; IDSO had served its purpose and outlived its usefulness. The London directors bowed to his decision, and Sillitoe retired once more to Eastbourne and to the terrors of further obscurity.

Chapter Nineteen

Endgame

Shortly after the Sillitoes had first moved to Eastbourne in 1946, during the early days of Percy's association with MI5, they had a house built. It was a conventional suburban dwelling with three bedrooms and a bathroom upstairs, and a study, drawing room, dining room and kitchen on the ground floor. Dollie had little difficulty in managing the house herself with the help of a daily cleaning woman. The house stood directly opposite a church in St John's Road, and the weekly bell-ringing, both on Saturday mornings when the bell-ringers practiced and before matins on Sunday, was the cause of a dispute between Sillitoe and the vicar which threatened for a time to be a repetition of the 'Barking Dog' case at Kilmalcolm.

The loud crash of bells twice a week was more than Percy could endure. He invited the vicar to the house and told him that the noise was driving him berserk. A hot debate ensued and neither party would give in to the other. Sillitoe threatened to obtain a court order if necessary, and the minister replied that the ringing would continue. The ringing time was lengthened and Sillitoe became more furious. 'Bloody arrogance', he called it. In retaliation, he organised a petition to force the church to curtail its bell-ringing activities. A local newspaper, publishing the story, gave prominence to 'Sir Percy Sillitoe's leading role in the dispute' and of his threat to take legal action. As a result of the newspaper story, the dispute was brought to the attention of the vicar's superiors, who very sensibly worked out a compromise and prevented the matter being taken to court.

Sillitoe was, at the time, still with MI5. His frequent trips abroad in connection with his job, and the curtailed bell-ringing, made life at home at the weekends bearable with only the occasional gripe about having his peace disturbed. However, when he retired and became depressed through inactivity, the bells got on his nerves again.

Meanwhile, as long as he was working on the diamond-smuggling investigation and had various other things to occupy him, he was reasonably tolerant. When further years of retirement appeared on the horizon, he faced the prospect with renewed frustration and anger. As matters turned out he was spared the ordeal, because no sooner had he severed his ties with the Diamond Syndicate than he was invited to meet with and help another large commercial organisation, the De La Rue Company. In fact, he was to remain in demand until the end of his life.

In recent years, the criminal community had discovered a lucrative source of income in the collection of payrolls, and there had been an outbreak of attacks by strong-arm thugs on people bringing cash from the bank. Unarmed and for the most part unescorted, the payroll clerks and similar personnel who also performed this duty were highly vulnerable. They followed predictable routes and timetables, and were therefore easy prey. As this type of crime increased, the press and official sources offered abundant advice, but they could not provide the actual protection that alone could have solved the problem.

De La Rue's scheme, based on an idea which J. A. Shepherd-Barron (the present Chairman of Security Express Limited) had while working in America, was to provide a secure payroll delivery service for the benefit of large organisations. Of Sillitoe's involvement, Shepherd-Barron says:

> 'When I had the idea of setting up such an operation in the UK I reckoned we needed a well-known security name who would be able to achieve Home Office and police backing for such an enterprise, which was novel in this country in 1959. I actually came across Sir Percy through some friends of mine in New York whom he had known over the years. We asked Sir Percy to be our first chairman in a non-executive capacity for the first couple of years.'

The De La Rue plan, involving specialist personnel and armoured vehicles, was not a new one, but it had not been widely exploited, mostly for lack of investment capital. This De La Rue were prepared to provide, so the task of 'selling' the service and of attracting a sufficiently large clientele to make the venture self-supporting, were secondary considerations to building up the organisation and training suitable personnel—hence the interest in Sillitoe, in addition to the reason explained by Shepherd-Barron.

Sillitoe attended a luncheon to listen to the proposal of Shepherd-Barron and his associates, liked the idea immediately and agreed to participate in setting up the new organisation, which was to be called Security Express Limited. The venture was both costly and ambitious. It required a large outlay of funds for the production of armour-plated delivery trucks and to meet salaries and operating expenses, with no guarantee that customers would flock to their doors, even though there appeared to be a crying need for such a service. Operating out of a small office in the city, Sillitoe and Shepherd-Barron began the task of recruiting a field staff, developing plans for a procedure to follow in the collection and delivery of the payrolls that they expected to be carrying in no time at all, and scouring the field for prospective customers. After weeks of making elaborate plans and putting the service into a state of readiness, Security Express was still without a single client and Sillitoe was disenchanted with the whole idea.

'We might as well shut up shop,' he said. 'We're not going to get anywhere.' This sort of attitude was typical of his mood when things failed to go the way he expected, so easily was he discouraged.

Suddenly, there was another surge of hold-ups. Within a few days, Security Express was swamped with calls; the groundwork which the small staff had so carefully carried out bore fruit at last. The armoured trucks, unused for months, now were so busy that it was necessary to add to the fleet.

One of Sillitoe's conditions of his becoming Chairman of the new company, was that one of his sons, Anthony, should be made managing director, a condition Shepherd-Barron eventually agreed to with some misgiving because he disapproved of nepotism.

Reflecting on Sillitoe's term as Chairman of the Board, Shepherd-Barron noted, 'He acted as chairman in a grand way, although at times I must say he made me a bit anxious, as I later discovered that owing to his predilection for publicity in his MI5 days, he was not as popular as I had hoped in government circles; but his personality carried over all obstacles.'

Throughout the next two years business steadily increased, and Percy had enough work to maintain his interest in the affairs of the company. In the autumn of 1960 a Scottish office was opened in Glasgow, with an official opening attended by the Lord Provost and other dignitaries. Returning to the city where he had spent over thirteen years of his career, Sillitoe was able to call on a number of his old colleagues from the Glasgow police force to lend a hand, and ex-Detective Superintendent R. Colquhoun* was engaged to manage the Glasgow operations.

On the night of the opening of the Glasgow operation Sillitoe, in the company of Sherherd-Barron, was involved in an amusing incident. It had been a long evening; first, for the benefit of the television news cameras, there had been a dummy run of the first armoured truck in Scotland, and then a long formal dinner. Afterwards, the two men took a stroll in the cold night air along Sauchiehall Street, the scene of many a brush with the street gangs in the old days. They were stopped by a dirty, unkempt figure leaning against a lamp post who asked them for a light. Sillitoe didn't smoke at that time so his companion offered a light. It was then that the old villain recognised Sillitoe.

'Ach!' he said, 'you're the old bugger who put me away for ten years in the thirties—go on, have a cigarette!'

There was a pregnant pause. Percy took a home-made cigarette from the dirty old tin he was offered and began smoking. 'Well, I hope we made a man of you,' he said.

'Aye!' came the reply, 'I've been straight ever since, and look where it's got me.'

'Well,' said Sir Percy, 'here's a couple of pounds to help you on your way.'

The Wells Fargo Armoured Service Corporation had been persuaded to join the UK enterprise at the outset, with a forty-nine per cent shareholding in Security Express; this was during the period when Wells Fargo was owned by American Express, with whom De La Rue officials had friendly contact. The US held shares were bought back from Amex in 1963 when Amex got involved in the Great Oil Salad Scandal and, it is believed, needed every bit of available cash it could get hold of. From that time on De La Rue has held the total equity of Security Express. Sillitoe's major contribution to the operational success of Security Express was in establishing a national radio network for control

* Author of *Life Begins at Midnight*, John Long & Co., London 1962.

purposes, a facility their friends in Wells Fargo did not have in the US.

The old warrior was now seventy-two, and was losing interest in the fortunes of Security Express. He was showing his age, with greying hair and a slowing down of his once jaunty walk. Because of his respiratory problems he no longer took exercise on the golf course, and there was another outbreak of trouble with his game knee, which became stiff and sore, making walking painful. However, he still managed to attend the annual dinners of the societies of which he was a member, such as the Old Comrades Association of the City of Sheffield Police, and took an active interest in those national movements which interested him. For instance, he was a staunch supporter of the Society for the Return of Capital Punishment, being one of its founder members. But despite his willingness to lead an active public life, it was clear to those who had followed his eventful career that he was fast going downhill. In the late summer of 1961 Dollie persuaded him to take a holiday with her, the cost being met by Security Express as a parting retirement gift.

'I'm going on a Caribbean cruise,' he said when questioned by reporters, 'because I've not been feeling well for the past month.' This was true. He had suffered an attack of pneumonia some weeks earlier and was far from recovered. When the Sillitoes returned to England some three weeks later, Percy was at last content to seek idle days in retirement, doing little beyond pottering around the garden of his Eastbourne home and leafing through the *Daily Telegraph* and *The Times*.

He had not given up complaining about his situation and would dearly have liked to be more active, but even he realised that he was no longer a young man with energy to burn. As a warrior in retirement, he was like a sword in a shop window on which one may gaze and wonder what scars the burnished blade has to hide. For more than half a century he had fought crime in its various guises and upheld the law as he understood it, not simply those prescribed and written laws of society which must be obeyed but also those within the domain of duty and public spirit and 'good form' which he himself interpreted as '... the collective wisdom of society', or what Lord Moulton once described as '... the domain of obedience to the unenforceable'.

Sillitoe was in many ways a superior and vain man, but in no sense was he consumed with pride. He never used high office to achieve personal gain and privilege, but was extraordinarily tenacious in his pursuit of those public officials who did, such as the policemen of Sheffield and the municipal councillors of Glasgow. For his compassion and humanitarianism towards the men and women who worked under him and to the unfortunate and underprivileged, he was indeed a man deserving high admiration. This sense of compassion, together with his stern disciplinary attitude towards his subordinates, he constantly maintained. Those enemies of society whom he was employed to pursue were never considered by him to be beyond redemption, for he was as constant in offering them a helping hand as he was in succouring their more law-abiding fellows. When we consider his attitude to ordinary people who exercised their right to challenge the establishment and society, we cannot help but recall his noble gesture at the beginning of the great hunger march of 1934, when he organised a collection to present to the march leaders before the column set off for London.

Just about the time when he appeared to have completely recovered from his illness and was refreshed by his Caribbean cruise, he again fell ill. This time it was his knee, which had been getting more painful. After weeks of growing stiffness, accompanied by pain, the knee began to swell, as it had so many years before in Tanganyika. There was also an accompanying skin infection which was diagnosed as cancer. The joint was so painful that he was quite unable to move and had to be confined to bed, but he was not told the true cause of his trouble. During the two months of life remaining to him—the cancer, quickly invading bone tissue, spread rapidly—he became once more 'the world's worst patient'.

A nurse was engaged, an arrangement which met with his approval because he had little patience with Dollie, who throughout his life was the recipient of his anger and frustration whenever he was ill or in pain. One day he asked for soda water to add to his orange juice and there was none on the bedside table. Dollie said she thought they had run out of it but would go downstairs to check.

'For Christ's sake get water,' he told her angrily. 'No, don't. Just clear out! You're getting on my nerves! Clear out and let the nurse get it!'

Despite these outbursts of anger, Dollie was still Tod's tolerant companion and made excuses to the children for his short temper.

She could not endure seeing him in pain and frequently implored the attending surgeon to 'Do something, anything, to put Tod out of his misery'.

Percy's elder brother, Hubert, moved into the house as soon as he received news of the illness. This merely added to Dollie's burdens because Uncle Hubert, as Richard Sillitoe confirms, was not a man to fetch and carry for himself. The visitor expected to be waited on, even though he came with the best of intentions, to be at hand in his brother's hour of need. The Sillitoes' elder son, Anthony, was a frequent visitor while Richard, though he was about to leave the country for Canada, was at that time living with his parents. For those last two months it was a busy household.

During the afternoon of Thursday, 5th April 1962, Richard, as usual, was at his father's bedside. His father seemed to have made a sudden and remarkable recovery: he was of a clear mind and feeling none of the excruciating pain which had been his constant companion—a tormenting one—over the past few weeks.

'My God!' he said, 'I damned well nearly died, I was so ill,' and he went on to speak of his relationship with his children. He said, 'I know I haven't been the best of fathers to you children, Richard, but I'm going to make it up to you. I've always been too busy worrying about my job to pay much attention to you children, but when I get over my knee trouble I'm going to come to Canada and set you up in business.' He put his hand on Richard's knee and his son thanked him for his promise. It was a kind thought.

'Don't worry about me,' Richard replied. 'I'm quite old enough to take care of myself and I've got enough money to set myself up in something.'

'No, but I mean it, I'm serious,' his father assured him. 'I know I haven't been the best of fathers to you, but I'll make it up to you when I'm on my feet.'

They agreed to leave it at that and parted on the best of terms. It was during the evening meal that the nurse came down to tell the family that Sir Percy had gone into a coma. By the time they reached his bedside he was dead. The witchdoctor's curse had almost come true; it was the knee ailment which had killed him, and that was as the witchdoctor had predicted; yet Percy survived the first attack in Africa and had lived a full life—as though in defiance of the curse.

A small, private funeral was arranged. Dollie would not attend the actual cremation, but other members of the family and a few close friends, together with two or three official mourners, accompanied the *cortège*. The old chief's obituary was carried by most of the national newspapers and the local papers of those communities in which he had served. It seemed strange to Richard Sillitoe, considering all that his father had done in the service of the British police system, that he went to his Maker with so little fanfare. According to Richard, of all the policemen with whom his father served, only two attended the funeral: one came from the London Metropolitan Police, a force with which he served not a single day; the other was Bill Deacon, who had spent more time working with Sillitoe than any other man. The third official representative was from the Home Office.

On the day of the funeral, the sky was heavily overcast and a fine drizzle was falling. The small *cortège* moved slowly from the house on St John's Road and wound its way through Eastbourne to the crematorium. Almost at the end of its journey, the procession came to a busy crossroads where a single policeman on point duty held up the other traffic to let the hearse pass. Then, almost as an afterthought, the young man turned and raised his hand in a salute.

Appendix

The following confidential report, addressed to R. N. Duke, Esq., DSO, an official in the office of the Secretary of State for Scotland, was written following Sillitoe's first visit to the USA to attend the 40th Annual Convention of the International Association of Chiefs of Police, Chicago, and is a condensed version.

City of Glasgow Police,
Chief Constable's Office,
Headquarters,
21 St Andrew's Street,
Glasgow, C.1

Confidential:
CH/59/24. September 13th 1933
Personal:

Dear Mr Duke,

You will probably have heard that I recently visited Chicago at the invitation of the International Association of Chiefs of Police. The opportunity to learn something in other American cities besides Chicago was too valuable to miss, so I sought the assistance of Mr Dixon, who very kindly passed on to me some very useful information he had obtained from Mr August Vollmer, who was formerly Chief of Police at Berkeley, California, and now is a Professor of Police Administration in the University of California.

I feel it is essential that I should (first send you the report) to save publicity which would be unavoidable if (it) were submitted to the Police Committee; my report to them can be in the nature of any recommendations that you and General Dudgeon think worth while supporting.

The Convention at Chicago was of great assistance to me, even if only for the purpose of making contacts with chiefs of police whose places I wanted to visit and thereby making things very easy for me in saving time. From Chicago I visited Los Angeles, Berkeley, San Francisco, Sacramento and Portland (Oregon), New York and Philadelphia.

Wireless

I was immensely impressed with their wireless development and feel for that reason alone that my visit was worth while. It was a revelation, for example, to see and hear in police cars the highly efficient receiving sets of almost diminutive proportions in comparison with the cumbersome apparatus that has been demonstrated here. I have brought back with me a typical American type of receiving set used by police cars which I have installed in one of our cars. The complete outfit, including customs duty, cost about £14.

(There follows a detailed technical explanation of the Chicago Police radio network and that police department's efforts to scramble messages to police cruisers, to prevent unauthorised listeners monitoring radio transmissions.)

To digress a little, the Berkeley police organisation is the most modern and model police force I have ever seen. The strength is 58 all ranks, for a population of about 90,000. To patrol the city's area of $9\frac{1}{2}$ square miles, the whole force (uses) motor cars which they provide themselves, but upkeep and maintenance are met by the police authorities. A police officer on patrol may have a trained police dog (in his car); they also have police telephones (and) a system of signalling lamps at all intersections to (call) a patrolman to (contact headquarters). Response to any call for assistance is (therefore) amazingly efficient.

Everything in Berkeley is done under the guiding genius of Professor Vollmer, whose idealism in police efficiency has almost come true. It starts with the selection of the recruit. The candidate is subjected to a battery of tests to determine his intellectual fitness for the position. Attention is also (paid) to physical and temperamental qualities. Scientific laboratory tests are given; a neurological examination follows, tests to debar the physically unfit, and psychiatric (tests are used) to disqualify temperamental misfits. The result is that Berkeley is already becoming the nursery for future chiefs of police in other parts of America.

Modus Operandi System of Identification

The central bureau for the whole of the State of California for criminal identification and investigation is at Sacramento, and by law the police (must) furnish to the (bureau) *on standard forms* particulars of all felonies committed, describing the nature, character and all peculiar circumstances of each crime committed in their jurisdictions. The value of such a bureau is immediately apparent (in that it) permits intimate study of (all) police reports in the shortest possible time. For this purpose a mechanical tabular has been adopted.

(There follows a detailed explanation of the Hollerith Mechanical

Tabulator, which is an early form of computer or data retrieval system.)

Scientific Laboratory

(At) Chicago I visited the Scientific Crime Detection Laboratory at their North Western University. You may have heard that they have a psychological department, under the direction of Mr Leonarde Keeler, who has perfected an instrument called a polygraph, popularly known as a 'lie detector', which is used in the examination of candidates for posts of trust. I understand that various banks in Chicago are now using this service for every employee added to their staff. It is used also when persons are suspected of petty thefts in a store and in petty cash thefts in banks. They tell me that their results have been extraordinarily effective and that the machine is increasingly useful. Briefly, the parts consist of three units, one recording continuously and quantitatively the blood pressure and pulse, another giving duplicate blood pressure and pulse curve taken from a different part of the subject's body and the third unit recording respiration. Indubitably it has proved of great use in certain cases, although a practical demonstration in my own case was not too successful and I do not propose, at any rate at present, to recommend its use in Glasgow.

To sum up, therefore, I am of opinion that should it ever be decided to send anyone to the United States to study their methods, particularly as regards selection and training of personnel, wireless, recording systems and the scientific investigation of crime, they could not do better than go to Chicago, Berkeley and Sacramento. The excellent training school at New York is of course well known and well worth a visit en route.

Finally I should like to recommend for your consideration whether it would not be worth while to set up a committee in Scotland, similar to that which I believe has been done in England, aiming at closer cooperation between the Police forces of that country in dealing with crime, when the possibility of starting a recording system in this country on the lines indicated in this report might also be discussed, but perhaps before anything else we ought to come to some definite conclusion as to what we are all going to do about wireless up here.

With regard to the latter, I tried to establish the principle that controlled (the number of radio-equipped patrol cars required) in each American city I visited and I discovered that the number was based (on patrol areas and police ability to respond to) a call for assistance within a space of three to five minutes. Before, however, making any recommendation to the police authority here, the whole question of the type and number of transmitters required will have to be studied very carefully. For this purpose I think it might be as well to obtain as soon as possible the authority of the Corporation to appoint a whole time technical expert, similar to what they have in America. I will, however, wait to hear what you and General Dudgeon have to say about the possibility of forming a Committee (could we not have one in co-operation with England?), although I am perfectly prepared to go ahead myself if you like. I could be in London on the 26th of this month and we might have a chat about things then if it were convenient to you.

Yours sincerely,
(Signed): *P. J. Sillitoe*

Bibliography and Sources

There was no principal source of information for writing this book because, apart from ex-Superintendent Bill Deacon who served under Sir Percy Sillitoe in Sheffield, Glasgow and Kent, no one who worked with Sillitoe during any one period, or at the most, two periods, of his career had knowledge of others. One has had to fit the pieces together. I made liberal use of his memoirs and scrapbook. Also, his son, Richard Sillitoe, has been consulted throughout.

The following printed works have also been consulted:

Argenzio, Victor. *The Fascination of Diamonds*. Allen & Unwin, London 1967.
The Army List of 1900, courtesy of the Royal Canadian Military Institute, Toronto.
Chatterton, E. Keble. *The Königsberg Adventure*. Hurst & Blackett, London 1932.
Cloete, Stuart. *The African Giant*. Collins, London 1957.
Colquhoun, Robert V. *Life Begins At Midnight*. John Long, London 1962.
Dane, Edmund. *British Campaigns in Africa and the Pacific, 1914–1918* Hodder & Stoughton, London 1919.
Deacon, Richard. *A History of the British Secret Service*. Muller, London 1967.
du Plessis, J. H. *Diamonds Are Dangerous*. Cassell, London 1960.
Fleming, Ian. *Diamonds Are Forever*. Jonathan Cape, London 1956, and *The Diamond Smugglers*. Jonathan Cape, London 1957.
Gibbs, Peter. *The History of the B.S.A.P.* British South Africa Board of Trustees, Salisbury 1972.
Grant, Douglas. *The Thin Blue Line*. John Long, London 1973.
Hyde, Montgomery H. *The Quiet Canadian*. Hamish-Hamilton, London 1962.
Lockhart, Robin Bruce. *The Ace of Spies*. Hodder & Stoughton, London 1967.
Longford, Elizabeth. *The Jameson Raid*. Weidenfeld & Nicholson, London 1965.

Mitchison, Naomi. *The Africans, A History*. Anthony Bland, London 1970.
Page, Bruce; Leitch, David and Knightley, Phillip. *Philby*. André Deutsch, London 1968.
Patrick, James. *A Glasgow Gang Observed*. Eyre Methuen, London 1973.
Pearson, John, *The Life of Ian Fleming*. McGraw-Hill, New York 1969.
Sillitoe, Sir Percy J. *Cloak Without Dagger*. Cassell, London 1955.
Sillitoe, The Rev. Hubert. *The Sillitoe Family Tree*. A private publication.
Shankland, Peter, *The Phantom Flotilla*. Collins, London 1968.
Webb, R. K. *Modern England*. Dodd, Mead & Co. New York 1970.

Report of the Royal Commission. *The Gouzenko Report*. Queen's Printer, Ottawa 1946.

Various letters, reports and correspondence from the private papers of Professor August Vollmer, courtesy of the Director of the Bancroft Library, University of California, Los Angeles, California, USA.

Index

fn = *Footnote Reference*

Abercorn, Duke of, 30
Abliss, Sir George, 80
Aitcheson, Judge Lord, 147
Aldred, Guy, 130, 134
Amundsen, Capt. Roald, 8
Archer, Jane, 180
Arnot, Sergeant, 109–10, 154
Attlee, Clement, 175, 179, 184, 186

Baring, Sir Evelyn, 189
Barton, Captain, 34–7
Beatty, Chester A., 196
Beit, Alfred, 11
'Blaize, John', 193
Bodie, Colonel (Billy), 14
Bowman, Bull, 141, 144
Brink, Major-General J. A., 195
British Campaigns in Africa and the Pacific, 33
British South African Company, 11–14, 21, 30
British South African Police, 10–11, 14, 16, 19; enlistment of Sir Percy, 8–10
Browne, 98–9
Buchanan, Bob, 197
Burgess, Guy, 117, 187
Burke, 'Deaf', 133
Byng, Lord, 96

Campbell, Hugh, 162–3
Cargill, Sir John, 104–5
Carson, 158
Chamberlain, Neville, 160
Chapman, Major, 168
Churchill, Sir Winston, 175
City Imperial Volunteers, 6

Clegg, Sir William, 75
Clifford, Sir Charles, 84
Cloak Without Dagger, 2–3, 10, 35, 178
Collard, John, 183, 193
Collins, Sir Godfrey, 162
Colquhoun, Ex-Det. Superintendent R., 208
Cornish, Captain W. F., 190
Criminal Justice Administration Act of 1914, 57
Crockford, Inspector, 97
Crowley, Chief Constable F. J., 80
Currie, 98–9
Cuthbert, Johnny, 82–3

Daily Herald, 196–7
Daily Mail, 196
Daily Worker, 186
Daly, Commandant Colonel James F., 160
Dane, Edmund, 33
Dawson, Constable, 89
Deacon, Bill, 100, 106, 128, 157, 159, 167, 212
Deacon, Richard, 179
Deramore, Lord, 70
DeRocher, Jacques, 175–6
Dewick, Trooper, 190
Diamonds Are Dangerous, 198
Diamonds Are Forever, 1, 192–3
Diamond Smugglers, The, 193, 199–201
Diamond Syndicate, The, 194, 196–197, 204
Die Transvaaler, 194–6
Directorate of Security Services, (MI5), 180–2

INDEX

Dixon, 213
Dixon, Sir Arthur, 85
Drost, Father, 51, 54
du Plessis, J. H., 198–201
Dudgeon, Brigadier-General, 150, 213, 216
Duke, R. N., 213

Ede, Chuter, 176
Else, Superintendent, 85
Empire Exhibition, The, 157

Farrelly, Constable, 92
Finlinson, Asst. Police Chief, 120
Fleming, Ian, 1, 192–3, 199–201
Fraser, Hugh, 162
Fuchs, Klaus, 187, 190, 193
Fullerton, William, 141, 144–6

Gallacher, William, 129
gangs, in Glasgow, 141–7; in Sheffield, 89–93
Garvin, 92
Gemmell, Bailie, 163
Geraghty, 91–2
Gill, 158
Glaister, Professor John, 155
Glasgow Evening Herald, 9
Goddard, Sergeant, 95
Gouzenko, Igor, 176, 181
Grant, Ex-Inspector Douglas, 160
Grant, John, 152
Gregor, Dr, 157
Griffith-Boscawen, Sir Arthur, 81
Gutteridge, PC George, 97–9

Hall-Dalwood, Colonel, 75–6, 90–1, 122
Hammond, Sergeant, 106, 143, 156
Himmler, Heinrich, 157
History of the British Secret Service, 179
Hitler, Adolph, 138, 157
Hollis, Roger, 180, 183
Hollis, Superintendent, 98–9
Hoover, J. Edgar, 117, 124
Horton, Corporal, 36–7
Hughes, PC, 144
Humphreys, Mr Justice, 94

International Association of Chiefs of Police, 116, 191
International Diamond Security Organisation, 197–204

Jackson, Sir John, 7–8, 21
Jameson, Sir Leander Starr, 14, 30

Keeler, Leonarde, 215
Kell, Major-General Vernon, 180
Kelly, George ('Machine Gun'), 117
Kelly, Mayor, 116
Kelly, Sir Thomas, 103
Kennedy, 98–9
Kennedy, 146
Kenyoni, 51–4
Kilpatrick, Chief Constable, 61–2

Lambert, Jimmy, 82–3
Langmuir, James, 123–4
Lee, John R., 39
Leeper, Sir Reginald, 194
Lenin, 129
Lettaw-Vorbeck, General von, 32–4, 38, 41–2
Liddell, Guy, 179–80, 183
Life Begins at Midnight, 208 (fn)
Lloyd, F. E., 16
Lloyd, Harold, 120
Lobengula, Chief, 12–3
Looff, Admiral Max, 39
Loxley, 91–3
Lunn, 91–2
Lynch, Roche, 85

McCarthy, Senator, 186, 190
McCulloch, Malcolm, 111
MacDonald, Sir Alexander, 72
MacDonald, Rev. Hugh, 131
McGlinchey, James, 103 (fn), 133, 137, 149–50, 159
McGlinchey Papers, 103, 130
Macguire, George, 163
McIntyre, Peter, 134–5, 148
McKay, Sergeant Daniel, 144
McKinnon, 29
MacLean, Donald, 117, 184, 186–7
McNamee, Andrew and John, 146–7
McPherson, PC, 89

220

INDEX

Marais, David, 196
Marshall, William, 189–90
Maxwell, Sir Alexander, 167
May, Dr Allan Nunn, 181
May, Sir George, 102
MI5, *see* Directorate of Security Services
Miller, Angus James, 151–2
Moffat, J. S., 12, 16
Money, Sir Leo, 95
Mooney, 92
Morrison, Herbert, 175, 184
Mostly Murder, 149 (fn)
Moulton, Lord, 209
Murray, Colonel, 41
Mwami, 51
My Silent War, 178

News of the World, 99
No Mean City, 141
Norfolk, Duchess of, 83
Northern Rhodesia Police, 19, 24
Northey, General, 38–40, 43
Ntare, 'King', 51–4

O'Hara, 158
Oppenheimer, Sir Ernest, 194, 197, 202, 204
Oppenheimer, Harry, 204
Oppenheimer, Otto, 194, 202
Oppenheimer, Philip, 203

Peel, Sir Robert, 96
Petre ('The Clincher'), 148
Petrie, Sir David, 180
Phantom Flotilla, The, 39 (fn)
Philby, Kim, 117, 178, 180–1, 183, 187
Pick, Professor Frank, 196–7
Pictorial Weekly, 87–8, 93, 121
Police Athletic Association, 82–3
Police Pension Act, 61–2
Polinius, Marcus, 166
Pontecorvo, 187
Popkess, Captain Athelstan, 85
Powrie, Miss, 174
Prichard, H. Hesketh, 8

Ramensky, Johnny, 148–9, 175

Rand Daily Mail, 196
Ready-Money Football Betting Act 1920, 84
Reid, Aggie, 141–3
Rhodes, Cecil, 11–3, 26, 30
Rhodesian Patrol, 16
Ritchie, Bailie, 136, 163
Roberton, Bailie Violet, 160
Robinson, Sergeant, 89–94, 106
Rogerson, Mary, 156
Roosevelt, President Franklin, 123
Rudd, 12
Rudemeyer, Brigadier C. I., 198
Ruxton, Dr Buck, 156
Ruxton, Isabella, 156
Ruxton Murders, 155–6

St John, Captain, 15
Salisbury, Lord, 12
Sandy, Lt William, 6
Savidge, Irene, 95–6
Scott, Sir Francis, 6
Scott, Captain Robert, 8
Security Express Ltd, 207–9
Senura, 51
Shankland, Peter, 39 (fn)
Shaw, Neil, 163
Sheffield Daily Telegraph, 84, 94
Sheffield Herald, 80
Sheffield Mail, 76
Sheffield Star, 80
Shepherd-Barron, J. A., 206–8
Shippard, Sir Sidney, 12, 16
Sillitoe, Anthony (son), 65, 110, 164, 171, 174, 207, 211
Sillitoe, Audrey (daughter), 58, 110, 157, 160; birth, 54; husband, 164–5, 174, 191
Sillitoe, Bertha (mother), 2–4, 6, 9–10, 14, 48, 60 (fn), 111
Sillitoe, Bertha (sister), 2, 50
Sillitoe, Dollie (Lady) (*see also* Watson, Dorothy), 3, 9, 14, 55, 58, 60, 101, 149, 169–70, 194, 205, 209; children, 54, 65, 110; engagement, 28–9; and family, 65, 69, 99, 115, 174, 191; first meeting with Sir Percy, 27; funeral of Sir Percy, 212; marriage, 48–

INDEX

Sillitoe, Dollie—*contd.*
50, 127, 164, 194, 210; pregnancy, 50; in WAPC, 160

Sillitoe, Rev. Hubert (brother), 2–3, 8, 14, 21, 50, 191, 211

Sillitoe, Joseph (father), 2–5, 10, 48–49, 60 (fn), 111

Sillitoe, Sir Percy, appearance, 5, 21, 150; autobiography, 2–3, 10, 35, 178; birth, 2; C Division Specials, 132–5, 138, 158; career: British South African Police, 8–10, 14–21; chief constableships in Chesterfield, 70–9, East Riding of Yorkshire, 70–4, Glasgow, 101–66, Sheffield, 75–100; Colonial Officer, 50–5; Communist Organisation Report, 175–6; and corruption in Glasgow, 161–4; De La Rue Company, 206–9; Diamond Syndicate, 192–204; Directorate of Security Services, 176, 178–191; early, 7–8; Empire Exhibition, 157; and football violence, 153–4, and forensic science, 66, 85, and gangs, 89–93, 140–7; Hull City Police, 59; International Diamond Security Organisation, 192–204; and IRA activity, 157–8; Kent County Constabulary, 167–77; law, studying, 59, 65; MI5, 176, 178–191; Northern Rhodesian Police, 21, 23–6, 29–31, 47–8; Security Express Ltd, 206–9; sweetshop, 193; World War I, 34–47; World War II, 167–77; character, 17, 20, 30, 48, 51, 58, 67–8, 85, 101, 111, 124, 127, 150, 165, 209–10; childhood, 2–8; children, 54, 65, 110, 154, 164–5, 191, 207, 211; death, 211–12; education, 3–7, 59, 65; engagement, 28–9; family, 2, 110, 191; father, 2–6, 10; friends, 24, 156–157; homes, 2, 6–7, 58, 127, 152–3, 170, 205; and hunting, 25; illnesses, 26, 40, 54–5, 165, 199, 209–10; knighthood, 161; languages, 17, 30, 43; marriage, 48–50; mother, 2–4, 6, 9–10, 14, 111; nickname, 8; politics, 78, 209; and the press, 8, 80–4, 87–88, 93, 95, 121, 124, 143; prison work, 131, 147; retirement, 193, 205–6, 209; report on USA trip, 193, 213–16; and Rotarians, 68–9, 111; travels, 188; Caribbean, 209; trips home, 48–9, 55; Northern Rhodesia, 18–21, 23–26, 28–32, 34–48; South Africa, 40, 194, 198; Southern Rhodesia, 8–11, 14–18, 20; Tanganyika, 50–5; USA, 115–25, 191; and women police, 159; Women's Auxiliary Police Corps, 160; World War I, 34–47; World War II, 167–77

Sillitoe, Pursey, 2

Sillitoe, Richard, 2, 9, 19, 55, 65, 149–90, 181, 194, 211–12; childhood, 110–12, 153; and father, 154, 211; illnesses, 154; in Merchant Navy, 164, 171–2, 174

Sinclair, Dr, 5

Sinclair, Colonel Hugh, 5–9, 14, 21

Sinclair, Mrs Hugh, 7–8

Skardon, William, 183, 187, 190, 193

Sloane, Tod, 8

Smith, Bertha, *see* Sillitoe, Bertha

Smith, Charles, 146–7

Smith, Mary, 147

Smith, Sir Sydney, 149 (fn), 155

Soane, Sir John, 2

Spicer-Simpson, Commander, 39–40, 47–8

Spilsbury, Sir Bernard, 85

Stennett, Lt Colonel, 24, 28–9, 34, 36–7

Stennett, Mrs, 24, 28–9, 41

Stephenson, Sir William, 193

Strain, Bailie James, 108–9, 135–6, 161–2

Sunday Graphic, 156

Sunday Mail, 143

Sunday Morning, 121 (fn)

Sunday Times, 193, 196

INDEX

Surpell, Michael, 184, 188
Swinton, Lord, 180
Sybille, François, 82–3

Taylor, Bailie, 163
Taylor, PC, 97
Templar, Field-Marshal Sir Gerald, 188
Thin Blue Line, The, 160 (fn)
Thraves, Frank, 77–80, 83, 93
Tombeur, General, 41
Trenchard, Lord, 64, 79, 96, 103, 149

Vance, Colonel, 165–6
Vernon, Superintendent C. E., 71, 73
Vollmer, August, 114–15, 117, 120, 140, 174, 213–14
von Falkenstein, Count, 33–8

Warnock, Asst. Chief Constable, 123–4
Warriner, Charlie, 29–30
Watson, Bernard, 26, 28
Watson, Cecil, 26–7, 40
Watson, Dorothy (*see also* Lady Sillitoe), 26–30, 40, 47–50
Watson, John, 26–9, 49, 55, 57–9
Watson, Mrs John, 26–8, 50
Webster, Dr James H., 66, 81, 85–6
White, Inspector James, 145
White, Sir Richard Goldsmith, 179, 183
Williamson, Asst. Chief Constable, 101
Wilson, Major, 13, 28
Wilson, Thomas, 163
Women's Auxiliary Police Corps, 160